"CHOCOLATE-COATED PiRANHA"

THE TRUTH, THE SCANDAL AND THE LIES

Mike Smallman

I Love You This Much©

Editing, design and typesetting by UK Book Publishing

www.ukbookpublishing.com

ISBN: 978-1-7385068-0-4

I Love You This Much©

DEDICATION

Dedications can be difficult to do, particularly so in this case as my book is about life and there are lots of people (positive and negative) who have passed through my life. All people that have made this book possible. This book couldn't have been written without the corrupt ones; the ones that were frightened of losing their name, the ones that manipulated evidence, all the ones that I could list... get the idea? The peaks and flows of happiness, sadness, trauma, anguish, disappointment and elation have been contributed to by these people.

How does anyone get through such a traumatic life? It's simple: having rays of sunshine in the people that you meet make it possible: raucous laughter with a man you've never met before in a prison cell. Feelings of hope, belief in my own spirit and in the true story.

So, I dedicate this book, in a certain way, to myself: my hope, spirit, and enthusiasm, my belief in myself and my never-ending passion to achieve a positive outcome. All of this, coupled with the time I had with my children who have suffered because of my actions and because of my determination. It's only fair to say that in many ways they took the brunt of all the stages in my life. They dealt with it in the way they did, possibly considering if similar things could happen to them; simply because things like this can happen to an ordinary person like their dad. It must take a toll upon their belief of what is possible and impossible in their lives.

A dedication of this nature to my children is simply to say this book is the truth and I really do understand your feelings and thoughts from when things unfolded right up to the present day. Above all, this book is to help you understand who your dad really is. I also dedicate my book to the greater population in order that they too can see what goes on in the world relating to their life. Hopefully they, like me, will come positively through what is affecting their life. It's a dedication of hope for everyone.

Life isn't over till it's over. So hopefully, the people who read this book gain hope from it and use that hope to proliferate hope around them. I too need hope — continuing hope — and hope that all the negatives and positives that have happened in my life have a positive and meaningful outcome. I'd also like to mention here that I hang on to every sinew in my heart, mind and in my soul that maybe, one day, I'll see my princess again.

CONTENTS

FOREWORD

The very first time I heard about Mike was through our mutual friend *Andrea* in 2018. I had what I can only describe as an immediate heartfelt connection. It was a spiritual nudge that came with an inner knowing that one day we would meet, become friends and end up working together. Here we are in 2024, the year that Mike is finally publishing the first part of his mind-blowing, rollercoaster of a life story into this book. It's a hell of a story that will create ripple effects in more ways than one.

So here we are, Michael Smallman's book, in his voice, using his words and with his very personal account of his life, a plethora of gut-wrenching, extraordinary, traumatic, staggering, uplifting, heartbreaking experiences. With uncharted territory, we are offered a truly inspiring story that will encourage countless people to keep strong in the face of adversity, to carry on, to never ever give up, and to have faith in the human spirit.

For you, the reader, this is a powerful, thought-provoking read. It will be easy to see just how quick we are to judge and assume the worst in others. To see that we each have it within us to overcome anything, to dig deep and find compassion, forgiveness and acceptance. Then to know love to be the strongest power, as it really is.

If this true, no holds barred, often hard-hitting story doesn't move you, I seriously don't know what will. This is a detailed, factual, honest, explicit, harrowing, sometimes graphic in nature, and often hilarious description of just some of Mike's experiences in his life. We travel with him through his past to the present, with life in 2023. The book touches on early childhood, being raised by loving, but poor, parents in a family of eight. It includes the harshness of life on the streets of Moss Side in Manchester; of being hounded by a predatory paedophile, whilst at the same time also attacked by an extremely violent bully who regularly beat Michael senseless. Even then the young entrepreneur emerges and makes his mark in more ways than one. His life story includes young love and loss in tragic circumstances, the road to recovery, meeting and marrying a woman he loved dearly, having two wonderful children, creating a strong, happy family unit and building a business empire. It touches on the success and the lifestyle that ensued and the loss of it all through imprisonment for a crime he says he did not commit. The book delves into the detail of that and includes the utter horrors of life within the prison system, and the road to recovery, again and again and again.

You will have the opportunity to read extracts from the newspaper reports and read hard evidence that provides and supports Mike's version of events to help you draw your own conclusions.

What Mike has experienced could happen to you or to anyone you know. One minute you're flying high, the next in total utter despair, where the life you knew and loved is annihilated and gone forever.

For those not so keen on reading, this and the books to follow, I'm sure there will be a film, which will have movie audiences stunned into silence, introspective, humbled, horrified, reaching for tissues one moment and possibly peeing in their pants the next when Mike's humour, one of his many great attributes, emerges. Unlike most

Hollywood blockbusters, however, Mike's story will not require any extra or fictitious dramatisation as it has more than enough gritty, heart-wrenching and dramatic life content.

There are many deep messages and much wisdom within these pages to share. The book might not be for the faint-hearted but it's an awesome read for anyone who has a heart. It demonstrates that peace and happiness reside within.

No amount of compensation can change Mike's greatest loss, the thing that mattered the most to him, his family unit. Getting to know him more as time passes by, I'm certain any compensation he may be offered, including revenue from this book, he would use to help and support other people, including those living the nightmare that is prison life hell.

In the Summer of 2021, I was fortunate enough to meet one of Mike's friends who had served a prison sentence, a lovely, gentle man. During that lunchtime he shared with Mike how three other prisoners who had been released at the same time as him had all taken their lives, unable to survive 'on the outside'. How tragic is that? Men who had once been someone's son, brother, father, husband, friend or neighbour, who through whatever had happened to them, ended up in a system and unable to see a way to life beyond. As with many systems, including the judicial system, the police system, the government system, the media machine and more, we must, in time, learn many lessons to enable change.

You don't get to reach the significant business success that Mike reached, without vision, imagination, determination, courage, ambition and other key indicators that drive an entrepreneur, including all the knock-backs. Conversely, you don't get to go through what this man has experienced without a bigger purpose or mission.

One that we cannot always see, but a higher plan that is there slowly unfolding.

I am proud to be part of Mike's team, 'Groupies' as he calls us. Can we ever put ourselves in the shoes of others? Perhaps we can only imagine. Well, I will stand by this man's side any day, as will any of our team, and no matter what follows the publication of this book, we are there for him.

This healing journey for Mike has no vendetta, no wish to harm, and every desire to support others in their lives, to help create peace, success and happiness. With our weekly Monday gatherings to help get this book written and out there, the book never loses its momentum.

It takes a minuscule flame within to bring about transformational change for the good of all. We can all access that flame for ourselves and for future generations. Let us begin...

With love,

Jayne

ACKNOWLEDGEMENTS

For the people that know me they will be aware of my colloquial greetings and acknowledgements. For men I use the word 'cock', and for women I use the word 'chuck'. So I'd like to say to everybody that was involved in helping me write this book, 'cheers, cock!' and 'thanks, chuck!'

Now, there was only one 'cock' that helped, but little does he know how much. Adrian Graham has supported me as his friend in many ways, with encouragement and with his skills to create, so big thanks to you, 'cock'. Now, the 'chucks' are more numerous; a list of ladies most of who I call my 'crazy groupies', the list is many but here are a few...

Leslie Herman Jones, Leslie Gore and Jayne Goldstone: all three with good constructive criticisms, ideas for tangents and all the elements of a directional push-me, pull-me, jiggy-joggy mind-provoking input. Also 'chuck' Jayne for her catering, her spiritual feelings and resoluteness at being a friend.

Sheila Venamore aka 'The Duchess' for her ears, carefully listening to my narrations, her searches through documents and her inspiration that helps drive my art.

Two more 'chucks'; one is Celia Oates for patiently re-aligning her ears and listening to the digital recordings to type some of the chapters whilst I was constructing the book.

The last chuck, Andrea Atwell, who has led the way for month upon month in fields and in cafes, on the floor in my flat, listening continually, typing, formatting and guiding, but above all, understanding my personality and the way I wanted the book to come together. If I'd had the money I could have employed people and paid them to do similar things for me. But for everyone concerned, the payment I offer is eternal friendship and the largest amount of gratitude. All of this was there to get my story told.

...And finally, to Merlin the pooch, who sat, slept and farted through meetings to add to the ambience of the crazy group of people that came together to help, through the book, mend my broken heart.

PREFACE

You may be wondering why a skinny, poorly boy from Manchester who became known as the biggest education fraudster in the world would want to write a book. You may think it could be best for him to just hide in the background, or even become someone else. Well, I had to put things right, put my side of the story forward just one more time.

You see, if you googled me, it would say that I ripped off tens of thousands of people for millions. It would tell you that I stole £5.8m from Prime Minister Tony Blair and it would go on, and on, telling you what a very bad man I am. However, as you may well know, what the newspapers report isn't always the truth. I can't say that the newspapers lied because at the start of my character assassination they were told lies by others. This book isn't me shouting about my innocence. It's about the many phases of adversity in my life, from a boy to a big businessman and my huge, sad downfall.

This is a page from the (disgraced) News of The World national newspaper. It was printed as a result of dishonest discussions with City & Guilds...

During my trial and throughout all the preceding investigations, my voice became that of the 'small man' that was unimportant and not listened to. When it suited people to deflect their stories upon me, I was the 'small man' to carry the hefty weight of the blame upon my shoulders. This quote, verbatim, from my barrister, was written within the grounds of my appeal against conviction:

"...It is submitted that the issues in the case were obfuscated, and the Appellant deprived of this case being fairly put to and considered by the jury, with a result that the verdicts returned are unsafe."

This means that the issues were made obscure and therefore unintelligible, leaving the jury bewildered and resulting in an unfair trial and a miscarriage of justice. My voice was unheard throughout my trial and appeal and throughout the years ahead, until now. This book is for my voice to be heard and to show you, the reader, that whatever life throws at you, you can get through it, deal with it, and ultimately rise above it.

My life story makes people laugh and it makes them cry. It sometimes takes people's hope away, making them doubt themselves, society and the systems in place, but then it gives it back. This book covers a particularly difficult part of my life story, but I'd like to say it's not all sad, depressing stuff; au contraire, there are loads of funnies in it too. I do, however, compare life for an individual to being a dog.

When you are born, life puts its collar and lead on you and begins to drag you down all the avenues where you don't really want to go. If I was a dog, my owner would attach a lead to me and drag me wherever they wanted me to go. They would feed me the food that they want me to eat and prevent me from doing the things I instinctively want to do. They would shut me up when I made too much noise and they would punish me when they thought I had done wrong. They would restrict my life of freedom just for being a dog, because they can, because they want a dog. As dogs we may feel we must wag our tails from time to time and pretend that life is treating us well, but life and its restraints would still have its lead on us, no matter who we are. It's fair to say that some dogs are bigger and stronger and pull back from time to time, but this dog, me, never, ever stops pulling at that lead.

The basis of my book is me popping out of my mother's stomach in 1963, a healthy baby at the time. Life then put its collar and lead on me and dragged me down a road which led to so much grief and sadness that there had to be a contra side to it. That was the ability to smile through anything and never give up on the way to success.

Abused as a child and having lost loved ones to a car crash at an early age, life for me was a catastrophic existence. Life continues to try to pull me by the lead into low life, but I don't succumb. I have always pulled back and still do. I had made a life that was so successful, so diverse, that it led others to pull back on their lead. It inspired them not to conform to the jerk in society that has taken their lead. It dragged me to courtrooms, to near self-destruction, to the loss of every kind you could imagine. So, the intention of this book is to keep inspiring people to pull on their lead, to go in the direction that they feel they want to, not the way the lead is pulling them and to make that life shine a light on the world.

The journey of my life is relentless, but I'm always pulling on the lead in order to find freedom. This book is one of the ways I'm pulling on my lead. I've still got the 'never give up' attitude. I can smell freedom. It isn't death. Freedom or imprisonment is a state of mind. We can be physically imprisoned or even mentally imprisoned, but we are always free to wish, hope and even believe life is sanguine. Freedom is a choice of how to deal with and respond to physical or mental incarceration. It gives a greater understanding of why we go through the things we do. We don't live our life in the things we do, or in the environments, in cars and taxis and buses and trains and buildings and relationships or walking by the owner's side. We live it in our minds.

A phrase I completely relate to came from Churchill. He said, when you're in the mire don't stand still or you'll sink. Just keep going and eventually you'll come out the other end. In my own way I keep going and I'll never, ever, ever give up.

INTRODUCTION

Mike has asked me to write this introduction as, for once, he appears lost for words. I am sat here in a coffee shop reading through the final draft of the book before it goes to a publishing house. I would like to say I could help with that, but I believe that the need for this book to reach as many people as possible and to engage many in the world to look at their own life stories and investigate their own approach to life leads the book to the door of an international publishing house and an agent that understands Mike and how he works. Primarily there are needs within the book for people to look at every aspect of human behaviour and question themselves honestly about their own fears and how often, subconsciously, fear drives behaviours that we aren't proud of.

Many people are involved in Mike's story, and many more in future books still to be completed, but to say that Mike holds a grudge would be wrong. He holds compassion and friendship on his sleeve with a large dollop of forgiveness that melts hearts. I do wonder if people were often placed in situations like this in life how they would cope. I wonder if that happens and I simply just don't realise it, but nonetheless this book, and those to follow, make for provoking discussions and frankness within every written piece that may help, and hopefully will engage, those who can help to change our systems for the better.

I will introduce Mike first as a friend and a businessman I met through interesting circumstances whilst he was in prison. That's for another book, I'm sure, but for now I'll just say, he can inspire a world to make a difference. So, in life I wish him all the best in his future with this adventure, but in business I wish him a myriad of opportunities to do what he does best, to make people smile.

This book, the first of many, leads people to understand the nature of our underpinning systems, many of which are operating very well to bring humanity to a level of appreciation for life, simple and easily lived, given choices and the means by which to survive with support. The few that have some level of corruption or disease within them, I know from discussions through the making of this book have simply just to be changed with open, honest discussions about what leads people to do what they do when they are faced with dilemmas of significant natures. For the most part it appears to be fear.

So, with that in mind I asked Mike, what would he really like to do with the information in this book and he says – quite rightly so – to make a difference. That said, I would like to offer one more thought before you read on… a journey of great results often comes from adverse beginnings, complex jigsaw pieces falling into place and a will of great spirit to keep on going and never, ever, ever give up. Those who meet Mike will know this is what got him through the entire experiences to follow in this book.

Happy reading.

Andrea

CHAPTER ONE – THE HOLE

ere I am, 59 years, one month and one day after I first popped out on September 2nd, 1963. I'm here with the crazies and Merlin the pooch. The crazies are here to help me write the book, as we sit eating vegan food, yuck! The only one who got some meat was Merlin and he got my out-of-date ham. It cost me 69 pence, but it was all right — I had a bit myself. I'll tell you more about the crazy groupies later.

When I made my entrance into the world it led to a mass of things.

I was sort of contrived; spirits, the Universe, God maybe, asked me to have my life on Earth before I was conceived. It was written. It was contracted and I agreed to it. I agreed to be spat out into the Universe for a reason. That was to have a life that would take me around the world, upside down and inside out. It was all in order to show people how to go through adversity: things that you might want to hang yourself for, be exceptionally disappointed about, but still have the ambition and the motivation to go where you intend to go. To show that with a 'never give up' attitude, no matter what life kicks in your face you can pick yourself up. You can brush yourself off; not necessarily to start all over again. To continue on the road of ambition with the 'want', 'need' and love to do something. Perhaps without understanding why you do it. Why do you do it? Why does anybody do it? I don't know, but for me the deal was done before I went 'pop', and that was September 2nd, 1963.

The Beatles were No.1 with "All You Need Is Love", and all I needed was love. All I wanted to give was love, and 59 years, one month and one day after that, all I want to do is to give love and to show what love is all about.

Someone said to me "If you get an opportunity in the future as a speaker you could express this sentiment to millions". That's my intention, but let me tell you, every day I'm stood on a stage and all I try to express is my love. No matter how I'm feeling, what's gone on, what is to come, how pissed off, depressed, or poor I am. It's a way people should also endeavour to interact with everyone and everything in the universe. Generally I do it through laughter, acting the goat, being silly. A lot of people notice what I'm doing underneath it all, many more don't. My thought processes that go on are all attempting to make something bigger, something better. It's good that a lot of it's not noticed. The subliminal awareness of people that have known me a long time, and even with passing strangers, allows a future penny drop moment.

Quite some time later, on 9th December 2008, Judge George Moorhouse slammed his hammer down on his maple gavel and declared that I should go to prison for seven years. I had my wife beside me. She got 15 months. Fifteen months of prison for doing nothing, but for being my wife. Some would have said that she should have got a medal for being my wife, but she didn't, she got 15 months in jail for money-laundering – they said. If being good at your job and getting paid for it is money-laundering, we should all be in prison, because that is all she did. As for me, what did I do? My 'crime' was finding out about a problem within the government. My 'crime' was not being quiet about it. My 'crime' was trying too hard to be someone a bit different, a bit more special. I will profess my innocence until the day I die.

After years on bail, years putting my defence case together and a 91-day trial, a seven-year prison sentence was given to me. I made a 45-minute pleading speech. It can be read in 'The Daily Mail'. They printed it almost word for word. They said I fell on my sword. I didn't. I was just pleading for freedom, for myself yes, but that was never going to happen. I was pleading for freedom for my wife and the protection of our children. What I'd said to the judge was, "Irrespective of what you want to do with me, please don't send my wife to prison because my children will suffer and my business customers will suffer."

Having both parents in prison at the same time isn't a good thing for anybody's children. It certainly wasn't a good thing for mine. I said to the judge, "Please don't send my wife to prison." I begged him. That's why they say I fell on my sword. They said – by begging – I admitted to the offences, which I didn't. They misinterpreted that. I was just pleading for my wife's freedom and for my children's protection. It went on for 45 minutes. Most people in the gallery, including the press, were crying. They could sense my passion, even if they couldn't sense my innocence. The loudest cry was from my brother-in-law. Looking back on it, I don't think he was crying for me. He was crying for his sister being sent to prison. And he did cry. He was sobbing. It was the loudest noise in the room.

After my little speech the judge said, "Have you finished?" I said, "Yes I have" and silently, with my eyes, I said, "Come on, do your worst". And he did. He said to me, "Stand up." I already was. He was really intimating for my wife to stand up to take her punishment, together with mine.

Three months earlier, 12 people were fooled. That's the jury, and they were fooled. Throughout my 91-day trial one young man, probably 18 to 20 years old, sat there sleeping with his hoody up. Seemingly they were all manipulated by one lady. If I could have a crystal ball, or a medium, or whatever, it would be one that could tell me something like this: I'm certain it would tell me that the lady foreman of the jury was planted there by the police.

It took the jury two minutes to find my co-defendants – apart from my wife – innocent. It took them six days to deliberate that I was guilty. The astonishing thing here is that my co-defendants had written all the cheques and had led the company for years. They were innocent and yet I was found guilty! Six days of deliberation tells me, reading between the lines, that not everybody on that jury thought I was guilty; that it was a split decision. However many, I'll never know; but it took them that long to come to a collective decision which the Court was happy to accept.

The connotations of me being found not guilty would have rocked the government. I had to be found guilty and so I was. So, after my begging speech, the judge said, "Stand up. Your business, your customers will suffer, your children will also suffer. I am sentencing you to seven years in prison, and you, Mrs Smallman, 15 months in prison. Take them down."

At that point I put my hand in my pocket and pulled out something that had sat there for quite some time. Something I have in all my pockets, in all my trousers, in the bread bin, in the car, wherever I went. It's invisible. It's what I call Mike's Magic. I take it out to help people. For the first real time in my life, I needed some myself. I pulled my hand out of my pocket, looked briefly at the Mike's Magic and bit a piece off and swallowed it. Really there was nothing there. Mike's Magic is a fictitious thing from a visual and tactile point of view. It's a state of mind, it's a remembering not to go down the hole. I ate a bit, swallowed it, and thought to myself "Right!". I turned to my wife and smiled at her. She was in shock. I said to her, "Don't worry, everything is going to be okay." Because it needed to be that.

She too, like me, didn't expect to go to prison. The body of evidence didn't suggest that we were guilty. In the end we were 'guilty' because the jury said so. These 12 people, totally uneducated in business, were fooled. They were manipulated by all in the Court: the prosecution barristers, the judge and even my own defence, who were weak to challenge salient points.

Now, this part of the book isn't about my innocence. It's just setting the scene for the things that had happened before, and after, the time when the judge smashed his hand down. As I said to my wife, "Everything will be fine", I smiled at her. We turned to each other and the prison officer handcuffed us together. The door was unlocked and we were politely asked to walk through it. We walked down about 60 concrete steps, into what could only be described as the dungeons of the Court. One step, very slowly walking down…no rush. We were handcuffed at the wrists, connected through steel. Holding hands, connected through flesh and skin, heart, sorrow and desperation. We connected in such a way that I couldn't feel the pain. Probably a little bit like when you have a limb chopped off. It might hurt the minute it gets chopped off but a couple of minutes later you can't feel it. The adrenaline is pumping around your body in such a way, it's killing all the pain.

We almost floated to where we were going next, not knowing what's going to happen. Not least what's going to happen to our children. For me, not knowing what's going to happen to my wife and, of course, not knowing what's going to happen to me. We took our time down those stairs so we could be together for as long as possible, holding hands, squeezing our hands tight. Then at the bottom the female prison officer smiled. I gave my wife a kiss and told her again: "It's going to be alright."

They took the handcuffs off. She went left and I went right. I presumed that what happened to me for the next hour or so also happened to her. They put me in a cell no bigger than a small toilet. It didn't have a toilet though. It had a bench with a newspaper on it. I opened the newspaper and on page four was the continuing story of me. It was 'The Sun' newspaper. I didn't read it. I already knew the end of it.

The door went. They asked me to come out. They catalogued my property: a pen, a little bit of money, cards, driving licence, phone, belt, clothes. They catalogued everything. They put me back in the cell for a couple of hours while we waited for the meat wagon, the bus, the transportation, call it what you will. Basically, it's a steel box with an engine and upright coffins in it.

The noise inside was horrendous. It was cold, it was cramped, and it was uncertain. There were obviously other people in the bus. The noise was them shouting at each other. They shouted about what they'd done, what they'd got and what they were going to do with the drugs they had up their arse. Shouting that they were going to make a small fortune. They thought it was good for them to be in prison. Possibly because they would only be in for a short time, and they could make some money.

The bus seemed to take forever to get to the prison. Then it stopped at the security gates. I could hear their radios. The gates came up like a big roller. The bus drove forward into a neutral area and the gates came down behind us.

Two officers came on the bus, counted all the people inside, me being one. I smiled at them, because there is one thing I'll always have, even underneath the frown is a smile. Always inside is a smile somewhere to be found. They started by unloading the lads that they knew that had been there before. One by one they unloaded them and marched them into the prison to start their process.

They left me to the last. I don't know why, but it seemed like forever. Even though it was probably only a minute or two. In that time I was sat in that coffin-like cubical. I was locked in with no space to stretch my legs or even stand up. I think that time must be a little bit like when you are on your last breath, when your whole life flashes in front of you. All 45 years of my life flashed in front of me: where I grew up, how I got to be in that meat wagon and everything between those years. I was in total and utter bewilderment.

I wondered about how a young lad from Manchester can go through all the things that I had been through in my life to end up in a prison coffin, waiting to be unpacked and repacked into the warehousing. That is what prison is, it's warehousing. It is not supposed to be purely punitive, but it is. It is supposedly restorative, but it isn't. Certainly not for most.

While I sat there in the meat wagon, waiting to be unpacked, I just couldn't comprehend how it had all happened. All I believed was that I had seven years to serve, and I couldn't understand why.

They opened the door to my meat wagon cubicle about two inches. There was a chain on the door, so it could be open just enough for me to put my arm out. They put a handcuff on it and then the other end of the handcuff was put on the prison officer. They unlocked the door and marched me out. Down two little steps, across a bit of tarmac where yellow lines were painted. I was told to walk between the yellow lines. Supposedly, if I didn't walk between the yellow lines

I was trying to escape. Or at least that's what I gathered; cos why else have the lines?

We went up four steps and turned right, into the reception. The other lads were being processed in front of us. I was the last one. The door slammed behind me, and it was locked. I could see the prison bus disappearing out of the window, and I could see the security. There was a big steel door to stop me walking out into this yard. Then there was a drawbridge-type door and a wall that seemed about 20 foot thick, with another drawbridge door at the other side of it. Around it all was razor wire — which apparently is illegal; it certainly is in Europe. Hey ho, I'm just a 'fraudster' and they need razor wire to keep me in. I'm not a fraudster but it does say so on the internet. It does say so in the documentation of the Courts. So I must be?!

The first thing the man said to me is "are you okay?".

So I got one of my smiles, smiled at him and said, "Of course I am."

He said, "Do you know how long you've got?"

I replied, "Yes, I've got seven years."

Then he said to me, "Do you know why you got it?"

I said, "Yes I do."

He asked, "Why? What was your offence?"

"There wasn't an offence," I replied.

So, he kept going. "No, come on. What was your offence?"

I said, "There wasn't an offence, but you can put the word *fraud* down."

He did.

He wrote it down and asked me to move into a square where they take a photograph. I was then moved to another square where they took my DNA with a swab. No, they didn't stick it where you might think. It was just on my cheeks on the inside — mouth cheeks, that is!

They took everything off me that I still had, which was not very much. I never had a watch. They asked me where my watch was, and I told them I didn't have one. They asked me if I was healthy and well. They put it all in. All the things that they needed to put in a book to create my prison file. Then they asked me to go and see the nurse.

The nurse asked if I was going to kill myself.

So, I said, "Why would I want to do that?"

"Well, people do. People who have got six weeks do. People who have life sentences for murder and are never going to get out do. So we ask it of everybody."

It was an assumption by society that everyone who is going to prison has a mental health problem and in that is a great irony. No mental health problems would be taken into consideration. Not in my case or in anybody else's that I'd meet in all my time in jail. We'd done a crime as far as the court was concerned. We just needed to be punished for it and the law says that the four walls of the prison is the punishment. It doesn't sentence you to what happens inside it though. What happens inside it is more punishment than you could ever wish to have. Not least being separated from the people you love and the life that you had built and wanted to continue to live. The punishment is your removal from freedom in society. What happens inside is supposed to be the restoration of you: the repair of your 'faulty character'. In reality, the punishment goes beyond the walls and is tainted with violence, bullying and degradation. It's laced with filth, drugs, and depression in every negative way you can imagine.

The nurse did her thing with me and took my blood pressure. It was through the roof. She said, "I'll check on that again tomorrow." She was a nice lady. She was called Karen and I got quite friendly with her over the years. Not in any relationship way, just in a friendly way.

I went back to the reception counter where another officer asked me if it was my first time. Although it wasn't — because I had done a few minor, silly things as a kid 25 years earlier — I said "It is".

He asked me to walk to the right where there were two prison lads who had got the job of handing out equipment: a blue plastic bowl, a white plastic knife and fork, a blue plastic cup and a blue plastic plate, a new toothbrush and a razor to shave with. I found out the next day the razor was that blunt you couldn't even spread butter with it if you tried.

I was then asked to go into a cubicle and take off all my personal clothing. They gave me some prison clothing: tracksuit bottoms and two stripe trainers — that's what they are called as they have two stripes on them, a bit like a little plimsoll or pump. Whilst I was naked I had to put all my things in a box. The box goes into storage for the day I was going to get out.

They asked me to bend over and they looked up the hole of my arse as if it was the eye of a telescope. It was as if they were going to see something on the other side. Obviously, the only thing that came out of my arsehole was sunlight. There were no drugs up there.

I put my stuff on. The trousers of the tracksuit were 18 sizes too big and the top of the tracksuit was about 18 sizes too small. It all made me look very odd. I wore them together with socks and underpants that around 50 blokes had worn before me. Let me tell you, it was soul-destroying. My dignity had gone out the window, along with the sunshine up my arse. Then they led us all off together for a night on the reception wing. We seemed to walk forever. It was a huge place. There was 1200 men there, or thereabouts. They were all naughty boys of every description: murderers, rapists, paedophiles, people who hadn't paid their speeding fines.

They took me to a wing and handed me over to another prison officer who was in charge of the wing. He opened the door to cell number 3. I walked inside and a young lad called Scott was sat in there. He was six foot four inches tall with muscles everywhere. He seemed alright. As they slammed the door behind me I noticed that there was excretion, snot and lots of writing up the walls. I looked at the mattress. There is no other way of describing it — it looked like it had been shat on four times, pissed on ten times and wanked on 500 times. It was disgusting. The officer came back and gave me a green sheet which wasn't that much better. I covered the mattress with it. There was no pillow, no blanket, no top sheet but I sort of made the best of it.

Scott said, "Hey mate, I saw you on the telly! All the lads saw you on the telly. They reckon you've got millions stashed. I bet you're gutted, aren't you? I bet you're really gutted."

Instinctively I just said, "Yes, I am. Totally and utterly gutted!"

I was braving it out – being the hard man. Inside I was falling to bits.

He said, "You got seven years, didn't you? Do you know that you've got to do the whole of the seven years?" He was lying to me, but I didn't know it at the time. I believed him.

So, there's me thinking I've got seven years to do and how could I live in a shit-hole like this for seven years? Furthermore, how could I go without seeing my family for that length of time? Without seeing and doing all the things I loved.

He kept saying: "All that money you had! All those cars! All that property! Everything! I bet you're gutted." I was, but it wasn't because I'd lost all those things. It was because I'd lost my family. All I wanted was my family back. I just wanted my little girl Grace back. I wanted my son Christopher and my wife. I was thinking to myself, what if my wife, Angela, is in a room like I'm in, with shit and snot up the walls and God knows what in the bed? I didn't think about the money, the property or anything. I just thought about my family. What was going to happen to them? What was going to happen to us as a family? So I laid down on the bed and just stared at the bunk above. Scott was fidgeting.

There was a bonus – well, almost a bonus. 'Coronation Street' came on the telly. There was a twelve-inch telly in the room. Everybody has one, to keep you quiet, to entertain you, to take the edge off everything. I watched 'Coronation Street' as if I was at home. I was blanking out the 91 days of the trial and the years and years and years of preparing for the trial. I forgot, just briefly, that I was there for seven years.

I fell asleep. It was probably only for a couple of hours before I woke up again. Scott was doing something. I realised that he was actually lying under his bed. It was a metal tubular framed bed on a different bunk to me. It was a grey-pinky colour with chips all over it and it had pen marks where people had written their names. I sat up in bed thinking, I'm sure he was above me a minute ago, but no, now he was under the other bed in the room.

There were three beds, one single and one with a bunk and a window that couldn't be opened. It had a dirty great big crack in it. There was a heating pipe about six inches long in diameter. It ran the length of the back of the room and into the next cell. Over the years people had chipped away at the wall where the pipe went through it to next door. Scott was shouting through it to the next-door neighbour in the next cell. "Have you got any, mate?" Or words like that.

I'm thinking, have you got any what?

A lad next door says "Yeah" and pushed something through.

The ingenuity of it! If you can imagine a six-inch round pipe going through a wall with a little gap at the top, about a quarter of an inch. How do you push something through that? He unrolled a toilet roll and, like a train, he slowly slipped it through the gap until it poked through into the next door's cell. The lad next door gently pulled it all the way through. It was still attached to the main toilet roll. At the other end he placed 'whatever it was' on top of the toilet roll and folded it in half. He shouted to Scott, "Go on, you can pull it!"

Scott slowly pulled the toilet roll back, which dragged 'whatever it was' into our cell. I'm thinking wow! Nine inches of concrete between two cells and he's just broken into next door's cell with a piece of toilet roll and brought back some goodies. I'm watching this and, to be honest, it had distracted me from my grief because it was so fascinating.

Next he sits in a metal framed chair and gets a spoon out. He shouldn't have had it; you're only allowed plastic ones, but he had a metal one.

After he had broken up whatever it was, I presumed heroin, he heated it with a lighter and asked me if I wanted some. He then got a syringe from a cigar tube that was up his backside and sucked the juice up from the spoon. He injected himself in the arm. He asked me again if I wanted some, and I said, "No, mate. It's not my sort of thing."

He said, "Oh well, never mind" and then he spent the next four or five hours crushing up tablets, anything that he could find. Maybe they were Paracetamol or Ketamine. It was whatever he could get hold of. Strange, isn't it? He was injecting it, snorting it, smoking it, and all I could think is what the fucking hell am I doing in here?

At that point I thought to myself, 'What do I do? Where do I go? How do I do it? How do I get out of here?' I thought how I was going to appeal and take it around the world. How I would blow the world up and burn down the Houses of Parliament. Anything to get me out of here.

Seven o'clock in the morning the door opened. Every door opened on this little wing of 40 men. All of them had been in prison for just a couple of days. They had come directly from the courts. Everybody started off on this wing. There was no discrimination. It was the same for all of us, no matter what they had done. All were just a number next to a surname that was chalked on the wall on the outside of the cell.

Scott says, "It's breakfast. Get your plate."

Everybody walked down to a hatch serving the grub. To be honest it wasn't too bad: egg, bacon and tomatoes, lovely! As you pass with your plate, they slap your food on it. God knows what body fluids it had in it. Then you take it back to your cell and have it on your bed. Sometimes you eat it while your cell mate has a shit four inches away from the bedhead because that's where the toilet was. There was absolutely no privacy. You're chewing their smell when you're chewing your food. So, when I needed a shit, I would hold onto it for as long as I could, but when you've got to go – you've got to go. Sometimes I would manage to have a shit when my cellmate was asleep or was called out of the cell. It was a little bit like having a baby. You don't want to have to push your child out of your bits with everyone looking at your bits and messing with them, but it's got to be done. So all dignity goes out of the window. I suppose it's a bit like that anyway. Having a shit in front of someone you don't know, while they are having their breakfast. So that morning I just ate it right there and then.

Eleven o'clock comes and me and Scott had held a few conversations, nothing very dramatic. Underneath his drugs and his criminality that surrounded his drug problem, he was a nice lad. I learned in the years to come, that pretty much all of them were nice lads. They had a mum and they loved their mum. They had a dad and they loved their dad. Those that didn't have a dad wanted a dad. Some wished they hadn't been abused and let down by society. They wished they hadn't been brought up by the wrong person and they wished all sorts of things. There they were, in there with the drugs and all the criminality and they were stuck in it. The system is supposed to be restorative — but as I say, it isn't.

The door opened and they wanted me. I was thinking, fucking hell, why don't they just leave me in here? Even though I was with a hardened criminal, who was built like a brick crap house, who had drugs in every orifice of his body, I felt safe. Now I had to come out there into the big wide world of the prison! I found out it was just the nurse to check my blood pressure. It was still sky high.

After that they took me to another wing. They asked me to pack up all my kit and I'm thinking where am I going now? They told me I was going to C wing in House Block 1. On my way there I was passing people, officers, inmates, civilian staff. One or two of the inmates said, "Have you just come in?"

I said, "Yeah, I've just come in."

They asked, as I was walking past them, "Where are you going?"

I said, "House Block 1, C wing" and they'd say "oh my God! Don't go in there! Don't let them put you in there!".

I thought, Why? I was filled with ideas as to what could be in there.

What was in there could only be described as Hell. There was about a hundred men. All most of them wanted to do was take drugs, fight – fight anybody, it didn't matter who it was – and make noise that would penetrate your soul. Hundreds of decibels of shouting, bawling, screaming, arguing, fighting and clunking. Everything was just mayhem!

They locked me up on my own. One of the officers said, "You don't come out of your cell on your first day, you'll be out again tomorrow."

I just lay on the bed thinking what am I doing here? I didn't believe it. I couldn't believe it was happening to me. There was no justification for it. Where did I go wrong? What did I physically do? How could it be like this?

About six o'clock at night they opened the door. I thought I wasn't supposed to be coming out, so I stayed in the cell. I was lying on my bed in my prison kit; boots on – which were two sizes too small. I was wondering if should I go out? It was like there was a thousand chickens outside; squawking, fighting, creating all sorts of mayhem…. so I stayed in my cell with the door open about a foot and a half.

After about 20 minutes it went dark, like someone had turned the lights off. They hadn't. There was just the most ginormous man that I'd ever seen in my life stood in my doorway. He was bigger than the doorway. The next thing I noticed was that he had only half an ear. A big chunk had been bitten out of it. I could still make out the teeth marks. Someone had nibbled at the other ear as well. I have since found out that the person doing the biting is the one losing and needs to do something drastic to get back on top.

He had hands three times the size of mine and I'm a fairly big fella, but this man was an absolutely ginormous man. He had one of those faces, enough to scare a lion. He looked as hard as hardness could be. He looked like he could bite my head off, literally. He was horrible. He was huge. He left the door open and took a pace forward into the cell. He told me that he had seen me on the telly and in newspapers. He said he had followed the trial and he knew that I had millions stashed but he didn't want the millions he thought I had. He just wanted the goods that I could buy. In a UK prison there are pieces of paper with a list of about a hundred things you can buy if you've got any money: cigarettes, sweets, chocolate, crisps, the odd bits and bobs, stamps and stuff. He told me this 'thing' was coming in the morning; this piece of paper under the door. He said, "Fill it in. Don't get anything you want; get the things I want." He told me if I didn't get the things that he wanted – basically tobacco – that he would give me a 'prison smile'. He called it a 'Holme House smile'. That's the prison I was in, but it happens in all prisons. As he said it, he pulled out his prison toothbrush, which in the back of it had two razor blades melted into it. They were about four millimetres apart. He suggested that if I didn't do what he wanted, he would cut me from ear to ear. It couldn't ever be stitched up because the distance between the two blades was too small and it would leave a slither of skin between them.

What he didn't know was that I was brought up on the streets on Moss Side and I'd seen hell. He didn't know that I was – let's say – exceptionally streetwise on the outside world. He just thought I was a big, fat, softy businessman who he could intimidate. He didn't know, but I knew who I was. I never forgot who I was. I never forgot that I had a paedophile messing with me for four years, or a bully for a similar amount of time, breaking most of the bones in my body. There was no way on this fucking earth that he was going to take over from them.

As I was lying on the bed, I was very vulnerable. If I had stood up and matched him face to face, he would have killed me because he really was massive. I had one leg off the bed, with my two-sizes-too-small prison boot on. They are made of very hard plastic, very uncomfortable to wear but very hard, brown, shit brown, not even a nice brown.

He was staring at me for a few seconds, waiting for me to say something. I said to him "I don't want no trouble mate, I'm in here for seven years. I just want to sleep it all away, and, to show good faith, there's a box underneath my bed at the end, it's got two Dairy Milks in it."

He thought it was my way of showing good faith – to take his threats in order that he wouldn't beat me up, cut me, pull all my teeth out, or whatever he was going to do. That's what he thought, but it wasn't really. There was no chocolate in the box. I just wanted him to bend down so I could put my prison boot right up his nose. I lifted my right leg so fast and so hard. With the force of his body weight coming down, and the force of my boot going up, I hit him right between his lips and his nose. He just fell on the floor totally unconscious. There was blood everywhere — all over my foot, all over my green prison trousers, which five hundred people had worn before me. There was blood up the door, up the wall, on my bed, everywhere. He came around within a second or so and shuffled himself out of my cell. That was a relief, cos I think if he had got up, I might have been dead. He was very big.

After he went out, I slammed the door shut and it locked. I don't even know what happened to him after that, not properly anyway. I just got a towel and wiped up all the blood and lay on my bed. Thirty-six hours in jail and already I might kill somebody, how's it going to go? Am I going to get the block? I didn't even know what the block was, apart from what I've seen on the television. What's going to happen? Am I going to get another ten years?

The little flap on the door opened about half past eight. There was an officer out there. I think it was an SO (Senior Officer) and he says, "Are you alright?"

I just went, "Yeah, I'm fine." I found him a smile. "Is he alright?"

He replied, "He's in the hospital at the minute."

"Am I going to be in trouble?"

He said, "No, the bastard deserved it 'cos he does it to everybody." He went away and shut me flap.

I learned over time that an officer that leaves your flap open has a heart. It's just a flap three inches wide by about eight inches tall with double security glass in — not that you could crawl through it if you smashed the glass — but it still had security glass in. They leave it open because it lets a little bit of light into your life. A little bit of light so you can see what's going on out on the wing, see who's out there. It extends your life out from the prison cell in the room, into the main body of the wing. It's an act of kindness to leave the flap open, and conversely, it's an act of bitterness, of nastiness, to shut it. Shutting it is like trapping you back in there again and you can't look out, can't see the people that you've gotten to know.

Two minutes later he returns, opens up the flap and he says, "Mr Smallman, he's alright, he's back, you broke his nose. You're going to be alright you are, you'll be alright."

That was probably the nicest thing that anybody had ever said to me. I didn't believe I was going to be alright up until that point, but now I knew I was because he told me I was, I could look after myself. He walked away, leaving my cell flap open.

The third day, my second full day in Holme House, there was nowhere to go and nothing to do. The television was on. God! I had a crush on Linda Bellingham for some reason, I don't know why. She was on at four o'clock every day. She was there on the TV, keeping me company, with all the other ladies in that programme. I forget what it's called now... 'Loose Women', yeah that was it. Anyway, six o clock at night the door opened and there was a railing which I could look over. I didn't realise I was three floors up and you could see all the other two floors below, into what looked like the bowels of a ship but with nothing in it, or a submarine maybe. Quite claustrophobic. I could see all the men, darting about, one or two playing pool, a couple fighting, others exchanging drugs and stuff.

I looked up across the space between the landings and he was there, a very big bloke with a bit missing out of his ear and the biggest plaster you could ever wish to see on his face and all across his nose.

CHAPTER ONE - THE HOLE

I thought, 'fucking hell, I'm going to die in a minute!' Just then he walked over, but he walked over with a lot of calmness, he wasn't angry, not at all. He came over and shook my hand. He was called Kevin and we had found real good solidarity. I can't say we were friends because I've never seen him since I come out and friends you would do, but we had a solidarity. I had such an effect on that man's life that he stopped hurting and bullying people after sitting in my cell, having coffee and talking his life away. But that's for another book.

CHAPTER TWO
- THE TWO STEVOS

I t was seven o'clock in the morning on the fourth day. It was a Friday. All the cells had been unlocked. The men who had got jobs in the prison had all been led out to where they had to go. The ones in education were left in their cells for another two hours. After that, everyone who didn't have somewhere to go or a job to do got locked up again. My door was opened, and I was told that I had a job. I was to be a wing cleaner.

There were two other wing cleaners on the wing. Both called Stevo, because their last names were Stevenson. They were only distinguishable by their size: short-fat Stevo and skinny Stevo. Short-fat Stevo had a wife and a kid but was just a kid himself really. He was in for six weeks and was getting out in a week's time. It was a bit of a holiday for him. Skinny Stevo had been in all his life; in and out, in and out, like a fiddler's elbow. He was a psychopath, he just hadn't killed anybody yet, as far as I knew.

So here we are on the wing, we were the three wing cleaners. Let me tell you if there ever was such a juxtaposition of attitudes between two people the next 24 hours demonstrated it between me and skinny Stevo.

Everyone's locked up on the wing, but as cleaners we were allowed to stay out. Continuous mopping, mopping, mopping, with some more mopping – just so we didn't get locked behind the door. It was like having some sort of control and the wand of control was the mop. What a wonderful mop! All that was needed to be out of the cell and not be locked in was a mop, and a bucket of course. Nothing was really needed in the bucket. Looking busy was the main thing. If you looked busy, they didn't really mind. Every 20 minutes or so we could go and sit on our beds and have a cup of prison tea. I could only just stomach the stuff; it was horrible. It tasted like the scrapings of dandruff off someone's head, swept up off the floor for added flavour before making a tea bag with it – and yes, I know what that tastes like cos I've licked someone's head before.

The canteen was due to be delivered later that morning. That's the canteen that the big bloke with the poorly nose tried to take off me. I had chocolate coming, coffee coming, some yummy Tetley tea bags, a bag of sweets, two packets of biscuits and the all-important writing pad and ten stamps. It's all I could have, and it all came to bang on £15, which was the amount of money I was allowed to spend. It was an event like Christmas.

Just before the delivery was due, we all got banged up behind the doors and then some key people — just like Santa's helpers who were prisoners — would work with the guards to distribute the plastic bags. Every bag was sealed, with all the goods in. I just had to wait and wait, while a hundred bags on the wing (that's 1200 bags for the whole of the prison) were put outside of the cell doors. Once they were all distributed, the two lads that were helping would get behind their cell with their bag. They were allowed to take it in themselves because they were already out. Then one by one a prison officer would unlock a door for 20 seconds to allow a prisoner to get their plastic bag filled with the goodies: biscuits, coffee, stamps and tobacco, if you smoked. I could hear him go to the cell next door to me...and I'm next. Stamps! I could write to me wife; I could write to me kids! But he just walked past. There was no bag for me. I didn't know why. Maybe I got my canteen sheet in too late, or it got lost, or they just forgot to put it out. Anyway, as he walked past and didn't unlock my cell, I started to bang on the door, which is something I thought I'd never do. After three days of everybody else banging on the doors I'd been thinking fucking hell, I'll never do that! They're idiots! And there's me banging on the cell door like one of the idiots. The screw that had walked past opened my flap and said, "What you banging the door for?"

So I replied, "Where's me canteen?"

He said, "There's none for you."

I've got to say right then, me not getting a couple of biscuits, me jar of coffee, a little carton of milk, a bag of sweets, the stamps, a couple of pens and me writing paper was more devastating than the judge giving me seven years in prison. At least when the judge gave me seven years in prison and my wife 15 months, while still holding her hand, there was no contemplation of what was happening to me. But now I knew, my little hole or escape route to the outside world in a letter with a first-class stamp on it, wasn't there. It would be another week before I had another chance of getting a stamp, or some phone credit on the card to make a call to see how my kids were.

I was devastated to tears. I sat on me bed thinking I really was on my own. There's nothing. I can't talk to anybody. I can't write a letter. I can't tell my wife her how much I love her and how sorry I am that she's in this mess. I can't tell my kids that everything's going to be alright... fine and dandy.

Some time went by and there's me feeling sorry for myself. All the lads had got their bags in. It was about an hour before lunch so they let the cleaners out. That meant me, short-fat Stevo and skinny Stevo were let out to mop the floor again and again, and again, and again. Both Stevos could tell that I was down, and I really was. I wasn't six foot one and a bit anymore, I was four foot two. My chin was on the floor and me heart was out me backside. It wasn't just because I didn't get a bag full of goodies; it was more than that. It was that link to the outside world had gone. They asked me what was wrong, and I told them, just what I've told you, that I didn't get me canteen bag and I can't write to me wife, can't write to me kids, can't write to me sister, can't do this, can't do that, can't do the other and can't even have a fucking cup of tea or coffee.

I'm sat on me bed, and they are stood there just listening to me and then me name gets shouted. "Smallman, go to the gate!" I'm thinking fucking hell, they've found me canteen! So, I ran to the gate. They hadn't found my canteen; I just had a doctor's appointment that I didn't know about. So I was at the doctor's all of lunchtime. The men had got their meals. The staff brought me a sandwich while I was in the hospital wing waiting to see this doctor. Just as a point of funniness, if there is such a word, he was called Doctor Death. That was his name. He was a nice fella. He says, "Do you want something for your blood pressure?" and I says, "No, it's just cos I'm wound up with all that's happening and I don't want no drugs".

Doctor Death sent me back to the cell after lunch. There was only one cell open, my cell. The other two cleaners hadn't been let out of their cells. The screw that was organising the wing on that afternoon said, "We're not going to lock you up, just get your mop and we will let the other two lads out later." As I walked into my cell, I saw there was a white plastic carrier bag on the bed, folded. It was obvious there were things inside it but on the fold it said, 'from Holme House Salvation

Army'. I opened it and there were six stamps, half a bar of chocolate, some ginger nuts, half a jar of coffee, a pen (which was chewed at the end), some sweets of around 20 different varieties, half a packet of polo mints and a full writing pad and some envelopes.

The Salvation Army didn't work in the prison. Stevo and Stevo, over lunch, had gone around the wing to the hundred or so men that they could get access to and told them my story. No doubt skinny Stevo did the talking cos short-fat Stevo was frightened of his own shadow. These were criminals of every shape and size, murderers, bank robbers and drug dealers, but one thing I learnt that day is that it doesn't matter who you are, what you have done, you are still a human being. At least if you can call yourself a human being that means you've got humanity, and not just humanity, camaraderie. All of us being in the same boat, all (for the most part) were looking after each other. On that day, at that moment in time, I pledged to myself that the seven years I still believed I had to serve, I was going to do it whilst helping as many people as I possibly could.

It was Stevo and Stevo that had done the leg work, but all the lads that they had access to had put something in if they had something spare. All the lads in the wing, all those 'nasty, horrible' people that some people say should be kept in there forever, had shown humanity, camaraderie and love to some extent. Let me tell you now, the feeling of relief that I could have some goodies, that I could write to my children and wife was enormous, but the overwhelming feeling was that I had friends, people who were looking after me. Needless to say, the way I eat chocolate, sweets and biscuits, it was all gone very quickly.

I spent hours writing letters on that pad; I even kept the cover for about ten years, but I lost it along the way. I wish I hadn't. Inside the cover and on the back of the pad I had drawn lines. Each day was a single line for the days of a month, and I turned each line into a little picture. If it was Christmas Day I'd turn the line into a Christmas tree or, on my birthday, I'd turn it into a smiley face; same with the kids' birthdays. Every day I'd draw a poor drawing of something to represent it. When one lad hung himself with a sheet, I drew a noose and when another lad slashed himself I drew a razor blade. Each little line on the cover of my writing pad became a visual diary. I had no dates on them but there was a story behind each little line of what happened on that day. If I was having a visitor, I would put it as a V. Every day I counted them, sometimes many times a day to see if I'd miscounted and might have a day less to do, but funnily enough there was always one less every day. One-thousand, two-hundred and twenty-seven days of my sentence – and that was only half of it!

Luckily enough for me, the other joyous thing, alongside getting my Salvation Army bag, there was a note passed under me cell door signifying my release date. It wasn't seven years. I only had to do half of it. So, within an hour of receiving that little bag of goodies I'd had my sentence reduced by half! Wow. That half a day took me through the next three and a half years, and probably still takes me through some parts of my life today. I was dancing and that's why I only did 1227 lines cos that's what it's calculated that I had to serve.

The next day the lads had gone out to work – the ones that had jobs. Me and the Stevos were out in the wing mopping and mopping and mopping. At one point we stood on the 'threes' (the landings) and we were there just chatting. I turned to short, fat Stevo and said, "Can you smell something burning?" He sniffed and said he could. Then I turned to skinny Stevo and he wasn't there. He'd moved along to get out my way because it was me who was on fire! He'd set the bottom of me prison sweatshirt on fire and there were flames as high as me shoulder! Luckily enough for me I had a thick T-shirt on underneath and, before it set me on fire, I was able to pull the sweatshirt off and throw it over my head and over the railings. It hit the metal nets that were there to stop officers being thrown over and hitting the ground floor, which could have killed them.

That's the juxtaposition I was talking about: from absolute abject wonderfulness, camaraderie, call it what you like, to a psychopath. There was no real reason to do it. He did it just cos he could do it. He wanted to just because he found it funny. I don't think he had any intention of hurting me, but he probably felt he could bully me a little bit. Anyway, I chased him around and couldn't catch him. Screws shouted from their observation point, 50 metres away – there were cameras everywhere. "Stop fucking about and get back in your pad!" They knew something was going on.

After about half an hour they let us out again to do some more mopping. One of the luxuries of being a cleaner is when all the lads are locked behind the doors, you've got the wing to yourself and, if you've got a decent officer on, they don't mind whether you're mopping or not. As long as you're not messing about and causing trouble you can go and have a game of pool or snooker cos the table is in the middle of the wing.

Me and short-fat Stevo were having a game and I was stood up, waiting to take my shot while Stevo was taking his shot. I suddenly felt a pressure around my neck. Skinny Stevo had pulled himself up on the wire nets and got his legs and boots wrapped around my throat. He was trying to choke me and was doing it quite successfully. My eyes were rolling back in me head. I don't know where I got the presence from, but I put one hand on the sole of his shoe and the other on his toes and I twisted his ankle round as far as I could take it and it snapped. The pain must have been horrendous for him. He let go of the wire above and fell backwards. His weight pulled his boot off his foot leaving it in my hand and he scurried away to the other side of the pool table with his broken ankle. I was going to kill him. I'd had enough. I was outraged. I had gone beyond losing my temper, but in the few seconds it took me to get to the other side he had scurried further away, just giving me the few moments that I needed to calm myself down. I swore at him an awful lot and I went and locked myself up in me pad.

Eight o'clock at night, or thereabouts, the same SO as before came to my door and said, "He's back from the hospital. You broke his ankle and it's going to take some time to mend" and again he said, "Mr Smallman, you're going to be alright!". We both had a little chuckle and he added, "The little bastard deserved it anyway."

During that single day the juxtaposition from being choked to death and set on fire by the same person who had instigated, or at least partly instigated, my goodie parcel, shows that you don't ever know who you're with or how they're going to behave. Nevertheless, I was alright. The screw once again told me so and I was alright because I didn't have a broken ankle. I also got a brand spanking new sweatshirt out of it, which was a little bit of luxury. It didn't fit but it was clean and no one else had worn it, which was a big bonus.

In the prison the laundry system is not one that protects any ownership of any item. What you had to do with your dirty washing is throw it over the balcony onto the nets. Two lads would then go and pick it off the nets. I would never know what I was going to get back. Because I now had a brand new sweatshirt, even though it got dirty, I would never throw it over the nets. I just washed it in the sink and put it on my pipe to dry. I knew that I was the only person ever to wear that sweatshirt and I didn't ever let it go. Until three and a half years later, upon my release, it was my sweatshirt. Over time it got smaller and smaller and so did I. I lost three stone. I used to have muscles everywhere. God knows where they've gone now.

One of my jobs as a cleaner was to climb over the railings and go onto the nets and collect all the washing. Once a week we would pick up hundreds of pairs of jeans and t-shirts and sheets. We used to bundle each separate item in their piles into the sheets making a huge bail of jeans or whatever. We'd then drag them off the wing into a benign area which was like a very wide hallway between offices. All the wing cleaners from all ten wings would bring their bails of washing and together we would assign each bail into mountains of separate pieces of clothing and bed linen. The good thing about this was it got me off the wing for an hour and I would meet lads off other wings which is an advantage to security. Knowing people from all over the prison was a priority for safety, especially when in the gym or other communal areas. The bad thing about sorting all the washing was the likelihood of catching scabies or some other nasty disease, and many of the lads did.

Sorting the washing wasn't fun. Some pieces were covered in shit and body fluids of all types; there was absolute filth within the jeans, the t-shirts and other garments. But imagine this, just like a person from a third world country picking through the rubbish to try and make a living, we were there picking through this rancid washing trying to find better kit to wear than we had ourselves; something that wasn't as worn or something that fitted. So perhaps being set on fire to get a new sweatshirt was worth it after all. Thanks, Stevo.

CHAPTER THREE –
THE PISS TEST

A fter three months in Holme House, a very tall screw-like gentleman tells me to pack my bags. I was moving to a new prison. In my heart of hearts I'd hoped I was going to the open prison at Kirklevington, even though I'd only been in a couple of months. I wasn't. They were moving me a greater distance away from my family, because I was shouting about my innocence to everybody who'd listen to me. They wanted me out of the way. The only good thing about it was they were moving me to a category C prison. Let me explain. If you are a very, very naughty boy like a murderer or a big drug dealer or you've got more than ten years to serve you are very likely to get sent to a category A prison, directly from your category B. All cat B prisons, in general, service the courts. So, whether you're a big, bad person or a little softy one, you're going to start off in a Cat B prison when you first get sent down. Now a Cat A prison is the highest of high securities; all doors everywhere are locked. You're likely to have dogs on the wing – not just sniffer ones – but ones with big teeth. You're likely to live there for a very long time, so long that you're able to access extra facilities, such as the ability to cook for yourself. You may share a cooker with a couple of other inmates, a proper cooker, or a deep fat fryer or some other kitchen appliances that are kept in an area on the wing. Needless to say, because of the type of criminal, many a time the odd face or hand will have been shoved into the deep fat fryer.

During the time I was in a Cat B I was thinking that they were sending me to a softer prison than one, cos a million horrible things had happened at Holme House in that first couple of months. I went down to the reception and picked up all my stuff. They signed me out. The screw got my file, and I was locked into the coffin-bus one more time. I was off to a place called Everthorpe, a Cat C near Hull. Now a Cat C is just like a Cat B with regards to the security, but you have a little tiny bit more freedom. Generally speaking, they are working prisons. Everybody has to do a job or follow an education while they are in there.

It seemed to take forever to get there. The coffin stopped off at another prison to pick someone else up. Cramp was setting into my legs because of the confined conditions. It was awful. There were three prison officers on the bus, together with four other lads. I didn't know any of them. When we arrived we were taken off one at a time. I was the last. The screw on reception seemed to be a nice sort of fellow. The first thing he said was, "we only use first names here, mine's Richard, welcome to Everthorpe".

It was a shithole. Total utter shithole, but it seemed like the place to be. To some extent it was! Even though I'd only just arrived and had no experience of the place, there was a good feeling about it. Yet, unluckily for me being the last one off the bus, the fifth one, it meant that I had to have a piss test. Absolutely my worst nightmare. The prison officer could see the dread in my face and explained to me that he was sorry, but went on to say, "you are number five and yes, it's you that has to take the test".

They test you to see if you've got any type of drugs in your system that shouldn't be there. Because of my history – of performing in front of men so to speak – it was almost impossible for me to have a piss on demand. It seemed that my appendage for peeing just did not work. I could have drunk 20 gallons of water and still wouldn't have delivered any piss. Before I knew it two hours had gone by. Richard, the screw, wasn't getting annoyed, but was a bit fed up as I think he was wanting his dinner. I could have a piss anywhere in private. I could go in the prison, when everybody's disappeared, but I was in this little room about three foot by two foot, with nothing in it but a toilet, me and a little plastic cup to collect 40 or 50 ml or more of piss. Richard the prison officer wasn't in the room. There was a tiny little observation window that meant someone was watching me. It was there to make sure I didn't take a pre-prepared bottle of piss, from up my arse, that had been collected earlier in the day from a non-drug taker.

If I'd have got my appendage and wrung it out, nothing would have come out of it cos I couldn't deliver while they were watching. They watch you through mirrors or slits in the door and they watch you pissing — if you can piss, that is!

Three hours had gone by, still nothing. Three hours and 45 minutes had gone by and the screw kept coming in and feeding me water. He says, "I can't feed you anymore because it dilutes the drugs in your body — if you've got any drugs in your body that is." I'm thinking, 'Oh my God, what am I gonna do?' I'd missed my lunch and I'd been told food at Everthorpe it was much, much better than it was at Holme House. In reality it turned out to be a lot worse, if that was possible.

Four hours and 20 minutes passed. Twenty minutes more than I was legally allowed to have to deliver a bit of piss. All this, just to see if I'd taken something – drugs that many prisoners used to bide the time away, to quash their sentence, to get hooked upon, to choke on their vomit, or whatever else they did.

After four and a half hours, the screw had had enough so he had a choice to make. His first option was to send me back to Holme House because I'd broken the rules...*You can't come into this nice, Cat C, prison because you have 'refused' to deliver*...How can they say that you've refused when you just simply can't piss because you've got a psychological problem? I can't even piss in a public toilet, unless I go in a cubicle. I can't stand next to men having a piss, let alone being watched. Anyway, this screw was a nice screw and he chose his second option. He pulled his appendage out and whilst I was holding the little plastic cup he pissed in it and says "that'll do nicely"!

Before he sent me on my way, we filled in two forms. I signed to say that it was my piss. We had a little laugh together and I said, "I'm sorry I couldn't fill the cup." He knew I wasn't being awkward. He had been doing this job for nearly 30 years. He understood the things that make you wanna stop pissing and things that make you wanna start pissing and he did his best to get something outta me. He had fed me gallons of water. The irony of it was that he had put his job on the line for me, cos if anybody had found out what he'd done – and his real name wasn't Richard by the way – he'd have got the sack and maybe even imprisonment himself. But because he had been fed up of waiting for me and, furthermore, being a decent, intelligent man he could clearly see that I had no drugs inside me. He could tell that I was stressed with the situation, and he was kind enough not to take the piss out of me (literally!).

Sometime later, about three o'clock in the afternoon, another screw came along and marched me off to a cell on the induction wing. It was quite clean. I was surprised. It was mayhem just like the other place, but even bigger. There was around 120 men or more on this wing. They had all just arrived in Everthorpe. It was total chaos. They locked me up and my flap was shut. I spent the next half an hour on and off the bog. Pissing out gallons of the water Richard had fed me. I knew no one was watching me now. All I could do was piss and piss and piss. If you've ever held your piss for long enough, you'll know what that's like but when you've held your piss, even though you wanted to get rid of it, and tried your darndest but you couldn't, the relief when you can is massive. It was an elation! I also knew I wasn't going to have another piss test for a couple of months at least. They were supposed to be random, but I don't think they were.

I was on that wing for about six weeks. I met a few people and made a few friends. My reputation of being an all-round superstar and good egg had come with me in the file from Holme House. After six weeks or so, we – all on the induction wing – got moved on. A screw came in and took me out of the cell. He tells me I'm going to the new wing and that in the meantime I'd become an 'enhanced' prisoner. A prisoner who's really nice, really good, gets to be 'enhanced', which means you get to go to an 'enhanced' wing: E wing. In an E wing you might be able to make a piece of toast in 'association time', which is out-of-cell time, if you can get to it before the other 120 men blow the toaster up!

To my surprise and dismay, he marched me from the 'enhanced' wing, onto B wing. B, ironically, was for Beirut. It was absolute chaos, it was awful. They took me inside the wing into the SO's office and I was complaining that I shouldn't be going in here. They asked me if I would just go in and have a word with the SO. She opened the door for me and asked me to sit down and she said, "Mr Smallman, you've come with a reputation that all the lads like you, you've got a lot of respect from the officers, and you seem to have a calming influence on people. So please don't go to E wing, but you can if you want to." She explained: "Stay here on B wing, you'll be a great influence on the wing because we can't control it properly. There's bullying, there's stabbings, there's fights, there's drug dealing and there's all sorts of mayhem." They really couldn't control the lads on the wing, it was too chaotic.

She said if I stayed on B wing, as a bonus I could have any job that I wanted. She suggested that I could have the job as wing painter, so I could stay out of my cell almost all day, help myself to their coffee, have a brew… it'd be easy on the wing. I said to her, "Love, I don't even paint my own house so I ain't fuckin' painting yours." She said, "What do you want to do?" I said, "I want to be in the gardens."

Not to go on about it too much at this point, but within half an hour I'd got a job in the gardens. I started on the Monday and made such an impact on the gardens over the next nine months that they won the Windlesham Trophy that year. The Windlesham Trophy is a reputable Royal Horticultural Society (RHS) award. As a result, the prison was asked by the RHS to develop a show garden for the Tatton Park garden show which is one of the most prestigious garden shows in the country. I was asked to lead the way. I can say this, with safety now, that me and Mr Jackson, the garden screw, sat in his office and I dictated all the begging letters to industry and government departments. We wanted to raise the £70,000 that was needed to design and build the garden. We got enough support in response to those letters and the garden went on to win a gold award and best-in-show in Tatton Park 2009.

The knives in the bridge design were donated from the local Police.

The newspaper stories don't say my name for legal reasons, but they praise Mr Jackson, aka Jacko, for its development and design. He left the service and went on to become a top landscape gardener and well done to him! The prison couldn't leave me out of it, however, because I was obviously such a big part of it. So they printed a book specifically for me. In the book were all the departments and industrial companies that contributed to the garden financially and with products. The front cover — which is all I have left of this book — says it all about my involvement.

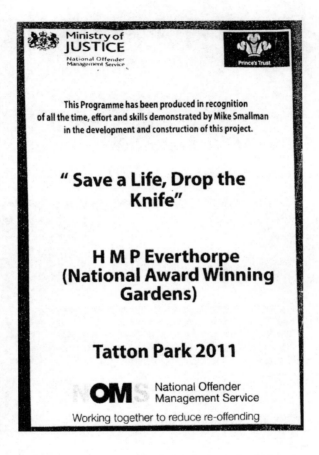

Being a former entrepreneurial businessman, I had the organisational skills to calm a war zone. I came up with a plan that suited everybody. This meant they could still trade in their drugs and tobacco, and get paid, without having to apply violence and intimidation to get the money. I suppose business on the inside isn't that much different to business on the outside. I won't go into details but within days the wing became much quieter, almost no fighting, almost no bullying and it was a great wing to be on. I was to be in there for 18 months with a hundred-and-one stories to tell, but again, it's not for now. I had my appeal going at the time and after about nine months on this particular wing I got shipped out to Pentonville — the prison that services the appeal courts. Eleven hours in the coffin to get there. Eleven hours of absolute hell.

Pentonville was an even bigger shithole. The wing that I was placed in had 750 men and I was the only white one. For the first time in my life I was able to see things from the perspective of a minority. The two prisons I'd been in before were very much predominantly white people. I felt how a person of colour could potentially feel in that situation. I felt so intimidated. I'm a great believer that we are all the same: white, black, brown, yellow, whatever the colour of our skins. I'm a great advocate that we are all simply humans. However, the social experience of being the minority, in the extreme, left me feeling exceptionally vulnerable. You see, many people's individual attitudes are the same – that we are all human – however, when the individual is within a collective, they are influenced by concepts of the social society and behaviours change. The individual's concept [that we are just human, whatever our colour], is lost. It was horrendous! I wasn't there very long. Only ten days and in those ten days I didn't come out of my cell once. That was good because I really believe I would have been at least beaten up, if not killed, if I had.

I had a three-day appeal in the courts. I remember getting delivered at the Royal Courts of Justice on a Thursday. There was a lovely lady there. At the time I was around 14 stone and she made four of me. She was very big, very wide and dare I say it — not wanting to offend anybody who is fat—she was fat! She was ginormous. She was the court officer, so when they called me up from the cells it was her that I was handcuffed to.

The courtroom that I was going into was Court Thirteen, which was up four flights of stairs. I remember walking up the stairs with my broken glasses on. They were all stuck together — DIY prison-style. Actually, what I'd done is that I'd made my own sticky tape. Another prison tip… what you do is you cut a piece of paper, or bed sheet, into a long strip, get your sachets of prison powdered milk and put a small amount of water with it to make a paste. Then you spread the paste on the paper, or sheet, or whatever, and then wrap it round the arm, or frame of your glasses. Within an hour the wet powdered milk dries, and you have the most indestructible glasses ever. They looked a mess! I almost had to put one eye left and one eye right to see out of them. The one thing I do remember is chatting to that lady. It was so human — so normal. After going up the first flight of stairs she had to stop because she couldn't breathe. We had a lot more stairs to go. I had a little laugh to myself because I thought if she faints and rolls down those stairs I was going with her and there was nothing I could do to stop it because she was so big. We eventually got to the top and I was put in this little room that was hanging over the court.

I could see the court, but they couldn't really see me through the entire three days of shite that came out. Thereafter, the three judges agreed to my three appeal points. One appeal point was that City & Guilds — probably the biggest educational accrediting body in the world — had lied. They hadn't told the truth in 2001 to the national press, they hadn't told the truth in 2002, 2003 and 2004 to the police, and they continued to lie to the jury and the court in 2008. Today in 2023 they are still concealing the truth about the accreditation and their relationship with me and my business, the National Distance Learning College (NDLC), throughout. Considering I was found guilty of a £16.8m fraud that was associated entirely with City & Guilds and the accreditations we offered on courses from the NDLC, surely I should have got my sentence and my conviction quashed because the judges agreed with this appeal point? They said, and this is documented in the court reports, "We agree with Mr Smallman's point that City & Guilds had lied about his businesses accreditation;

CHAPTER THREE - THE PISS TEST

however, that doesn't make Mr Smallman innocent." Also, as a side note, accreditation isn't even a legal requirement and wasn't a legal requirement for the government grants, associated with the fraud I was accused of, to be received. But nothing that I could have said would have made me innocent in their eyes. If there was nothing to make me innocent, it wouldn't matter what happened with the other two appeal points.

You'll be able to make your own judgement about this in a later chapter. When you read the evidence in the later chapter you will find that, for approximately a three-year space of time before the trial, City & Guilds was in an open, and so called honest, dialogue with my NDLC and its staff. So, if you consider the possibility of me, or my business, being guilty of an accreditation fraud this would mean that City & Guilds are at the very least complicit with the 'crime'. Their involvement throughout would make them guilty as well! However, City & Guilds and I are not guilty as no deception to the public took place on either side. They, and I, had the good, honest intent mentioned, but at some point in time City & Guilds had realised their inadequacies, their ineptness, in the accreditation of the NDLC courses. When the national press got involved they didn't have the guts to simply say that 'we, as City & Guilds, have been working for several years with Mr Smallman and his business and accreditation is signed off and progressing' — albeit at a ridiculously slow pace! They chose to lie in order to deflect the national press scrutiny of them and subsequent media frenzy that could have destroyed their reputation.

The second appeal point was that to continue the investigations to the point of 'finding' something 'amiss', the Department of Education had funded Cleveland Police illegally. Simply because other police forces didn't want anything to do with it. The Metropolitan police, or I assume the Met police as they came from London, were involved with two prior audits that had taken place whilst my business was running. They found me, found my business, to have no fraud in it, not even any non-compliance! Fair to say everything was right, it was a perfect business. There were no negative comments and that was with the Scottish Executive, and separately the Department of Education, sending a very high-level auditor in with a very high-level accountancy firm…and someone presumably from the Met police. You can see the conclusion of the investigation in the documentation below.…no fraud, no-noncompliance!

Audit reports redacted by the authorities to protect identities.

ILA/05/02

THE NATIONAL DISTANCE LEARNING COLLEGE

Paid £63,120   Outstanding Batch 63 = £0

HIE Learner Monitoring Activity

Additional Work Undertaken by HIE

- HIE contacted 3/7 trainees sampled and in all cases the learner had received learning materials and/or undertaken the learning. They had also all made a contribution towards the cost of the learning.
- Two learners could not be contacted (directory enquiry search failed to find number for ▓▓▓ and ▓▓▓ was not available despite several attempts.)
- 4 substitute learners were contacted by HIE and in all cases the learners had either undertaken or had received learning materials and had contributed towards the learning.
- ▓▓▓▓▓▓▓▓▓▓▓▓▓▓▓▓▓▓▓▓▓▓▓▓▓▓

Conclusion

Fraud / Possible Fraud

- There were no issues that would suggest fraud/possible fraud

Non-compliance

- There were no issues that would suggest non compliance.

What was found out during this audit, which reviewed the 180,000 students of the NDLC, only three had complained. Now in anybody's business book that's an absolutely fantastic success in terms of a key performance indicator. Just to say though those three complaints could well have been simply because things had been lost in the post or some other such administrative problem, or it could have been because the government had stopped their funding. The main point here though is that no fraud was found and no non-compliance.

ILA/05/02

THE NATIONAL DISTANCE LEARNING COLLEGE

Paid £63,120   Outstanding Batch 63 = £0

HIE Learner Monitoring Activity

Additional Work Undertaken by HIE

- HIE tried to contact 3 learners not contacted by KPMG and reconcated ▮▮▮▮ ▮▮ comments. ▮▮▮▮▮ confirmed ▮▮ had undertaken learning and had contributed ▮▮▮ ▮▮ also confirmed this. ▮▮▮▮▮ could not be contacted as ▮▮ was no longer at that address.
- HIE contacted an additional 13 learners. 12 had started learning and had contributed ▮▮▮ ▮▮ We confirmed ▮▮ did in fact appear on the cancelled capita list for NDLC.
- 3 individuals stated that although initially happy with the learning provided later assignments were not returned and they were unable to get support from the NDLC.

Conclusion

Fraud / Possible Fraud

- There were no issues that would suggest fraud/possible fraud

Non-compliance

- All 16 individuals contacted had started learning and had paid a contribution
- 3 individuals were unhappy that the support from the NDLC ceased.

For all intents and purposes, we were as near as perfect as could be.

Just have a look at this little excerpt of the judge's appeal report (*ref smallmanfinal29mar, page 22, point 123*).

123. Although the *ultra vires* point was conceded in Hounsham, it has not been conceded before us. As we have not had the benefit of submission on behalf of the DfES or the Police (Mr Wheeler being instructed on behalf of the Crown Prosecution Service), we do not propose to determine the issue. We shall simply assume without finding that, for the purpose of this appeal, the funding arrangement was *ultra vires*.

The judges said in their report *"We shall simply assume…the funding arrangement was ultra vires."* They agreed with the point that the Department of Education shouldn't have funded the Cleveland Police as it was 'ultra-vires' — which means an abuse of power; a government department to another government department, paying investigators to 'find something'…but it didn't matter! So therefore, it's OK to keep Mr Smallman in prison. It suited them that way. It just goes to show what's not good for the goose is good for the government.

If it was a really big company, a business, like say Google, paying the police, my conviction would have been quashed. I would have been set free. The principle being that an organisation that has a strong interest in finding someone guilty shouldn't be funding the investigation…funding a police force to investigate the problem. It was 'ultra vires', that's a fact! The judges said so! But it didn't matter in this case because it was the government (Mr Blair, Estelle Morris and the others) and the government probably decided it 'wasn't in the public interest' to find me innocent.

Let me explain what the government mean when they use the words 'not in the public interest' — it's a deflection. The underlying meaning is that it's not in their interest if things were to come out – it would tarnish them in some way. So, cleverly, they deflect the issue by using this statement. In this case, my case, the tarnish would have been £650m, or thereabouts, of taxpayers' money lost. Not only that, approximately 8,500 businesses had been impacted, many of which went bust, losing thousands of jobs and livelihoods because of a rushed through piece of legislation leaving the backdoor open for criminals.

I'll explain this detail later in the book, but when you're listening to – or watching – the news, listen for 'not in the public interest', they use it a lot!

The third point of my appeal was that the judge 'erred'. I'd say that he didn't sum up properly and that he didn't direct properly at all throughout the trial. A judge has a legal requirement to be unbiased, but he had a negativity towards me throughout, and it showed itself in so many ways. Nobody on the stand – prosecution or defence – incriminated me in any way. They all stood to answer to a Mr Wheeler, who was a very slick, charming, wordsmith manipulator of a prosecution barrister.

It appeared very much to me and to many who witnessed the Hearing that the barrister was not only leading the trial but had the judge 'in his pocket'. An example… prosecution witness after prosecution witness had got on the stand and had been asked by the prosecution questions like… "the 'dodgy' certificates that Mr Smallman was providing, would you like to look at them?" The witnesses, Sue Smith from EdExcel, another accreditation provider, and even City & Guilds themselves had looked at the documents and had said they're not dodgy certificates...they're just certificates of merit. I'd authorised Brian Dowd who was my Educational Director to sign them.

To explain, when somebody passed a module, the certificates were saying 'well done, you've got the certificate to prove that you've passed the National Distance Learning College's first (or second) module'. That would lead onto a City & Guilds qualification. Every college, university, and probably school, in the country gives certificates of merit on the road to the final qualification.

The case was – from the prosecution's point of view – that the merit certificates were fake, that they were dodgy City & Guilds certificates. Everybody from the prosecution point of view went on the stand and explained this was normal, everybody did it, and said they weren't dodgy certificates. One by one the prosecution witnesses knocked to pieces the prosecution's evidence. The judge wasn't doing anything about it and he wasn't saying anything about it. So, I shouted "do something about it"!

The judge adjourned the court and the barrister met me outside — as I was still on bail at that time — and I says, "If you don't do something about this I'll stop the trial and I'll sack you!" This was some 45 days in, of a £20m, or thereabouts, trial that the government were paying from taxpayers' money to get me there. Another interesting point in itself.

The junior barrister, cos I had two, went back on the stand and he said to the judge, without the jury there, "Mr Smallman is unhappy about the use of the phrase 'dodgy certificates'." He explained that many, many people had been on the stand, from the prosecution's point of view and had said that they were not dodgy, that they were run-of-the mill, every day, certificates of merit and they had agreed that there was nothing wrong with them. He asked if the judge could do something about it, to put the jury straight? The judge said he would.

So, there I was thinking 'wey hey it's going my way', something in my favour, this is good considering it was the charge! Anyway, the jury comes back in and the judge just says, "Ladies and gentlemen of the jury, it is clear that the last six witnesses... this person, that person and the other person... were asked questions by the prosecution about Mr Smallman's so-called 'dodgy' certificates and each one quite clearly said they were not 'dodgy' certificates, so I want you to disregard all that evidence, all of the implications that the certificates were dodgy." Back then, at this point in my trial I was thinking that the case was going to get closed down, it was going to get stopped cos it was clear from the judge's statement that they were not dodgy certificates, that there was nothing false.

Anyway, the judge finished up, after direction to the jury, by saying this... He says, "Is that alright, have I said enough?" Following that the prosecution barrister says, "Yes, you've put it right", and the judge says, "Well you still believe they're dodgy certificates, don't you?" therefore negating everything he'd said to the jury. I lost count of how many times the words 'dodgy certificates' came up again after that from the prosecution and the judge. My barrister didn't do anything. I began to wonder who my barrister was working for.

There were many different things, within my trial, which led me to believe it was false and corrupt. From the selection of, with the greatest respect, a naive jury for this complex case (naive to business and business law) which enabled the manipulation of the jury, to the withholding of key evidence that would prove my innocence, until just before the summing up.

An investigations file had been handed to the judge at the last moment of the trial, which I later found out included many and varied documents that proved my innocence. It was withheld from my defence team, and the court, until a perfectly timed moment...

right at the end of the trial... so that it could be acknowledged and documented that it had been submitted. The purposeful timing of submission meant it was not effectively used.

Some years later the file was handed to me as I was walking in the street one day, during day release. It was towards the end of my custodial sentence. A kind individual involved in the prosecution came up to me and handed me the file. They told me that they couldn't live with themselves if they didn't pass it to me. I haven't disclosed their identity due to implications for them. I'm assuming that they risked losing their job by handing me this file, but honesty and a burden of guilt, no doubt, motivated this act of kindness. I've included contents from this file in a later chapter for you, the reader, to decide.

But, as expected, at the point of summing up, when the file was handed to him, the judge said, "Thank you very much, I will go and read it and pass judgement whether it can be allowed in." He left and returned very shortly saying, "I will allow these few documents [taken from the file] to be given to the jury but there will be no reopening or bringing anybody back."

The jury was, by this time, after 91 days of trial, no doubt comatose and uninterested in whatever was passed to them. The judge also went on to say that there were certain documents that he would not allow as they were marked as Top Secret and therefore "not in the public interest".

There is a move to bring in Artificial Intelligence (AI) into courtrooms to increase the fairness of trials and to remove manipulation and distortion. To remove the emotional leading of the jury and the obvious implications of that. I say, bring it on! A trial, now, is nothing more than a competition between barristers. It's an act. It's a show for the subconscious to be led. Derren Brown, eat your heart out!

I'd love to see a re-run of my trial with AI. In fact, I formally invite this to those who are developing the AI technology and who may be reading this now.

At the end of the appeal and the hearing, they sent me back to Pentonville, to wait for the bus back to Everthorpe. The screws in Pentonville were awful. Nigerian most of them and for some reason they didn't like me. They didn't like me at all. Four or five days later an officer had come in and said, "You need to be up at six o'clock cos there's the transport coming for you to take you back to Everthorpe."

I was elated because the regime, the people, everything about Pentonville was disgusting. I was ill. I was scared for my life. I'd not had a shower in ten days and not eaten properly in ten days cos I'd just not dare go out of the cell.

Six o'clock came. I got myself ready and waited and waited and waited. By eight o'clock I thought I'm going to get on the buzzer because I should have gone… I should have been going back to Everthorpe. So I got on the buzzer and one of the Nigerian officers came and I says to him, "I'm supposed to be going back to Yorkshire, back to Everthorpe. There's a bus waiting for us." He says, "Wait a minute." There was a computer on the wing and he looked at it and said, "Nah, there's nothing there, there's no transfer, get back in your cell and stop pressing the buzzer." I protested anyway and they shoved me back in the cell and locked it. So, I gave it another 20 minutes and I went back on the buzzer. I was getting really irate. A different officer come, another Nigerian officer. I said, "I should be moving to Everthorpe today, and there's a bus waiting for me." He just went berserk! He went absolutely mad and shouted over to the other fellow who had locked me up earlier.

Outside the cell there was a square, which you had to stand on and put your feet right up against the skirting boards. I stood on that, and they told me to strip off and I did. I took everything off but me undies and then they ransacked the cell. I said, "What the fuck you doing? What you doing? I've got a bus waiting for me out there!" They got even more irate, and they went, "No you haven't, we're looking for drugs and there's something in here!" I lost me temper and they pushed my head up against the concrete wall and one of them drew a baton.

As that happened, a white Senior Officer came along and said, "what the fucking hell is this man doing there?" He was looking at the two officers that were doing the bullying and he says, "There's a bus out there, a bus waiting to take him to Yorkshire!" They said, "...but we just checked in the computer and there isn't! So we were just giving him a taster is what happened." The SO lost his temper and told the other two just to fuck off because the bus had been waiting down there three hours and if I didn't get down there I'd be there for another month until the next bus came along to take people back to Yorkshire.

I went into my pad dragging my clothes with me. I put them back on and did a dance. Never before had a man wanted to go to prison, albeit a different prison, as much as I did. I floated through reception.

In Everthorpe, later on, I got £70 compensation for losing about £5 worth of clothing which was really good. Got lots of coffee and biscuits for that! But I was ill. I was mentally – and therefore physically – absolutely destroyed. I had become very fit in my time at Everthorpe and at Holme House. I'd been in the gym, sometimes twice a day, and lost a bit of weight – well I'd lost a lot of weight! I had muscles everywhere, but I was ill. That ten days or so in Pentonville and the hostility towards me really showed me how vulnerable I was as an individual.

I was terrified, but I danced! I was so excited to do the ten-hour journey back, which wasn't quite as long as going had been. When I got to Everthorpe the same screw was there and he just says to us "you're not having a piss test, don't worry about it". He'd remembered from the months earlier that it was just not going to happen.

I went back to my wing, the B wing, the hostile wing. Whoever was out of their cell – and there were just about 30 of them out – just pounced on me! Like you do when you see someone rich and famous. They ushered me to my cell and wanted to know all about Pentonville. Did I get my appeal? What was it like? They festooned me with food and all sorts of gifts: chocolate mainly, soaps, everything. It was a brilliant sensation coming from a very, very hostile prison to a prison where everybody knew me, and everybody was glad to see me. Even the screws were glad to see me. "Nice to see ya back, Mike, nice to see ya back."

The things I got up to there were unbelievable. One day my cell mate, who I'd had for a short space of time and who was about 20 stone and about five foot one – so he was very wide and very round – came back from the kitchens where he worked and put his hands down his trousers. I thought, 'my God I don't wanna see what's down there', but he didn't pull his thing out, he pulled out some silver wrapping paper, quite a large parcel of it which he had stored between his bollocks and his arsehole. He opened up the few layers of wrapping and there were four ginormous slices of pork! Because he'd worked in the officers' mess, he'd pocketed and stashed the pork while nobody was looking. Exactly where he'd got it from, I don't really know. Maybe it was just off an officer's plate, but wherever it was from he had sliced it up and stashed it down his trousers in that most horrible place. Can any normal man consider eating something — a piece of meat — that had been stashed between another man's bollocks and their arsehole? He gave me two of the pieces and he just shoved his two pieces down his throat.

Twenty minutes later the screws came in and arrested him because they'd known something was going on and they'd moved him out. They left me there on my own with two pieces of pork which had been for quite some time in a fat bloke's orifice, or very close to it, and he'd been working in the hot kitchens for the last eight hours! If you know about pork, you'll know it's the one meat that you really don't wanna mess about with cos it carries bacteria like nobody's business. It was there wrapped in silver foil, and I did have two pieces of bread. What do you do? Well, when you're locked up at night in your cell and you're bored and your belly's rumbling cos you've not had any proper food and you're looking at it and you're thinking "Do I? Don't I? Do I? Don't I? Do I? Don't I?" – well let me tell ya, you do! You get your two dry pieces of bread and your two slithers of pork that have been in that unmentionable place — sweating between a 50-year-old man's big saggy sack and his arsehole — for many hours, and you absolutely devour that pork as if it was the nicest cut of meat that you've ever had in your life. Even if it was a bit salty. Delicious!

The next day my cell door opened, and they put a lad in. He was called Nabil, I gave him the name Bill for short. He was from Morocco. Funny lad, 23, 24, maybe 25-year-old and he knew all about me. I knew nothing about him. Strange that everyone knows all about you and yet you know nothing about anybody. It's maybe like when normal people watch celebrities. Who's on that show? Who's married who? Who's got a new Ferrari and God knows whatever else they might have? Criminals do the same thing cos they're all normal people, but they also like to look at the 'celebs' in the prison. As mine was the longest trial, mine was the biggest fraud of its type ever (allegedly!) I were famous. Infamous in the eyes of many outside the prison. I was the celebrity.

Nabil sat there on his bed. We were just talking away. I'd been gifted a chess set in me little bag of goodies from the Stevos. Two pieces were missing but it didn't matter, because all you'd do is use a little bit of soap or screwed up a bit of paper for the pieces that were missing.

Nabil also showed me a trick. In the bag was a can of beans – and this was long before the days of ring pulls. The first problem when you've got a can of beans in prison is, how the fuck do you open it? What you do is (if you can) find a marvel can with powdered milk. You take the metal bottom of the marvel can out, it's like a round circle of thin steel. It's thin enough to fold in half to make like a rounded edged triangle and you use the pointed edge to pierce the can and rock it round. It makes a difficult but sufficient can opener to open your beans. That's your first problem and Nabil taught me how to do that. The second problem, how do you cook your beans? If you're in a prison like I was, you have a kettle in your cell because they don't like opening doors for you to go and get a cup of tea, you just made it in your cell. If you were lucky, you could get a plastic bag without any holes in it and you'd put your beans in the plastic bag. You'd then put them in the water trapped with the lid, so it didn't touch the element and you'd let the kettle boil and leave it for ten minutes. You'd then have hot beans and, if you were lucky enough, you'd save two pieces of bread from your dinner. Dried bread, horrible stuff, but you could have a baked bean sandwich. Abject luxury! So, Nabil taught me how to feed myself in prison, with beans and the bottom of a marvel can to make a can opener. It also could be used, and often was, as a weapon to slit someone's throat!

In prison, collecting insignificant things like plastic bags, small ones with no holes in, is important to you. You could not only just cook beans, but you could also cook poached eggs, cos you could buy six eggs off the canteen. You could have boiled egg. You could pop that in the hot water and leave it for an extra minute than you would do normally, and you'd get a lovely runny egg. If you were very, very clever and a bit daring you could make toast with your kettle. You'd just put no water in it and you'd put the toast on the element but you'd have to watch it as it would set on fire, cause a short circuit and blow the whole wing lights. Absolutely brilliant!

Me and Nabil got on like a house on fire. He was a breath of fresh air. He was half my age and only living in the country maybe a year. He spoke good English but couldn't read or write it and one day he asked me to teach him how to read and write. So, we're there, with the lights on but the door locked and the wings quiet. Most people are asleep or whatever they were doing. No one's outside, bar the clocky — the night watchman, who occasionally walked past and had a peer in every couple of hours to see that you hadn't hung yourself or killed somebody – whoever is in your cell. We're there talking and talking and talking, and you might not find this very funny, but I laughed and laughed at this next little story.

I'm teaching him to read and write and I'm dyslexic! The tuition was functioning, and it was going very well, going really well but, to be honest, after a while I got a bit fed up so I said, "let's do a game. I'll write a word down and you've got to write words which are made from that word. They need to be three letters long, no more and don't look for big words". I wrote the word Manchester down, because that's where I was from, and I started him off by saying the first word — M A N — and he went 'man', really good! He could spell and read the word man. I taught him that. I put another few words down and gave them to him to continue while I watched 'Coronation Street'. So he's put five or six words down and he's pacing up and down while he's doing it. He was really concentrating on words of three letters that he could get out of the word Manchester.

He was getting frustrated because he couldn't find any more three letter words. He said, "Mike, help me. Give me a clue!" So I says to him, "In England we have a little saying, which is...'the cat sat on the…' what?" It took me a few times to say "the cat sat on the whatever?" for him to understand that 'whatever?' was meaning the missing three letter word. He was up and down for 20 or 30 minutes and he's saying "don't tell me, Mike! I'll get it". He's going "the cat sat on the…, the cat sat on the…, the cat sat on the…" and he's going on and on and on, trying to pull this three-letter word from Manchester out. Just so he could write it down and learn a new word. "The cat sat on the…, don't tell me, Mike! Don't tell me, Mike! Just don't tell me. I'll get it, I'll get it!" He was so funny, walking backwards and forwards, that I started laughing at him. He said, "no don't laugh, I'm going to get it! I know what it is. It's coming in me head". Then he said, "I've got it, Mike! I've got it!" I said, "Nabil, what is it?" He says, "The cat sat on the carpet!" We both realised it was wrong and we fell about laughing, almost wetting ourselves, cos here we were, in a prison cell, a dyslexic man trying to teach a Moroccan to read and write English! The cat did sit on the carpet, didn't it? It did! We all know that it was the word 'mat', but it was so funny! He really believed he'd got it, he really did!

He'd stabbed somebody. I don't think he'd killed them, but he stabbed somebody, and he was very sorry. He really was genuinely sorry that he'd done it. He told me it wasn't a malicious stabbing, it was a stabbing to save himself from being stabbed. Gang warfare I suppose. Every person, I don't care who it is, will flower their story up. But nevertheless, he was a good lad and it was so funny. You had to be there…'the cat sat on the carpet'!

A few days later we'd gone through similar things. I'd taught him to play chess and he'd asked if he could read the letters that I was writing. He had no-one to write to, nobody in Morocco, no-one to telephone, nobody in his life. He was reading my letters and he was crying at the words I'd written to my kids and to my wife. Out of all the sorrow and love…and everything that's ok in my letters… he picked out that the most common words that I was writing in these letters, no matter who I'd written them to, was "please believe me, I'm not guilty" cos I wasn't! I must have written this a thousand times. To my kids, to my wife, to my sister and others that "I'm not guilty".

They really believed, or even knew, that I wasn't guilty, but the biggest fear, from paranoia, when you're trapped in a prison, is that they begin to be poisoned by others with an axe to grind, by the newspapers, or the mother-in-law. So you have to keep telling them. You are also reminding yourself that you're innocent and that you're not guilty and you're stopping yourself from falling into the trap of accepting that you are a convicted criminal and possibly turning a new leaf in your life towards criminality. It's easy to become one of the lads, not just in your heart, but in your actions. Many do, it's just too easy to do it.

The letters had brought this to his attention, and he asked me, "Why aren't you guilty?" So I began to tell him that basically I used to be a big businessman with a huge company, that employed hundreds and hundreds of people. I had everything. I had racehorses. I had fast cars. I had houses here and there all over the world and not little, two-bedroom ones either, huge places in Spain and America. I began to tell him the story about how I got there. How I thought of an idea one day and took one and a half thousand pounds and a little banger of a car and turned it into a multi-million-pound business in just a few years. I told him how I became international entrepreneur of the year, how I stood on the stage to receive my award, with Richard Branson and many well-known others in the audience, which ironically is about the time all my troubles started. Because of that my award never got publicised, not properly anyway. I began to tell him why I was innocent and that I was going to set the Houses of Parliament on fire, metaphorically speaking. That I was going to prove my innocence in everything that had happened to me. I told him about the judge and the seven years and sending my wife to prison. I told him about everything.

He said to me, "So you really were this huge, big businessman?" I said, "Yeah, I was. I was the man who had everything."

CHAPTER FOUR – THE GUILT

Nabil was shocked. He just could not believe that a democratic government like Tony Blair's government, whether Tony Blair was involved in it or not, could actually make such a mistake and try to pass the buck onto somebody else. That 'someone' being quite unassociated with their problem and his cellmate. He couldn't believe it! He says to me, "That's unbelievable!"

Everybody I speak to now, I still believe they don't believe me, because it *is* unbelievable! It's a giant story and I know every criminal who is found guilty says they didn't do it – don't they? – but it's true, I didn't.

Nabil puts the kettle on again. It's about 11 o'clock at night. He tells me a story about himself when he was a kid, of having an abuser. It was a real talkative night that night. He told me that his uncle used to beat him up and play with his bits, but he didn't go into too much detail. Somewhere between wanting to tell him my story and wanting to let him know that he wasn't alone in his abuse, I began to tell him about when I was a kid.

I was born, as I've said, in 1963. I was a poorly child and I think that led to people thinking they could take advantage of me, and they did. Firstly a man, his name was Franny Borman*. I had kept this secret for years and years and years and I promised my friend Jimmy* that I wouldn't ever say anything about it. I'm now making an assumption that the people who need to know are still alive and the people who shouldn't know aren't with us anymore or won't read my book: mainly his sister, who was married to Franny. They'd tried for years for a baby and they'd just got one, and Jimmy didn't want anyone, namely his sister and the child as it grew up, to feel unhappy knowing that the father was a paedophile. So, I kept the secret for years and years. Now it's out, well sort of, because the names have been changed*. Franny, who for want of a better phrase, messed with myself and my best friend Jimmy.

Franny was a man, not very tall, five foot eight, but he was a professional boxer for some time so he could look after himself. He was in his forties so still young enough to give a back hander. Myself and Jimmy would have been about 11 years old.

We had bikes that we'd made ourselves from the scrapyards, half of one bike and half of another. We went everywhere on them. One time we even went without tyres on them and we got there. It wasn't very comfortable. We did lots of different things when we were kids but one of the things we didn't enjoy doing, that Franny made us do, was to go to various doctors' surgeries and get repeat prescriptions for him. Franny was a junky. Not of cocaine or anything like that, but of prescription drugs. What you or I would take as a pain killer would be two every three or four hours, maybe eight to 16 in a day, pushing it to the very top. Much more than that and you'd start to become ill. These pills that Franny took were called distalgesics. They'd rot your stomach. Franny built his resistance up so he could take 200 in a day to take away his pain. His pain was his liver and kidneys cos he'd been an alcoholic in the past and the doctor had told him that if he didn't give up he would die. So he gave up and turned to the pills cos his kidneys and liver gave him pain. The more we could get him the more he ate. We felt sorry for him cos there's nothing you could do. He was in genuine pain. The pain drove him to a point where every doctor in the region for miles around, where we lived in Manchester, knew him, cos he would change doctor after doctor, until no doctor would prescribe for him. That's when he started on us. He'd pay us, give us money, and he'd make me go to my doctor and ask for a prescription. He wanted a repeat prescription of me mum's medication, which were distalgesics. They were prescribed to everybody in those days, people who had pain anyway, as they do with similar drugs today.

We did this probably about 40 or 50 times over the years but that wasn't the worst thing about Franny. The worst thing about Franny was what he did. I hate to think what he did to Jimmy cos he had much more access to Jimmy than me.

My first encounter with these actions was when I was on my own one day. I was just riding my bike about, and I put it up against the wall at the post office to go in and get some sweets. On my way out, Franny was there. He took me bike and put it into the vestibule between the houses and the shops so no one could see, apart from me looking for me bike thinking it was nicked. He made it very easy for me to find him and he give me the bike, but he stood in front of it so I couldn't ride away.

He said to me, "I want you to go to Dr Henry's for me." He was a really nice man was Dr Henry, a very, very nice man. He dealt with medical problems with me and made me much better. That aside, Franny wanted me to go to Dr Henry's to ask for some distalgesics or whatever he could get on my mum's prescription. I refused to. He put his thumbs in the top of my belt, one on the left and one on the right, and he lifted me up by my belt so my feet were just barely touching the ground. He took me off the saddle so I was stood on the ground and he then put his hand down my trousers and held my testicles and squeezed them like you could not imagine. It's hard for a woman to understand what that feels like cos they haven't got any, and if a man's ever trapped one or two or sat on them, or whatever, then they'd know a bit about it – like Gazza did when Eric Cantona squoze his nuts. I was a kid and it did make me cry. It was agony, absolute agony! I did his beckoning and got his prescription.

Not wanting to go into too much detail about what Franny did to me, you can imagine how it escalated. The more freedom he got with me, the more he could feel he could do things, the more he did to me. He was a very dangerous predator. A predator with such evil in him. He was using fear to control kids, at the very least me and Jimmy. Who knows if more kids than us got it as well, but if you can imagine what a paedophile does, that's what he did. About once a week for four years, whenever he could get hold of me. Ever since, and now as an adult, I can't pee to order. Can't go in a public toilet. I hardly associate with men. Ninety-nine percent of my friends are now women. It leaves its scars. I regularly have flashbacks and there's many things I just can't watch on television.

I didn't know he was messing with Jimmy until one day I found out. It was the day of the biggest regret of my life. I found out when me and Jimmy were in his mum's front room. It was probably a Saturday, fairly late on in the evening. His mum had gone to bingo as she always did and then she'd be in the pub after that. Me and Jimmy had got a bottle of Guinness, which we shouldn't have had, and he had two fags.

I never smoked and he had one lit, but I was drinking the Guinness. It was disgusting, but I still drank it cos you did as a kid. We were discussing what we were going to do, what we were going to be, when we grew up. Jimmy said he was going to be a millionaire, have a Ferrari and buy a magnum gun. He had a fascination with guns. He used to watch Magnum PI and he collected them later in life, just plastic ones — fake ones — as far as I know, anyway. I said, "All I want is a little boy called Christopher and a little girl called Grace." I just wanted to be the best dad I could be and then twenty-ish years later I did have those two. But, as that conversation was going on, Franny came through the door. He shouted Jimmy into the kitchen. I went cold. Jimmy just got up and went, conditioned to the evil of the man. After ten or 15 minutes or so, Jimmy hadn't come back. There were rumblings and noises in the kitchen but I couldn't tell what was going on. I got very scared and shouted to them I'd better go cos my dad would be looking for me, just so Franny wouldn't stop me if he thought me dad would be looking for me. I crept down the passage, the hallway, past the kitchen door which was ajar, about five or six inches. I glanced to the right to look through it and there was Jimmy naked, stood on the table. Franny had something, well, let's just say he had something in his hand.

All I did was run all the way home, not knowing what to do. What do you do when you're not even a teenager yet and you don't know what the word 'paedophile' means because it wasn't used in them days? You don't know how to express it. You don't know nothing. Childline wasn't there in them days. You know it's wrong but you're in fear. I was in fear of what he was going to do to me. I was in fear of me dad thinking I was lying or doing something even worse and believing me and going and killing him, cos he would have done. What do you do? You say nothing. Can I just say it's the biggest regret of my life, because I know Jimmy got a lot more than that, a lot worse happened to Jimmy than me, simply because Franny had the key to the front door. Any time Jimmy's mum was out, Franny could come and do whatever he wanted to do.

By the time I was 16, that abuse had been going on for four years, at least four years. It's not the sort of thing you record in your diary, so I don't know exactly how long it went on. You forget, or at least you try to forget, most of it. Later on in life I went my way and Jimmy went his way and I started to live my life as a young man.

By the time I was 34 years old, I had the NDLC business and it was escalating, it was getting good so to speak. It was becoming a larger business and I was doing very well for myself, and I had the occasion to go back to Manchester. I was now living in North Yorkshire. I was driving to Manchester for a meeting at Trafford Park and the journey took me down the Mancunian Way.

On the way back I wondered to myself if Jimmy was still living in Hulme. Would he still live there? Now we're talking 18 years on since I've seen him, so I thought let's have a look. I parked up about six o'clock at night and I walked down the street to where he lived and knocked on the door. Jimmy opened it, a 35-year-old man. He's a year older than me and it was just like twenty-ish years had disappeared. All that time had gone and evaporated, it was just like I was calling round to play. So much distance had been put between our lives. He was still youngish. He looked just the same to me. It was as if it was only yesterday, the last time I saw him. He told me he was still doing the same job that he had done forever, and I'd become this almost millionaire and started doing all sorts of things and had got a family. I'd got Christopher and Grace.

He opened the door for me to walk in and we went and sat down in the front room. We didn't say anything. We said absolutely nothing. We just sat there on the same couch that had been there since we were little and he was looking at me. He had his hands on his knees and was leaning forward slightly. After what seemed like forever he says, "Me mum's dead." His mum was a very abrupt lady, but she was a very nice lady. He says, "Me mum's dead and the bastard's dead." As he said that a great feeling of guilt came over me, I felt that I could have helped stop his pain and I didn't. Do I tell him that I knew what

Franny was up to? As soon as he said 'the bastard's dead', I didn't know what to do, but I knew who he meant.

I knew what was going on with Jimmy but I didn't know whether he knew what was going on with me. What do you do? Should I have told him there and then that I knew what was going on with him, because I saw it? But then my guilt sets in and I was thinking I should have done something about it and he might think bad of me because I should have done something about it. So there was quietness and he then said, 'Franny's dead'. I said, "I thought that's who you meant." And then we talked and cried for hours about stuff…the things that he'd gone through with Franny. Then he begged me not to say anything, because he wanted to protect his sister. The bastard was dead. What could anyone do about it. Jimmy had to live with it; his sister didn't.

We'd had some beer. Jimmy always had beer. Five or ten beers later, we were still 'compos mentis'. We're not really drunk, we were having a laugh and talking about David Soul and 'Black Bean Soup', which was the double A-side to 'Silver Lady', another David Soul song that we used to sing in the Seventies, along with other music of the time. Like any ELO song, we knew them all.

Jimmy remembered something and said, "I've got something for you," and goes into what was his mum's parlour cupboard. He comes back out with an envelope which looked a bit grey and a bit yellow cos of time, the sun and dirt and god knows what else was on it. It was oldish. He says, "That's for you." I didn't know what was in it. It was quite fat. I opened it up and there was £940 in. I said, "What's that for?" He said, "Do you remember that day you said you wanted a boy called Christopher and a girl called Grace and I wanted a Ferrari and to be a millionaire? Do you remember what we said?" I says, "Yeah, if either of us won the pools we'd share the winnings." And six years earlier he'd won the pools. He'd won just short of £2000 and he counted the cash out, halved it and put it in the envelope waiting to see me again. That was probably 20 years on from the day that we promised each other and I'd not seen him for 18 of them. As you're reading this you're probably thinking 'wow, what a friend!', 'what loyalty!'. I didn't need the money. I didn't need the money at all as I was approaching being a millionaire, but I couldn't refuse it cos what a magnificent gesture it was of childhood friendship and promises. It was like we were still young boys, even though we were both in our thirties.

As me and my groupies are typing this book out they are asking me to express my emotions at the time, but I just can't. Cos if you can imagine when something so terrible happens to you and also to your best mate, a way of coping with it throughout your life is to void yourself of the linked emotional state that you should be in. You hide it, you shelve it, you pretend things didn't happen. So they didn't. To carry the emotions would be to expedite that man's actions and to carry them with me as a victim forever and, let me tell me you, I'm no victim.

We carried on chatting, going over all the things that we did as boys: the snogging of the two Paulas that we'd both had the pleasure of, at different times, needless to say. Later on I got back in the car and drove away with my little envelope of money and a big smile on my face, realising that there was somebody in the world that I could rely upon. I've not seen him since that day and that 25 years from now I don't think I will ever see him again because we are such different people, but who knows, maybe he will read this, you never know.

Another thing that happened to me when I was a kid was to do with a boy called Kipper. When Jimmy and me went to school together we were inseparable. He was in the year above me and together we were absolutely formidable, but he left and went to another school, a secondary school, leaving me alone for the last year of Cornbrook County Primary. We still met up every night, and we did what boys do every night, ride our bikes and whatever.

In that year a boy called Mark Kapenhurst, whose nickname was Kipper, noticed that I was now on my own as I walked through the park every day to go home. Kipper used to go Cornbrook but had left three years earlier. He was about four years older than me and he was one of those boys that had a body of a 35 year old man, muscles everywhere. He knew I had a sister who was born with Down's Syndrome and knew he could beat the shit out of me any time he wanted to and he did. Nearly every night. For a similar span of time that Franny was abusing us, Mark K, Kipper, was breaking my bones. It started off with just slaps across the face every other day and calling me 'spacker' or 'mong' or something derogatory towards my sister. I just brushed it off. It hurt and there were always tears in my eyes but I never cried or anything, which maybe I should have done. Maybe then he would have left me alone.

By the time I'd left junior school I was 11, and had started Greatstone Secondary Modern, where he was, but four years in front of me. Jimmy was at another secondary school which meant I had to walk alone on the same path as Kipper, get on the same bus as him, stand at the same bus stops as him, share the same school playground as him, and he was relentless. The school I went to was the closest school to Manchester United football ground. The top three years were right next door to the ground and the first and second years were half a mile down the road in an annex building. That's where I was. Kipper was in the bigger building near the football ground. Every lunchtime he would run for half a mile or so from the big building to the little building just simply to meet me before I got on the bus. I used to go home for my lunch, not for any particular reason, other than I didn't want to be at the school. I hated it and sometimes he'd get there before I got on the bus, or if I was in the playground, he would get me there anyway and often did. If the bus was late, he would do things to me that you could not really imagine was a good thing for anybody. He'd slap me to the ground. I'd put my hands up over my head and face and curl up. He would kick and kick and kick and kick, till he thought he couldn't kick me anymore, and that would mean a broken leg or broken nose for me. I've still got the scars now. I remember the bone sticking through my nose. Broken hands and fingers; but one thing he couldn't break was my spirit. It was impossible to break my spirit and he knew it, I'd just look up at him and smile as if to say 'you can't hurt me'. That, in the end, led to him urinating on me as well, which he did about 30 times over the years. Spit — he had the greenest greens that you could possibly wish to have — and spit upon me and he'd make sure he hit me lips.

It was a great childhood – not! Mum and Dad were lovely people but very poor and to some extent very old-fashioned in the way they made money and spent money. What could I do? I couldn't tell them that I had a paedophile messing with me. I couldn't tell them that I had a bully. They had enough problems earning money. Enough problems looking after my Down's Syndrome sister and my other three brothers and sisters. To them I was just the boy who fell over a lot, broke his bones a lot. These days I suppose things are different, but then I was in and out of hospital with no questions asked. Falling over and hurting myself was easily explained because I was a poorly boy with my lungs. It wasn't until I was about 16, when the paedophile and Kipper got their comeuppance. I dealt with it myself — as I, generally speaking, had to deal with almost everything, — and probably why, even though lots of people help me, I try to be fiercely independent.

Stood at the bus stop waiting for the 263, at nearly 17 years old. I was waiting for this orange and white bus to come along to take me to the Tropicana night club on Oxford Road in Manchester. I shouldn't be going as I wasn't 18, but I had a tash and I was tall, so I could pass. I had a suit on and here comes Mark. I call him Mark now, not Kipper — we're not at school anymore. He's a working man, still built like a brick shithouse. I'd not seen him for maybe six or eight months. My illnesses had disappeared for the most part and I'd put weight on. I'd become a big lad. I'd learnt an awful lot of Judo and he comes up as he'd seen me, and he wants some fun. The fun he wants is me bleeding, me being kicked as he had done in the past; he comes over and takes a swing, but I was a different person then. I was bigger and stronger, more trained — if you like — to fight. So I did this thing called the Tomanagi Judo throw and he went straight over my head. I hadn't thought about the Co-op window that was behind us! There was no safety glass in them days and he went straight through and landed on the glass. All his stomach was cut open.

I was arrested and I got my first offence. It wasn't for grievous bodily harm. I got off with it because there were CCTV cameras and they saw that he had attacked me and that I was acting in self-defence. What happened was I got charged with criminal damage and fined £69 for breaking the Co-op window. I never saw Kipper again, but I do feel sorry for him because I know why he was like the way he was. A year or two earlier I'd seen him cleaning some windows at his mum's house. It was summer and he had his shirt off and his back was cut to ribbons where his dad would beat him with a belt and buckle, like a sailor in the 1750s having had that cat o'nine tails. He was a troubled man, troubled man — troubled boy. It was just unfortunate that I was one of his kicking stones. Hopefully he's worked his life out and he's not doing it to his kids, and he's made a life for himself. It is what it is.

Franny, on the other hand, well who knows what happened to him after he met me coming out of The Grey Parrot. It was a pub we knew round the corner from where my mum worked. He saw me. He noticed I'd grown up a bit in the last year, so he made no approach, and he turned the other way as I was walking towards him. I think he'd got a little bit frightened, not least because I was that much bigger than him. As he turned the corner, to the left of the Grey Parrot, there was a van parked with all the timbers sticking out of the back, on the flat-back-lorry type thing. He turned the corner so sharply that he didn't have time to stop and one of the sticks, the pieces of wood sticking out the back of the van, stuck in his eye and removed it. I just carried on walking. I never saw him after that again, but I do know from the conversation with Jimmy that he had lost his eye. Now, whether that was divine retribution or not, I don't know, but I take it as one. He was a bad man and the world is a better place.

Now, as a big grown-up man I can't stand a bully and always react when I come across one. I feel a need to rid bullies from the world and always point them out whatever the circumstance – if I see four or five kids beating up one kid or if I see a man shouting and balling at a woman. I'm exceptionally aware of my own bullying antics, especially when I'm trying to prove a point. It's not really bullying but over-emphasising the point when someone doesn't agree with you. I suppose it could be construed as a mental bullying. At some point in my life I will be writing a book about bullying and pointing out all the actions of what bullying is and emphasising that ninety percent of bullies, physical and emotional ones, don't even know they are doing it. Believe it or not, at some point in our lives we can all be a bit of a bully.

All the way through prison I didn't allow one person to bully me. I'd grown up in such a way that I could talk for England. The number of times I tried to talk my way out of Kipper beating the shit out of me or Franny Borman doing what he did to me, probably allows me to tell the story now. It gives me a gift: talking, convincing – who knows.

One thing that I need to say is no matter who you are reading this, you will have brothers, mothers, aunties, uncles, sisters, sons, daughters, cousins, nephews, and friends of all ages. It doesn't matter how old they are, they don't have to be kids, but particularly with kids. Any of those people could be going through something similar. It could be sexual abuse from somebody they don't know, somebody they do know, a relation. They could be going through physical abuse, very common in marriages ain't it these days? They could be going through absolutely anything, but you don't know, and you don't know because they are ashamed, they are covering it up, they are frightened, they don't want to tell anybody. They would rather keep it to themselves to save you.

So, the moral to this part of the book is simple: you don't know what people are going through so make sure the people in your life know that you are there for them, that they know that you love them. Don't be frightened of saying it, over and over and over again, so many times that they get fed up with you saying it. And they say things like Dad will you shut up saying that I love you, or whatever the connotations are. Ignore it, say it, because those people that you say it to, might just need to know that you do love them, that you do care for them and you're concerned for them and worried about them, and all those things that you need to do for them, and it might just help them through whatever they are going through, that you don't know about.

Just as a point while me and my crazy groupies are putting this chapter together an occurrence has happened. And I hope that the same occurrence happens with you. And that is almost everybody has been able to say something about what happened to them as a youngster, some things that they've struggled with, and although it's to help guide me with the book, in some small way it could be a small cathartic moment for them, being able to talk about the unhappy parts of their childhoods. It also made one person realise how happy their childhood was. For my childhood, I didn't have a sense of belonging, too busy just surviving day-to-day life. That still continues to some extent now, but at least with a ginormous sense of purpose; things are looking up.

CHAPTER FIVE – CHILDHOOD ANTICS

I suppose you think it sounds terrible – my life as a child – but it wasn't all that bad. I had some great times with my mum and dad, and my brothers and sisters. There was one time as a child, it was Christmas 1973 and I'd just had my tenth birthday. About three weeks before Christmas me dad had asked me what I wanted for Christmas and I wanted a Go-Kart. I had aspirations of being a racing driver and only a few years later, from the age of 16 to 21, I raced Formula Ford. Formula F is a little racing car, with a 1600cc Lotus engine, that looks like a formula one, but isn't. It has no electrics, three gears and no clutch and your arse is two inches from the ground. I was very good at it. I raced at Donington Park, Croft and other such tracks with people who went on to become Formula One superstars.

Me dad was a lovely fella, a really lovely man. Worked hard. Didn't really play at all, just worked hard and loved his kids. I knew he was going to get me a Go-Kart, but no matter where I looked in the house over the next week and the weeks running up to Christmas, I couldn't find anything that looked like a Go-Kart. And I really looked. Then one day me dad came home, ran up the stairs and went into the loft space. I don't know what he was doing up there, but the next day when he'd gone to work, curiosity got the better of me because it does when you're ten years old, and probably still does today.

I got the old brown steps out, opened the big loft hatch and pulled myself up into the loft space. There was a box and it was big enough to put a Go-Kart in it, like a flat-pack-type-thing to make a Go-Kart. I carefully, with a pair of scissors, took the staples out of the top of the box in order that I could peek inside. I just really, really gently prised the staples away, trying not to rip it, trying not to damage it so I'd be able to put it back together again. Now, that was foolish, because if you take the staples out, the box is going to get ripped, and as I opened the box…it ripped. I said "shit!", or probably ruder words than that and there were more, but never mind, curiosity drew me into the box and I started to pull things out. First a wheel, then another, and I knew I was getting a blue Go-Kart! I'd wanted one ever since one of my good friends had got one. Unfortunately, he'd got his go-kart out of adverse circumstances.

Young school-friends called Jimmy Pannet, Brian Parkinson, Billy Parkinson and my best mate Jimmy*. We were all playing on a demolition site, houses that had been bombed in the war, 30 years earlier, that were due to be knocked down. The demolition men had taken all the wood from the doors and roofs and put it all into a cellar and set it all alight to burn it. When we arrived on the site all the wood had burnt down to embers so all we could see six, or eight feet below at the bottom of the cellar was the black of the charcoal. If you could imagine all the walls of the houses had gone, so the cellar appeared as a big open hole in the ground.

We decided to play daredevils. We got a long metal beam and lifted it across the pit of the cellar. The beam was about six or eight inches wide, and our dare was to cycle across it. Enough said. Jimmy fell off and suffered 80 percent burns. He got his go-kart as a part of his rehabilitation to get his joints moving again. His joints that had been melted and scarred by the hot embers. I've not seen him for many years but if he's reading this now I just wanna say, from memory, the way you coped with your injuries was inspirational and I'll never forget how sad I felt for you when it was reported that someone had nicked your go-kart. Oh, and Jimmy, Lynn Barber said I'm a much better kisser than you!

So, I put it all back together as best as I could, with the wheels in the right place. I tried to glue it with a bit of spit, cos that's all I had to stick the lid of the box back together again, but obviously I couldn't. I was just praying that me dad didn't notice that I'd snuck in, or maybe he'd think someone else had snuck in. I pushed the box back to where it was and left it. I put the hatch back up, put the ladders back where they were and forgot about it.

My mum and dad were very poor, but they did their best. On Christmas Eve they'd send us up to bed between eight and nine o'clock. Then they would wrap up all the presents. They'd get pillowcases and put lots of goodies in. Then as they went to bed, they'd put the pillowcase on the door handle outside the bedroom, one for me, one for Peter, one for Jeffrey, one for Susan and one for Christine. That way, if we woke up very early, we wouldn't be disturbing them and we had something to undo before we all went downstairs together for the rest of the presents.

Christmas Day came. At five o'clock, me and Peter — cos we shared a room — woke up and we said to each other, "Wonder what's out there? Let's go and get our pillowcase!" So, we opened the door but that Christmas Day there was only one pillowcase with Peter's name on it... just the one pillowcase! Mum and Dad hadn't put me anything there and I didn't know why. I just thought, "Oh well, they've forgotten, or maybe have left it downstairs. I'll wait and just watch Peter undo his." I enjoyed watching him undoing his. There were just some little things, daft things like an orange, a little plastic toy or a book, just cheap little things to keep us occupied while me mum and dad had a little rest.

At eight o'clock they'd go downstairs and put big stacks of presents, that they'd saved all year for, in piles. Things that they couldn't afford like my Go Kart. Then they'd call us all down and we'd all undo our presents, maybe ten or 15 of them. They would be in a big stack; in a big pile cos it was a special day.

That day, about half past eight, they called us all down into the living room and everybody, apart from me, had a pile of things to unwrap. They had everything from a jumper, pairs of socks to more fruit and some nuts. Anything to have the excitement of opening it up and they all got the big present that me dad had spent all his money on. Big boxes with all sorts of things that they wanted, telescopes —God knows what— whatever they wanted. The one thing that they'd wanted all year, they got it; but me, I had no pile. I just had to watch everybody undoing their presents, thinking 'what's going on?'. I was quite upset really. Ten years old and no pillowcase, and nothing downstairs. Everybody's happy and I'm just thinking 'what the hell's going on'! As a shy boy I didn't want to ask, but then again, I think I knew that I'd been rumbled.

Me mum looked at me and says, "Can you pick up all the papers?" She'd got a big black bin liner and there were mountains of wrapping paper, but none of it with my name on it. I picked it all up, put it all in the bag and put it out for the bin man.

Then we watched some television and I'm still thinking 'what is going on? Where are my presents?' – I didn't know. Anyway, as normal, me dad cooked Christmas dinner and he always got grumpy for two hours cos he didn't like anybody fussing around him while he was cooking. Me mum kept smiling at me. I didn't know what she knew, but she knew something.

We all sat down and had a fantastic Christmas lunch. Turkey leg. Me, ten years old and a turkey leg bigger than me, with gravy and carrots. I didn't eat them. I gave 'em to the dog. The dog didn't eat them either and just left them all over the floor. We did that for a couple of hours... Christmas pudding and all the normal things. We'd have a laugh and for that hour or so I forgot I'd got no presents, cos we were having a lot of fun, jokes in crackers just like you do. I don't really understand them now. I have my own jokes now and everybody laughs at them, especially the one about the dog: 'How long does it take a small dog to have his dinner?' Well, if you've thought about it for a little while I'll tell you the answer...it's 'Chihuahuas'. Do you get it, small dog, it's so funny. Are you laughing cos I am?

Anyway, after lunch the relatives come. Auntie Jo and Uncle Sid, Grandma maybe, a few others and we have an afternoon party. The relatives come in with bags and bags of presents, giving them out to the kids and the cousins cos they bring the cousins with them. More presents, loads for Christine, loads for everybody and guess what, nothing for me! Absolutely nothing for me. I'm thinking to myself what have I done, what have I done to deserve no presents, no pillowcase, no morning unwrapping, no presents off the relatives, none? I just can't work it out, or was it something to do with my snooping?

I'm half happy because everyone's about and we're having a good time, but deep down I'm totally gutted cos I knew for a fact that there was a Go Kart up in the loft. I knew that I'd have got other things, even if it was just a pair of socks from Santa or something like that. I would know that because it happened every year. But this year I got nothing.

All the Christmas wrapping paper was picked up off the floor again and everyone was chitter-chattering. More people had come along, me brother-in-law's mum and dad, one or two others. They'd brought little presents for all the kids, for everybody, swapping, exchanging. And nothing for me. I was beginning to get exceptionally paranoid. Maybe that's why I'm so psychologically affected now at the age of 59 and why I'm totally and utterly paranoid. Hmmmm, must talk to a psychologist.

Anyway, me mum does her usual spread on the evening, like a buffet, a cheap council house buffet. We loved it because we had Lurpak butter, which made everything taste so much better than the normal cheap margarine that she'd buy for a couple of pence a packet. We'd have ham and sausage rolls, crisps — three different types — cakes, and my mum's world famous trifle, which I could eat 50 or 60 gallons of without stopping.

Seven o'clock comes and the party games started. Me mum had a weird sense of humour. She'd get my sister's potty and fill it with tea and blindfold someone and ask them to put their hand in the potty. They didn't know it was a potty, and then when they felt the liquid she'd whip the blindfold off them. For a few seconds they'd thought they'd put their hands in the piss but it wasn't really, it was just tea! That was me mother. She was sick. She really was sick, but a lovely lady.

Me dad then suggested that we all played hide and seek. All the kids, and there's about 12 of 'em, including kids that were supposed to be cousins that weren't really cousins, they were just friends of the family. Me dad says it's my turn to be on and he sent me upstairs into the bedroom. I had to go and stand in the bedroom and count to 100. One…two…three …slowly and then come and find my brother Stephen who had hid somewhere downstairs. So I counted to 100 ever so slowly. It seemed like it was 500 cos I did count slowly and when I got to 100 I shouted "coming, ready or not"! Then me dad shouted upstairs for me to count to another 20 – "Stephen's not ready" – so I did. I counted to 25, just to make sure, and I shouted again, "coming, ready or not"! Me dad shouted upstairs "count to another 20, he's not ready"! So I did. I counted to 25, just to make sure, and I shouted again "coming, ready or not"! I ran down the stairs and as I opened the living room door, do you know what was there? A mountain of presents. There must have been a hundred, without exaggeration, a hundred! From me cousins, me brothers and sisters, me aunties and uncles, and the biggest one was a Go Kart all made up. I burst into tears cos I thought I wasn't getting anything and me dad came up to me. He picked me up and says, "That will teach you to go snooping in my loft."

What a Christmas it was! It taught me a lesson, and that was to mind my own business and don't expect anything as you might not get anything in your life. It also taught me something that will stand me in good stead in my business future and that was always to look at things optimistically from a pessimistic point of view. Expect everything but be aware that you might not get anything.

So life wasn't all bad, was it? Loving parents and good brothers and sisters, although they did beat me up sometimes. Life was good in places, and I grew up from that, learning all sorts of things. I grew up learning that I was going to be, it's wrong to say…'something special' but I'll say it… something special, something different. I had ambition. I had greed if you like, but it was really ambition.

I remember Boxing Day that year. We'd gone to my uncle Peter's house. He wasn't a real uncle, he was my mum and dad's friend, him and Auntie Maureen, his wife. She was the president of the Cliff Richard Fan Club. She loved Cliff Richard more than she loved her husband, more than she loved anyone, she really did. There was Gary, a strange lad, their son, and all of us were there.

My uncle Peter was a really nice man. He was born in India. He used to take all the kids under the stairs. He'd put a tea towel on his head and get a fishbowl and empty it, turn it upside down and pretend he was reading a crystal ball. Jeffrey, Stephen's twin, would go under the stairs, and then Uncle Peter would say, 'you're going to be a fireman when you grow up' and tell him a story about a fireman. Stephen, the other twin, would go and he'd be a butcher, a baker or a candle stick maker. Everyone would go in under the stairs for a ten-minute laugh with Uncle Peter. He would pretend to be a fortune teller, on the basis that he was born in India, and he would tell them what they were going to be when they grew up.

The thing was though, he'd never take me under. I'm pushing 11 years old and he'd never taken me under the stairs to tell me what I was going to be when I grew up. So when he came out and turned the light off from under the stairs, I said, "Uncle Peter, why don't you tell me my fortune?" He put his hand on my head, looked me in the eye, knowingly, and said, "I don't need to tell you your fortune. You know where you're going," and in that instant I really knew where I was going. I knew it then that I wanted a son called Christopher and I wanted a daughter called Grace and I wanted a lovely wife and I wanted to be a lovely husband and a lovely man. I wanted to do my best for everything and everyone. I knew I wanted to be a businessman, and I knew I wanted to be a millionaire, and I knew I wanted to go and do fantastic things. I didn't know what was to come and that's what this book is about. So it wasn't all bad, was it?

I remember a little bit later, I'm 15 years old and not left school, and I'd asked me dad if it was alright for me to go and start a little business. He says, "Yes of course you can. Do what you like." But later on he got a little bit jealous because I started earning more money than him.

Me and me mate Jimmy used to go around the blocks of flats and we'd bang on people's doors and say, "have you got any broken hoovers?". We had a Silver Cross pram, an old battered one, and we'd put as many old hoovers as we could get into it. We'd collected about 25 on the first night and by the end of the week we'd have 300, literally 300. We put them all in his mum's flat's spare room, which was a three-storey tenement building, and then we'd pull them all to pieces and make one from five. So we ended up with let's say about 50 hoovers, mainly hoover juniors, which were a bit mucky, but we made them work again and went round the flats re-selling them for £2 or £3, maybe even £4 or £5.

That was the first business. We made a fortune. You'd never seen kids have so many sweets and crisps, ice cream and days out: the zoo, the circus. We used to pay for everything ourselves. It was brilliant.

That business ran out quite quickly so, after about four months, I was reading the Manchester Evening News. There were some business opportunities, and there was a small ad in there that said "we buy old newspapers by the ton". So, we went round the flats again with the Silver Cross pram, knocking on all the doors for weeks, upon weeks, upon weeks collecting everybody's old newspapers. We collected so many newspapers that when we went to Mary's Chippy, she couldn't wrap her chips in newspapers because people had stopped giving them to her cos they were giving them to us. She was having to buy in secondhand newspapers, so to speak, or proper wrapping paper. She knew it was us and began to moan a bit about it, so we took advantage and, you've guessed it, we used to demand fish and chips for a huge pile of newspapers!

When we thought we had collected enough, what we used to do is stack them on the kitchen scales and weigh them by the stone or the pound, until it added up to a ton. This room, this box room at the back of Elsie's flat, was crammed full of newspapers, and we believed at this point we had about two and a half tons, so we rung the ad and we said we've got two and a half tons, can you come and collect it, and they did.

They came and collected it and we got £40 a ton, so on that occasion we got about £90. We thought we'd been cheated cos we'd weighed it, our scales were accurate, and my maths was good, but maybe not.

The second time, what we did to make sure we got value for each two-foot-tall stack was, we made sure the papers in the middle of the stack were very wet so they weighed more. Anyway, about four o'clock on a Friday afternoon after school, before the man come to make the collection, me and Jimmy were at his mum's and she was out at work. We hear a banging on the door, and there's a man in a coat, a flashermac coat and he had the trilby – even then hats were still unusual, not like they were 20 years before that – and he asked to see Mrs Norman. We said, "Well she's not in." He says, "Well you need to tell her that we need to come in and inspect the back bedroom." He was from the Council, and he wanted to inspect the back bedroom where we had our newspapers. We thought 'crap, what are we going to do?', so we asked him, "why do you want to inspect the back bedroom? Jimmy's mum isn't going to like that, she doesn't like people in the house", and he says, "tell her there's a structural problem, and the people downstairs on the floor below, have got huge cracks across the floor, so we need to inspect the bedroom to see what the problem is".

Of course, we realised what the problem was. It was the two and a half tons of newspapers pulling the side of the flats down. Anyway, he went, and he gave us a little card with black writing on white paper. We rung the man the very next day and asked him to get it, and within the space of 15 minutes we threw every stack of newspaper out the window and into his lorry. He paid us about £80 and went away and to this day, nobody knows why there were cracks in the ceiling in number six or the floor below.

Actually, a week later they turfed everyone out of the flats and everyone was in a strange flat for three weeks while they repaired all the damage that we'd done.

We were good boys and we really tried, but we did make a mess of quite a few things.

Another thing that we did was on bonfire night. At the age of ten or 11, you could readily go in a firework shop and buy what you wanted. We loved bangers. We used to throw them in the stairways of the tenements, and we can only imagine that it would scare the crap out of people, but it gave us a laugh from the top of the stairs as it echoed round.

One day, we had about 20 bangers and it was raining outside. So we lit them in the kitchen, one by one, and we burnt holes in all sorts of things. Jimmy's mum was going to go mad, not for that reason, but for this reason... we thought to ourselves 'how big a bang would it be if we tied about 20 of them together?' We curled up all the blue touch papers, so it made one big touch paper and wrapped a towel around them. We tied the towel to the bangers really, really tightly. Now, it was a bit frightening, so what we did was we put it on the balcony. It was a 1940s balcony made of brick. We put it in the corner and we put some bricks and half paving stones against it thinking that it wouldn't blow back. We thought that it would be strong enough not to. We didn't realise we had actually made a bomb, but we just thought it would go 'bang'. So we set it all up. Twenty bangers all wrapped in a towel and tied with string to make it really, really compact because we wanted to intensify the bang. We put the bits'n'bobs of rocks and stuff against it, lit it and ran in the kitchen and shut the door.

A few seconds later there was a ginormous loud bang and then a crash. We crapped ourselves. It shook the whole building. Car alarms were going off, but worse than that, when we opened the door to the balcony from the kitchen there was no balcony. We had blown the fucking balcony off the building – and this was made of brick! What were we doing?! We laughed and then panicked because Elsie was coming home, and she had a good right hook. What could we do? We just couldn't do nothing. So we ran out and didn't come back for about 12 hours until about three o'clock in the morning because we thought we were going to get murdered by Elsie.

It's only now, more than 40 years after, it's occurred to me the possible consequences that could have been. Imagine Elsie opening the door to the balcony to get the mop bucket or to hang out washing and stepping out onto what was not there and hitting the floor 30 feet below. It doesn't bear thinking about!

When Elsie saw me the next day and asked, "did you know what's happened?" I says, "no". She muttered under her breath, "Bloody Jimmy, you cheeky melt, you stupid melt!" He was banned from coming out but didn't grass me up. He just said he had done it himself, but I knew she knew. I knew me dad knew. He thought it was funny!

The things we used to do as kids were unbelievable. Anyway, we grew up, didn't we? We went through the nasty bits, but we still had a life, we still had a laugh. We were still funny.

I can't swim. I really can't swim but me and Brian Parkinson, Jimmy and a few others were playing on the bridge over the canal one day. We'd found a mattress. So we got the mattress and turfed it off the bridge to the canal, 20 foot down. This wasn't like a modern canal, this was a canal with dead bodies in it, bikes, cars and everything. It was a rancid swamp mess! Then, what we used to do, the four of us, is that we would jump off the bridge onto the mattress holding a big long piece of wood and we paddled the mattress to the other side of the canal before it sank. We did this regularly. But me, being a coward, I had a big, long piece of rope tied to me. That way, if I did go down they could pull me out again. The stories I could tell! They are so funny.

One of the funniest stories at this time was my two weeks' holiday in my auntie Joan's caravan in 1973. It was the year before I went to the 'big' school. We had gone down to the caravan in Robin Hood's Bay outside Rhyl in Wales. This is 1973, but the caravan was from about 1943. It still had gas lamps in it, gas heating and no toilet. It was just a caravan. It was awful having to walk to the toilet block through the dark and the mud. It was like a prison, it was horrible. Nasty, cold, dirty and smelly but it was still a holiday and we loved going to Rhyl. We went on the amusements here, there and everywhere.

One dog was in the caravan. It was about ten o clock. We liked to play cards for money, just pennies. This night, it was about 12 o'clock, after playing cards for a couple of hours. I said to me dad, "should I make everybody some toast and a cup of tea?" and he went, "yeah go for it".

It was just coming up to my 11th birthday in the September, so I was ten. I go into the kitchen part which just had one door between that and where they were playing cards. I thought about what I had to do… I put the kettle on, put the cups out and I began to make the toast. At home we had an electric hob and an electric grill. This was gas from the bottle outside and I didn't really know what to do with it. So I got a long piece of newspaper, turned the gas on, struck the match and failed to get it lit a couple of times. Eventually, after 30 seconds or so, I got a light on the match to light the newspaper with.

As I went near the gas ring the fire on the newspaper went out, so I had to keep trying to relight it. It must have taken a minute and half, maybe two minutes, to get it properly lit. I walked over with my piece of newspaper, but the gas had been escaping quite some time by then. So, I lean over with an outstretched arm to light the hissing gas on the stove. There was only one thing that was going to happen, and it did! It blew up so much, it blew the window straight out the caravan so hard that it hit the next-door caravan! There was smoke everywhere. Don't laugh when you read this but there wasn't a hair left on my body! It took my little boy moustache off, it took the hairs off me ears, it took my eyebrows off. Every hair, every lovely little blond hair on my head, had a curly black bit on the end of it where it was singed.

Everybody rushed in and saw the state of me, covered in black soot and the window out, but me mum and dad were mostly relieved that I wasn't blown up. Dead. No one was getting toast or tea that night. It was clear the next morning that me dad had spent all night fixing the window.

From that little story, within a few days I'd gone to me new school — the 'big' school where Kipper was — and met all me new school friends. That's when and where I got me nickname 'Singe'. That lasted about two years. Everyone laughed at it when I told the story. The only person that didn't laugh was me auntie Joan because her caravan was wrecked.

So it wasn't all that bad. Not bad all the time. Even though some of it was gruesome. You never know, in another book I might even tell you some more funny stories. There's a hundred and one of them. It was funny but real and those sorts of things kept me going through all the negative times. Cos there were lots of negative times to come.

CHAPTER SIX –
FROM THE ABYSS

After the paedophile and bully had got it, if you know what I mean, I'd grown up into being a big strong boy. My chest problem had disappeared, pretty much, and I became Jack the Lad. Anything that moved, that was me, cos I could. I was tall, extremely good looking — if I say so myself — and of course fit as a butcher's dog. I'd go out into nightclubs at 16 pretending I was 18. I danced around more handbags than any 70-year-old woman had done in the whole of her life. I loved the discos, the dancing, the chatting up and of course, whatever resulted from the chat-ups. Oh my God the stories I could tell.

I grew up, a bit. I got a great job and travelled the world. I learned my craft as a salesperson and marketeer and as a motivational speaker. (I'm taking bookings now!) I probably had five years of proper life where things didn't go wrong, too much anyway. I led a normal life, like normal people do. There's loads of stories to tell about that, but there was one story which wasn't particularly good.

It was when I was walking down the streets of Manchester, down a road where we used to go shopping when I was a kid. It was called Alexander Road, locally known as Alec Road. It was in Moss Side, a very rough place. As younger children we used to go to Woolworths and buy our records. Top of the Pops and Greatest Hits or something like that. They were 2 and 6 before decimalisation and then 30 pence, and 50 pence, and a pound as time went by. I was doing really well; manager of a little company, well, quite a big company really, and I was travelling the world.

It was a Saturday afternoon, and I was walking towards Woolworths, where in front of me I could see a young woman on the ground and a man standing over her. He was a little bit older than her but not too much. He was standing over her, kicking her. He was kicking her face and the back of her head was hitting against Woolworths' wall. I panicked a bit; I didn't know what to do. But then I found the courage to shout "what the fuck are you doing?", I shouted as loud as I could and I started to run over to them. If he hadn't stopped, I don't know what I would have done, but, anyway, he ran off. We never had a fight, he just ran off like the coward that he was.

The girl, the young woman, was in a bad way. Blood and guts everywhere. She was unconscious for at least a minute or two. When she came around, I had a little chat with her and asked her if she was alright. She obviously wasn't. So I helped her up and put her in my car. which was only a short way away and I drove to Manchester Royal Infirmary. I took her into Accident & Emergency where the doctors and nurses looked after her. They did a quick patch up just cos she needed to have a quick patch up. Then we sat in the waiting room for four hours cos she needed to get further attention. In those four hours I told her about my life, the story that I've told you about the paedophile and the bully and the other things. I told her all about my grievances and the pain and my batterings, and she told me all about hers.

The man that was kicking her was her husband. He was a violent man, a drunk. He was a soldier and every time he came home from his manoeuvres with the army he would drink and beat the shit out of her. He would break her bones, give her huge bruises, black eyes, broken ribs, you name it she got it. Her only respite was that he went away quite often, but every time he came back, she'd get it. This — me meeting her — as she was being kicked to death was her and her husband just doing what they did. Doing what he did. He didn't have a reason although he said he did, because she was always 'at it' whatever that meant. She wasn't, she was a nice young lady. He was just using it as an excuse to be violent. Anyway, within those four hours we had talked so much we had found an affinity with each other. We found a common problem, and that common problem was violence, and we were a sort of verbal sanctuary for each other.

In those four hours we fell in love. Every time we could be together, thereafter, we were. We were inseparable. We were always taking the opportunity to be together; a walk in the park, cinema, making love. Nobody, but in particular her husband, knew this was going on. It was too dangerous for her and probably for me, for it to come out.

We had an 18-month secret relationship. Nobody knew: not my brothers, not my sisters, not my father, not my mother. The lady was called Joy. We really did love each other. I think most people think they love each other but they don't really, they just like the idea of being in love. We had that common goal of freedom from violence, a common goal to be happy and I still have that today.

After a while, the inevitable thing happened and, whilst he was on manoeuvres, she conceived. Luckily for us, to some extent, when he was home, he was always drunk and he couldn't even remember if he had an arm or a leg, let alone whether he'd done anything. Anyway, sometime later it was there, a 'bump'. She was so frightened of this man she begged me not to say anything to anybody, so I lived the lie and the pretence that it was his baby, or his baby-in-the making, for quite some time.

Time passes and our little boy was born. I did get to see him. It was a very difficult time for me because I didn't know what to do. I just wanted to go and smash the husband's lights out. Maybe even kill him. I didn't, of course, but what we'd done previously, even before the baby was conceived, was save up for some time. We had a bank account where we were saving and when we had enough, we were going to go to a different country, maybe Spain or just to the South of England. We wanted to get as far away as possible from that man. We did occasionally achieve that…days out here and days out there, but we never got enough money to go away.

After the baby was born, about three weeks after, my mum gets a phone call. No mobile phones in them days, not proper ones anyway, none like we have today. It was the police asking me to go to Longsite Police Station. I wasn't in trouble, but they wanted me to go. So I did. I took myself off in my little car and went into the police station where there were two policewomen waiting. We went together into a side room, and they asked me to identify myself…who were my girlfriends? Who did I know? Obviously, I couldn't mention Joy because I was sworn to secrecy. One police lady then pulled a handbag from under the table and put it on top of the table and said, "Do you know who's this is?" I says, "yeah, it's Joy's," and they opened the bag and inside there was a photograph. It was a photograph of me with my mum's telephone number on the back and the name 'Mike'.

They looked at me with a little smile and one of them said "clearly you are the 'Mike' on the photograph". It wasn't a question. She was pausing with her words and her voice was cracking because I think she knew I had more than I'd said to do with Joy. She goes on to say that she was so sorry to have to tell me that Joy and the baby had both been killed in a car crash. A taxi crash. It was nothing to do with her husband. He was on his way back from Germany or wherever he was because his wife was dead, and his baby was dead. But it wasn't his. It was mine!

I didn't tell the police anything, there was no point. I just said, "thank you for telling me" and went. I disappeared. Went back home that day with a big brave face on. I am an expert at putting big brave faces on. I've been trained well by my life, to smile a lot. I waited a week and went to the funeral. Stood from a distance away. While I was there, I just thought of all the things that could have happened and might have happened. I had to come to terms with never really knowing my baby. Never getting the opportunity to tell anybody. I didn't tell anybody until I was in my fifties. One thing for certain, those events were to make my future children even more important, even more wanted, even more precious.

After the funeral I went back home and said to me mum and dad that I'd got a job in Tenerife. I hadn't. I'd got a £50 cheap flight and flew out. I did that because I didn't want to be there anymore. I couldn't live there anymore. I was, no word for it, but devastated, beyond devastated. It was probably worse than devastation because I couldn't tell anybody about it. I couldn't tell me mum and dad that their grandchild had just been killed in an accident, when they didn't even know that they had one. Everybody just thought I was daft... chucking in a good job and flying out to sell timeshare.

I got myself a little room and it was a really nice little room. Just a single room like a bed-sit type. It had everything I needed in it, even a lovely window, and I stayed there. I'd go out and find other people my age and I'd have a laugh or a joke, or at least tried to, but really I was just masking my grief inside. I began to drink. Brandy and Baileys.

Couldn't touch the stuff now, it would make me sick. I'd drink a bottle of both and then a bit more and then a bit more.

Within three weeks I was permanently drunk, permanently masking what had gone on in my life. Masking my sorrow and my grief. One day, I can't remember what time it was, I found myself waking up on my little bed-sit floor. It smelt of sick and it was all over me from top to bottom. I'd obviously puked in the night, all over the place. Then I realised I could not see anything. I couldn't see the hand in front of my face. It was pitch black. As black as you could ever imagine blackness to be. It was also totally and utterly silent. I couldn't hear a cockroach, the wind, a car, a voice. I couldn't hear anything. Not seeing anything and not hearing anything and being in the state that I was led me to believe that I was dead. Looking back on it, I didn't truly believe that I was dead, it was more that I wanted to be dead. I hoped I was dead… But, at that moment, I believed it to some extent. I listened and tried to listen to everything, but I couldn't hear anything. I'd accepted that I was dead. I'd accepted that the world had departed from me. I just closed my eyes and accepted it.

I must have fallen asleep; it could have been a day or more. I didn't really know what the timescales were. I had a sensation…a searing pain had developed in the middle of my forehead. It was bad. It was like a burning, drilling, intense pain. I opened my eyes and the light was so intense. Do you know when you've been in the dark for a long time and you go out into the light…it's intense. But this was 20 times or more intense. I couldn't see anything now. Not cos of the black stuff, but cos of the bright stuff. It was so bright it was unbelievable. It was painfully, painfully bright and the searing pain in my head was getting worse. Then I heard cars go past and people talking, and my eyes began to focus and I realised that I wasn't dead. I was alive and the pain in my head wasn't a hangover, or anything like that, it was the Tenerife sun coming through the window and it had burnt my forehead. You might find that funny because I do now, but I wasn't dead! For a split second, and it was a split second, a nanosecond, a sequence of things happened in my head. You can get a lot of thinking into a nanosecond, you can almost relive your life, like a dream. You can dream for what feels like five hours in your dream but really you've only been asleep for 20 minutes. You've had a whole journey, a whole sequence of things happen, but you've only been asleep for a short while. It was like that, do you know what I mean? A nanosecond of thought, thinking I'm not dead, but, if I just close my eyes again, I can be dead. I wanted just to lie down there and die. Not eat, not drink, not move. I'd shit and piss my pants as it came and just lose the will to live...the last little bit of will to live that I had.

Instead, something happened in me. It was a feeling in my belly. It was an urge to live, a will to live, a presence. 'Mike's Magic' was born that day and I understood that I had something inside me. It had got me through illness. It had got me through the paedophile. It had got me through broken bones. It had got me through everything that I'd been through in my life. It was my driving force. At that time, it was weak – as I'd lost the things that I loved, I'd lost everything – but one thing I didn't lose was the driving force. It was now telling me to get my skinny arse – yes, I was skinny once – my skinny arse off the floor and make a life for myself.

I stood up. I was vomiting. Not because of the hangover but because of the stench. I stunk. It was horrendous! There was dried up sick everywhere. I went in the shower, and had a shave. Put some clean shorts on and a clean T-shirt. I have never been so hungry in all my life, but not just hungry for food. Although I did go to the fridge and eat some green, mouldy Sutherland's salmon paste — it was delicious! It was the first food I'd had in my new life. This was my rebirth, so to speak. My second chance, although I'd probably had many second chances but not realised it. The hunger in my belly was for doing something with my life, for getting somewhere. Just like I had when my uncle Peter had put his hand on my head and I realised that I was destined for something totally and utterly different. Not knowing why or what, but I was going to go out there and live my life, and I did. In the meantime, however, I went out and, to be honest with you, I bonked everything that wanted bonking for six months.

I didn't care about anything. I didn't drink. I just lived and I've not had a proper drink since that day. What's the point? Drowning your sorrows is pointless. Even if it's just at the weekend.

Everybody has grief in their life, some at the beginning, some in the middle and some many times over. Sometimes it's different types of grief because you lose a lover, because they've found somebody else. Or you lose a lover because you don't love them anymore or you lose a lover because they die, however they die, it doesn't really matter but they're dead. The force to drive on is sometimes tampered by the grief. You get over the grief, or you don't, but most people do. I did and I was driving my life ten thousand miles an hour.

So many things happened in that next six months which will be a book in its own right. So many books, so much life. To cap this off though, I was walking down the street in Tenerife when two Guardia Civil pulled me up and said "passport por favor". Si, mi Espagnole es fantastico. In those days Spain — Tenerife as it is Spain — wasn't in the EU, or in Europe in that respect and you had to come in and out every six months to have your passport stamped. That was my first deportation. They picked me up. I left my little flat and all the things in it...I had cleared up the sick by the way... and they put me on a plane. I was banned from going to Spain, or any part of it, for ten years. They threw me back into England again where I went home to live with me mum, live with me dad. I got my job back and picked my life up in such a way... Well, read on!

CHAPTER SEVEN - THE RISE

I was explaining to Nabil that going through all of that as a child could have destroyed me, but it didn't. It made me stronger. It made me able to build the business that led me to be the man who had everything, and I really did have everything. I could buy almost anything I wanted. I also had a lovely wife, two amazing kids and what I believed to be good friends. It wasn't always like that; in the early days it was very difficult cos we had nothing really. I had a job working for a company called Kent College, they were based in Kent believe it or not. I was their north-eastern rep, manager, call it what you like. One day I went to a sales meeting and they said to me if I didn't improve my handwriting they would sack me. To cut a long story short I told them to stick their job where the sun didn't shine, like where mine shone from!

I threw the keys at the manager, got the train home and said to my seven-month pregnant wife, "I've chucked my job in and I'm going to start my own business." It was about time that I did. She asked me "what are you going to do?" and she was right to ask. I just did not have a clue. I rented a small unit in the Hemlington initiative centre in Middlesbrough for £120 per month, which was a bargain cos it was quite a big room in a modern facility. I sat in there deciding what I was going to do. I'd been involved with sales training and marketing and motivational stuff, so I thought to myself I would develop a company which would offer those facilities. I could offer the services of teaching people how to motivate themselves, how to sell, how to brand. I was good at that. I sat in there all on my own for two and a half days with the shutters down. Sometimes with the lights on and sometimes with the lights off. I read this, that and the other to see if I could get some form of motivation or inspiration. I thought to myself 'what am I going to call it?'. I decided to call the original business Assertraining, as in to be assertive and the training to be assertive, but with me and my dyslexia I spelt it wrong. I spelt it with one 't' cos it was one word 'assert'training'. With one 't' my lovely wife pointed out that it didn't say 'assert training', it said 'assert raining'. Never mind, it didn't matter, I left it as it was.

I'd incorporated the limited company and I was beginning to think about 'what skills do I need?' – I needed to be a bookkeeper because I couldn't afford a bookkeeper. I decided I was going to teach myself bookkeeping, so I did. I wandered along to the local library and borrowed a book called Frank Woods 'Teach Yourself Bookkeeping' (you can check it out, it's really good). So I did. I got myself my little 386 'piece of rubbish' computer and started to read the book. I couldn't type and the computer was useless, so I scribbled notes in my scribbly hand, bad spelling, bad everything and I asked my wife to type it up. She was a teacher and probably the best teacher I've ever met.

After a few weeks she said to me, "Do you know, Mike, you're teaching me how to do bookkeeping? You've written your notes down and it's like a course." In that moment I had like an epiphany. I wasn't going to teach people how to brand, how to market, how to motivate themselves or how to sell. I was going to teach them how to do bookkeeping. Just simple double entry bookkeeping. So I continued with the course, the course of teaching myself. This developed into a 16-to-18-page course on double entry bookkeeping. I then printed a few copies out. They were very bad. Badly spelt and badly put together, but they did get the information across. I created a leaflet which basically said 'teach yourself how to do your own books, save your accountancy fees…If you're a small business….do one of my little courses £32'. All they had to do was rip off the little coupon at the bottom, put their name and address on and send it free-post to my office address with a cheque for £32. I photocopied several hundred of these leaflets. Then me and my seven-months pregnant wife delivered them around the houses of Stockton and Middlesbrough, and we waited.

Three days later through the post came a brown envelope which was addressed to the free-post address. In the brown envelope was a white envelope which was addressed to the same address. It was just one envelope in a brown envelope ,which I thought was strange, but basically the Royal Mail was consolidating all the post for the free-post address. I opened the little white envelope and inside was one of my coupons with an address on it and a cheque to Assertraining for £32. My heart sank. Not because it was a bad thing, it was a brilliant thing, but what I had to do now was organise it properly. What if another one came? Who was going to tutor these people if they needed some help? I was going to give them a freephone number that they could ring if they couldn't understand part of the course. So, someone had to be there as a tutor.

The next day another two came, and the next day another three or four. By the end of the month from that first several hundred, or probably a thousand leaflets that went out, we got 20 or 30 responses. It was brilliant: we had a business.

I sat in my little office with my spreadsheets thinking about how many houses there are in the UK. There were 26 million at the time. Twenty-six million private houses, private letterboxes that I could put a leaflet through! From my scruffy little photocopied leaflet, I got 20 responses at £32 a time. Thats £620 for every thousand and it was costing me £50 a time per thousand to put them out through Royal

Mail, including the print. Wow! That was me becoming a millionaire! All I had to do was replicate my little idea. So, I did.

That September, 25,000 leaflets went out. I was inundated. I was continuing to write the course, I was tutoring, I was packing, I was doing everything. The need to employ somebody came up very quickly. I put an advertisement in the local job centre for people who would work for nothing, because the government would pay for them on a YTS scheme. For those of you who don't know what a YTS scheme is, it's a youth opportunities training programme, or similar scheme, for the long-term unemployed, or maybe they had the skills but were just unemployable for some reason. I was going to give them a chance, but they were going to give me a chance because they were coming to help.

The first person that came was a man called Chris Larkin. I say 'man', but he was a boy really, 22 or 23 years old. He'd just passed his 'A' levels which included bookkeeping. He came and he didn't know that he was going to be my bookkeeping tutor. He appeared to know more about it than me and he did have a qualification. So I employed him. His first job and my first employee.

Then I employed Emma. She was 17 years old, could barely read and write to some extent, but was a nice kid. She was going to be my administrative assistant, my very first PA. Then the third person was Brian Dowd, a religious man. He was the first man to bring IT, Information Technology, into the Cleveland schools. He was the first man to use a computer in the schools in the Cleveland, North Eastern area. He'd got his own problems, so he'd left teaching.

At that time I'd also started to develop my own computer course with my brother Jeffrey, cos he was a bit of a computer geek. I wrote four or five modules on how to set up a computer: how to open it, how to type with it; how to do a simple spreadsheet with it. Brian came along and took over and made it into a fantastic course which was accredited, at some point in the future, to BTEC, the Edexcel organisation.

Staff grew, sales people grew and in the first six months or so, we were a small business that had turned over about £250,000. I had great dreams of becoming a national distance learning college and applied to the DTI — the Department of Trade and Industry — to use the word 'National'. By this time we'd had sales people in Exeter and in Scotland, Liverpool and Scarborough, so we could justify in a thousand-page document that we were truly becoming a national college. After a number of months the DTI said we could use the name, so 'Assertraining' ceased and it became The National Distance Learning College. 'NDLC' was born.

Time moved on and expansion took place. We'd gone from 25,000 per week to 1.6 million leaflets per week. Within a year and a half, money was coming in thick and fast: from various government schemes and from students paying their £20 or £40 or £50 per month. The course had grown exponentially. We were accredited to various organisations: one for bookkeeping, to BTEC for the IT course, and new courses were coming on line all the time.

We had moved premises from the Hemlington initiative centre. I'd bought premises in Linthorpe Road and Borough Road in Middlesbrough. They were scruffy, down-at-heel places, but they were mine because I'd paid for them in cash. In addition, we'd begun to rent a large building called York House which was built by the shipping magnet Constantine in the 1920s. It's the most splendid building in the Middlesbrough area, and it was mine, or at least I rented about ninety percent of it. Mick Mculloch rented the other ten percent. Mick was an older fella, a real nice man who opened a large engineering company called Mask(E) Machines. We got on very well with each other. He also noticed that I was doing very well and tried to buy a proportion of my business for his son, but I'd refused it as he wasn't offering enough money. Mick was a well-known character throughout Middlesbrough and was part-owner and chairman of Middlesbrough Football Club. When my trouble hit later he was very supportive but had no power to help.

One funny thing about Mick, after my business had gone down and I'd left the building, he was left as the main tenant. He was coming and going on a daily basis. Unfortunately, he'd died in the office and I presume the ambulance took him away and he was buried some time afterwards. Probably, many weeks after the funeral, his sons needed to collect his car which he'd parked outside York House. When they arrived to get it they couldn't move it because the Council, or the road authorities, had built a bus stop right in front of his car allowing only a six inch gap! I believe his boys had to get a crane in to remove his car.

While we were there, York House was costing us, from memory, £40,000 or £50,000 a month in rent. When you're expanding to that extent you don't really think about it. You just go and do the things you have to do because the expansion begins to take over. A monster comes and you try to force yourself into consolidation periods, but when you're an entrepreneurial spirit like me, consolidation might only be a few seconds, a few minutes or a few hours. Then you move on again to bigger and faster places. I had spare cash above and beyond the expansion, so I threw it in different directions to new ideas, because I wanted to create a group.

I wanted to create something that's just going to blow the tits off the world. I became bigger than I actually was but I was bigger and better than most at doing these things. I was a fearless entrepreneur looking for the next best thing. Some managing directors are real entrepreneurs, some managing directors are paid employees, simply managing the business. What makes the difference between a 'managing director' and a true entrepreneur is the size of the bollocks and the length of the neck. Meaning, that managing directors simply do that, they manage and they direct. True entrepreneurs put their bollocks on the line and stick their necks out much further. Even if that means the bollocks are squeezed so tight your eyes pop out and your head gets chopped off and put on a stick. Oh! Finance Directors, let me tell you, typically know nothing about business and have the smallest bollocks and no neck. Secretly they get excited with the thrill of the business rollercoaster, but they'd never get on it on their own.

There was one occasion where we had more than half the country covered with salespeople. It was going to take me maybe two or three years to expand beyond that, but I wanted it now. I was probably acting like a petulant three-year- old! I'd decided I wanted it now! I didn't want to wait two or three years to become a truly international organization. Truly to call myself a millionaire. I wanted it now! So I rang my bank manager at Yorkshire Bank, a man called Peter Kenyon, who later became my MD, my managing director. He just seemed to be a good man, a good friend, a good bank manager. His career had grown as my business had grown. Every time I had wanted to expand (and I expanded generically without any financing), the bank wanted me to have a new bank manager. I don't know if Peter ever knew this or not, but I used to say to the big bosses at Yorkshire Bank "if I have to change bank manager again, I'm going to change banks". So Peter got a promotion every time my turnover reached a particular threshold.

I'd rung Peter up one Friday evening and I said, "Peter, I want a half a million pound overdraft", and he went "oh right!". He had to write a report; he didn't say 'yea' or he didn't say 'nay'. I think it was out of his hands, he'd only recommend it. He said he would write his report and give me a decision some time on Monday. He arranged to come into my building, into York House, some time on Monday. That weekend I hardly went home. Literally, I went home and drove back to work again. I was thinking how do I expand and get the cash flow that I needed to be truly international? To get all the salespeople, all the marketing, all the everything covered and all the cash flow that I needed without the use of an overdraft? Bearing in mind that once you have an overdraft with the bank, they actually own your business and they can have it back at any point in time. I didn't want to put my business in jeopardy, into such a place, certainly not at this stage. So I sat there, and sat there and sat there in my office with the company of a meat-feast pizza, or two, or three.

I looked at the structure of the business and the way we did business, and basically, a leaflet would go out, a lead would come in. I would give that lead, or one of my managers would give that lead, to one of my sales staff. That sales staff would drive up to the lady's or gentleman's house and would explain all about the course, whatever the course was. The courses had grown and the prices reflected that they'd gone up from £32 to say, in the hundreds, three, four, five, six, eight hundred pounds depending upon the size and the depth of the course. We allowed people to pay on a monthly basis, so we were maybe asking them to pay a £20 or £30 deposit and the rest over two or three years. So, effectively, the deposit was their first payment. It was so simple! It was so simple for me to get the finances I needed without the overdraft.

When Peter Kenyon came through the door on the Monday, I said to him, "Don't tell me, I don't need to know whether I've got an overdraft or not. I don't want it. I don't need it." It was so simple. I just sent a memo to all my sales staff not to collect one month's payment for deposit but to collect two. My cash flow doubled overnight; it was a piece of simple genius!

This gave me the cash flow to take that leaflet distribution beyond 1.6 million per week. It allowed me to increase the quality of the leaflet, to recruit an extra 30 or 40 salespeople and to go back to Peter to say "I want to lease 70, 80, 90 cars all the same, all with the National Distance Learning college printed all over them".

We got Rovers, they were lovely: £16,000, £20,000 a time. It was the biggest independent order that the Yorkshire Bank had had for vehicles. Needless to say, it went through the Yorkshire Bank's own leasing company. The big boss, Gary Lumley, signed it all off and just could not believe his luck – that his little bank had my business as a customer and had struck this deal. The Yorkshire Bank, incidentally, had just become part of the largest banking group in the world at that time – The National Australian Bank – and his big boss was coming over from Australia. I remember being invited down to the Bank to meet the big boss from Australia because I was The Yorkshire Bank's 'jewel in the crown'. I was their biggest independent company. Councils used Yorkshire Bank, as well as the Co-op and other banks. Organisations did, some big ones, but I was the biggest. I was the most up-and-coming. I was the 'Golden Balls' of the Yorkshire Bank. The growth had been exponential!

We were two years in and already we were turning over millions and millions of pounds. They loved me. They couldn't do enough for me. If I wanted something, like a personal mortgage, it was just there. I had it, and that's how I bought Yafforth Lodge, rather than using the business's money. I just got a massive mortgage and then another massive mortgage and my little empire, my personal empire of houses was growing. I often wondered how a bank can give a man, no matter how well he's doing, such a large mortgage, even though he's got historical county court judgements from when he was poor?

Then one day I'd decided, at the request of my accountants, which was one of the largest companies in the world, KPMG, that I needed to go and get directors. At that time I had 250 staff, a couple of managers and me. I was managing director, sales director, marketing director, branding director, distribution director, co-ordination director and communications director. I did everything. I even did the books. I did the tax returns. I did everything.

Richard Bottomley of KPMG, the big senior accountant and senior partner of the big international firm, said, "Mike, you've got to give some of it up, you've got to go and get directors." I thought to myself 'God, aye, yeah I have'. I've got to become the chairman and take a step back. So, I offered Peter Kenyon, my Bank Manager, the job of being my Managing Director cos he'd been with me for two years; he knew the business inside out and was ambitious enough to want the job. He said "yeah". Yorkshire Bank let him go pretty much immediately, not because they wanted to lose Peter but because they didn't want to lose me and, I suppose, it had their man inside. Being a proper banker he could put some real good structure into the company.

Peter joined; he was great. He says, "Mike, what we need now is a human resources director because you've got to stop telling people to 'fuck off'." He went on to tell me I've gotta stop doing this, I've gotta stop doing that, I've gotta stop telling dirty jokes at banquets. He said, "You can't do that. You're a big business now and you've got to conform. You also need a financial director because you're doing too much." I said, "Peter, fuck off! I am who I am, but I understand, so go and get a fucking HR Director and a Financial Director." So he advertises in the Northern Echo. Several people applied but the man that fit the bill the most was John Hornsby. He'd had 20 years' experience with Price Waterhouse Cooper, another big accountancy firm.

My God! Was that the beginning of the end? Was that the turning point? Cos when you're driving wild horses, but you have control of the wild horses, they may be wild horses but they are going to the destination that you want them to go. However, when you give the reins over to people that will make those wild horses conform, it's possible that they lose track, that they lose direction, that they lose impetus, because really the people don't know how to drive a wild horse. They know how to drive and train a conformed horse maybe, maybe not. Maybe it was the downfall, the turning point. Anyway, I did it.

John Hornsby, together with Peter Kenyon, both stood in the court for 91 days' worth of trial. They were both accused of running my 'so-called' bogus company. When it comes to thinking about my innocence, think of this. Would a 20-year-long employee of Price Waterhouse Cooper, the largest accountancy firm, throw his 20-year-old career in to join a bogus company? Would he do that? Would a bank manager that was rising in the ranks and had been in Yorkshire Bank for 17 or 18 years throw his career in to join and run (be the boss) of a bogus company? Well, the answer is 'no of course they wouldn't'. They joined because no.1, it wasn't bogus and, no.2, because they weren't going to let it become bogus.

For my part as much as I am a hare-em, scare-em type person, who will stick their neck out, I wanted it to be right. I wanted it to be conformed. I wanted it to be run in such a way that it would become a special company, a huge company, a company that everybody loved and believed in. I wanted it to be a brand that shone the shiniest shine. Roy Grimwood came on as Human Resources director. Alan Young came on as a Marketing Director, although he knew nothing about marketing – I just gave him things to do.

One day I was walking down the street in Stockton, having seen my sister. It was just before Christmas 1999 and just outside of Marks & Spencer's I saw an old friend. I say he was an old friend, really he was an old Judas. He worked with me at the Kent College and when I decided to leave by chucking my job in he said that I was going to set up against them. Which I wasn't, but because of that they withheld the money they owed me. He thought he could get brownie points or a pay rise maybe from Robert Webb, the owner of Kent College, but he didn't. He got the sack.

Three months after he got the sack, after being a Judas to me, I met him. He was going into Marks & Spencer's and he looked shocking! This was a man six-foot-five, 20 stone, a little bit older than me and very cheeky. He was a major player in the hierarchy of insurance companies in his day. He'd been about. He'd had good experience, particularly in sales. I saw a man who had let me down badly. He looked at me as if to say, 'My God! Was I going to kick the crap out of him?' I just said, "Hi Sidney, how ya doing?" He said, "I'm doing great... fantastic...", and I said, "do you want to go for a coffee?". I invited him cos I had the intention of giving him a job – not holding a grudge. He says, "No, I can't go for a coffee. I've got to go into Marks & Spencer's to take a skirt back that's too big for my wife [Christine], to get a refund for it." So I says, "Well I'll wait outside for ya." So he got his £20 back, came back out and he dropped the receipt on the floor. I picked it up and I realised the receipt wasn't a cash receipt. It was a gift card receipt. So someone had given Christine a gift certificate and he'd gone to a shop in Middlesbrough and bought the skirt. Then, within an hour he'd scooted to the one in Stockton to get a refund – a cash refund.

That told me instantly he was on his 'uppers'. He had nothing, and, possibly, the only thing they had to get them through Christmas was this £20. So I took him for a coffee and offered him a job: a very good job. I offered him a starting salary of £40,000 and told him he could pick his car. He picked a big Jaguar. He could start in the January as my General Sales Manager and he did do. He was good with the people and, for the most part, they liked him. Then I made him my Sales Director. The truth be known, he was my Sales Director in name, but he just did as he was told because he had no Sales Director acumen whatsoever. He was good as a manager.

Things transpired. The business goes from one strength to the next strength. I decide to diversify into all sorts of things, throwing ten grand at this and ten grand at that…all sorts of projects.

We had truly become the National Distance Learning College. We had about 80,000 students per year and huge turnovers. We were the biggest in Europe of its type. Then a man knocks on my door who I knew of from the entrepreneurial scene. He was an elderly man called George Horton and he'd semi-retired by selling his old folks' homes for several millions. I later found out they weren't his, they were actually his wife's. He was punting different businesses… a coal mine in Pennsylvania, which the owners wanted a couple of million for, which, by raising the money, he'd get a couple of percent of it. I nearly went for that one. There was another one which I can't remember, but one which was of great interest, it was a company called Red Balloo productions.

Red Balloo productions were the company that owned one of the fastest growing children's TV programmes, it was called 'The Lampies'. You can google it. It's not shown on TV anywhere anymore because of the bad taste of my conviction and things that the press were to say about me at a later date. It was an invention of a man called Dave Bonnar who was an ex-police inspector.

He, with one of his friends had developed Red Balloo Productions. They had raised money from various people from around the world, including my own accountants KPMG, to develop 'The Lampies', and another children's TV programme called 'Dr Otter'. They were doing really well. They had paid up Uli Meyer, who was the artist who had drawn all the characters for 'The Lion King'. They had commissioned him to draw up all the characters for 'The Lampies' and other programmes. They had made 32, I think it was, eight-minute shows. 'The Lampies' had just knocked 'Bob The Builder' off number one for the BBC. They'd taken it to various countries and developed all sorts of products, which they could sell, but they'd come to an impasse.

When businesses grow particularly fast – and, obviously, I knew this because mine had grown very fast – in order to maintain the growth of supply and demand of your products or services you need to be able to finance it properly. This is massively important, and they couldn't finance it. So, they'd asked George Horton to come and bang on my door for investments.

As soon as I found out what it was I instantly said 'yes' and arranged a very, very quick contract and a cheque for a million pounds. John Hornsby, who was later to give evidence in court to say that I'd made some foolish mistakes by investing in properties and in businesses, begged me for him to sign the £1m cheque. That's how much he thought it was a wonderful thing. Yet he decided at a later date, to save his own skin, not to give that evidence in court.

John signed the cheque at a little party we had and I became the Chairman, or so I thought, of probably the fastest growing entertainment creation business, certainly in the UK and quite possibly in Europe. The programmes had gone to the Cannes Film Festival and done very well …and so on and so forth. However, there was already a Chairman there who didn't really want to go. He was a minor shareholder. NatWest Bank was also a minor shareholder.

They'd financed a couple of million pounds before I came along. KPMG, my accountancy firm, had also given hundreds of thousands of pounds worth of services for a few percent of this up-and-coming children's TV programme-making company.

Now, I put my millions into Red Balloo Productions without doing the due diligence...foolish me! I'd took it that the half a million pounds' worth of due diligence that the NatWest Bank had done just a month earlier was good, was correct. So, on the basis of them, and their reputation, I threw my money in.

Mike Dawson, or Michael Dawson as he's better known, was the current Chairman and he didn't wanna give it up. He just did not want to give his chairmanship up and I didn't know why. I used to go and see him and he kept saying "we'll do the paperwork, we'll do the paperwork", but the paperwork never came. This is a revelation... it's a revelation for the police...he tells me that he's discovered that the two directors, including the founder of the business, had squandered about £1.5m on dancing girls, prostitutes and champagne and suchlike. He told me that the due diligence that the NatWest Bank had looked at was false and fake and that's why he couldn't hand it over to me. It was why he had taken my money to pay Uli Meyer off 'The Lion King' – to stop Uli Meyer taking the intellectual property of 'The Lampies' and 'Dr Otter' and all of Red Balloo Productions. At this point in time the shit had begun to hit the fan (and all this story was probably going over Nabil's head). The shit had begun to hit the fan.

The newspapers were all over me. This forced George Horton to come to me and beg me in a pub, in Newton Aycliffe, Durham, to please say nothing about what I'd found out. This was because the second director was his son-in-law. I've not mentioned his name because I keep my promise, no matter what. George Horton and his son-in-law was sat there through all my court case and never mentioned what I'm mentioning now…

That that director, Dave Bonner (an ex-policeman), squandered £1.5 million-ish of their investors' money and needed my money to cover it up. That led me down a road to refusing massive amounts of investments through Credit Suisse. The reason for this – contra to popular belief – is that I am an honest man. In some way I was protecting the investments of Credit Suisse clients whilst trying to protect my own investment into the production company. This was a £150m deal!!

The type of person portrayed in Google, the newspaper reports and the court would have no doubt taken this investment. No matter what, I was above board, and my refusal demonstrated that; but to this day Credit Suisse don't know why I pulled out of the investment. They believed I was the Chairman, but I wasn't because Mike Dawson wouldn't sign it over. Perhaps one of them is reading this book now, who knows.

Anyway, all my problems escalated and I just shut my mouth. Looking back on it, maybe I shouldn't have. Maybe I should have dropped a few people in the shit, because they should have done the seven years in prison that I got. Even though it was for different reasons. It's amazing really… when you find out who Mike Dawson is, and I'll tell you in a moment and you'll think 'Oh My God!'…

That a person such as Mike Dawson, who was a large businessman in his own right, can tell lies, withhold the truth from investors, who had put millions of pounds in and sequestrate — for want of a better expression — millions of pounds out of myself. He did this knowing that these two other men Dave Bonner and George Horton's son-in-law had just squandered and stole money from a limited company.

It makes you wonder why these people are in the position that they are in.

Let me tell you, Michael Dawson was the Queen's representative. He was the Lord Lieutenant of North or East Yorkshire. I can't remember which. He represented Her Majesty Queen Elizabeth at every event that happened in her name in North or East Yorkshire. But he, he alone, withheld the information of the embezzlement of the money from Red Balloo Productions from me in order that he could save his own investment in it. Right now, I don't know if he's alive or dead but if the police are reading this book now, I'll go on the stand and I will spill the beans, because I have had enough.

CHAPTER EIGHT – DEREK'S-MI-DAD

I once had a racehorse called 'Derek's-Mi-Dad' simply because I wanted to name a racehorse after me dad. No other reason. I did it for all my family members and extended family and so on. The horse was a shit racehorse, it was a bottom end racehorse. It was a horse I'd bought for next to nought but in no way did it reflect my dad. My dad was a wonderful man, a giant in his heart and he smiled through anything.

I have a story about me dad. I've got to tell you this story, because it's a nice story, a true story about him and the way he was with his kids. It's a particular story, which resonates with me about devotion and dedication to your kids.

My sister Christine who had Down's Syndrome was a lovely kid and a lovely adult; she loved everybody, but when me mum died several years ago Christine took a turn for the worse and couldn't understand where me mum had gone and why she never came home. It changed her slightly. Some days she was her old, sweet, lovely self, and other days she would be obstinate and an absolute pain in the arse to deal with. After me mum died, social services tried to persuade me dad to let Christine go into care, but he didn't want that. He wanted to look after me sister for as long as he could, and he did. He put up with the loveliness and all the negatives that had come out of me mum's death. Cos some days she realised that me mum had gone to so-called heaven, and other days she was waiting for her to come back from bingo.

One day, to reintroduce Christine back into normal life, they went to bingo in the afternoon, proper bingo, not the side shows on the fair. They had a good afternoon but on the way out of the bingo Christine went into one of her strops and planted herself on the concrete. She wasn't moving and shouted, "Where's my mum? Where's my mum? I want my mum!" Obviously, it was quite embarrassing for me dad. Here's this sixty-odd year-old bloke trying to drag this petite Down's Syndrome woman off the concrete to the short walk home. The more obstinate Christine got, the more obstinate me dad got. He began to, not drag her, but sort of pull her gently to try and get her onto her feet, but Christine was just getting worse and worse. She was shouting and crying "where's my mum?" over and over. Onlookers called the police, no doubt saying there's this older fella trying to drag this Down's Syndrome woman down the road and this woman is all distressed.

The police came along and, as in some cases and probably many cases, they didn't ask any questions. They just arrested me dad. As me dad's being loaded into the police car, Christine had kicked back and shouted "where's ma dad? Where's ma dad? I want my dad" and she was getting into a strop and a frenzy about her dad not being there. Me dad started fighting the police as much as he could, shouting, "that's my daughter, that's my daughter"! The police were saying things like, 'don't worry about it, we will sort it all out down the station'. They were not thinking of the stress it was causing my dad, and now my sister. They should have just left my dad alone to deal with my stroppy sister. The police put him in a car and took him down to the police station. They put my sister into another car and into the care of, I'm presuming, some sort of social care service.

Several hours later, my dad had been interviewed and Christine had been interviewed. The stress levels had gone up, all through the roof. The police and the social care decided to drive them both home and leave them to their life.

It shows you though, that little story is only a little story which is the beginning of the story of me dad. That the loss of a wife, or in Christine's case, a mum can have devastating repercussions. Whether you have Down's Syndrome or have some other, let's say some sort of life problem, then everyday things can become exceptionally distressing. It's a reason and a story that we should learn from. What we look upon isn't necessarily what is happening. We should always ask questions and investigate first in order that we don't increase people's stress and discomfort in life.

Anyway, time goes on a year or so and Christine is getting worse. Half a day lovely, half a day an absolute pain in the arse. She used to do things that would challenge the patience of a saint. Like everything that was not screwed down she would put down the toilet! It didn't matter what it was. It could be everything from a big cauliflower or cabbage to every toilet roll in the house, from a towel to her dolls and toys and God knows whatever else, me dad's wallet and ten pound notes. Everything that could be flushed down the toilet, or not, would be put in there. So me dad had to live in a house that was very, very bare, particularly near the bathroom. Another thing that she did was, if she was sent up to bed, or even to wash her hands, she would stand in the bathroom looking down the plughole with the hot tap on. She'd do this for four, maybe five, hours watching the water go down. If me dad tried to move her she would become aggressive, although there really was nothing of her physically. She would get very, very upset. She was focused on the water going down the drain. Sometimes it's a story for life, a message, isn't it? Sometimes it's what we do in our own life when we have a problem, no matter what it is, we watch that part of our life go down the drain. We don't act appropriately, we just let the problem drag us down the drain. Anyway, I digress.

On one occasion me dad was tired, he decided he wanted to go to bed early. If he wanted to get in his own bed before 11 o'clock he would need to send Christine to bed around seven o'clock. He knew she wouldn't be in bed until sometime after, after messing with the taps and the water, watching it drizzle or trickle or run down the drain. On this occasion me dad had sent Christine up to bed and she went willingly to give herself a little wash and to brush her teeth. After four hours of her being in the bathroom me dad had had enough. He marched upstairs, into the bathroom, and said, with a bit of a raised voice (we know this because Christine told us), "if you don't get in your bloody bed now, I'll tan your arse". Now me dad never hit anybody in his life and certainly not his kids. It was just an idle threat to try and get her to turn the taps off, get in bed and go to sleep. Anyway, as me dad says "if you don't get in your bloody bed now, I'll tan your arse", he had a huge stroke.

He collapsed, unconscious, on the floor and probably for the first time in years Christine did as she was told. She stepped over me dad, went to bed and went to sleep. Unfortunately, me dad wasn't conscious to see that his instruction had actually worked. When he woke up he found himself totally paralysed apart from his right arm which he had full use of and he could grunt. "Uggh" was all he could muster. This story is unbelievable, but it is absolute fact. He grabs himself — his paralysed 18 stone body — and grabs the floor with his right arm and begins to pull himself down the stairs. He was able to unlock the front door and pull himself onto the pavement to knock on the terraced house next door. There he was, banging, about seven o'clock in the morning. We know this was the sort of time because of the lady that answered the door. I can't remember the lady's name. She was me dad's next door neighbour. She opens the door and sees me dad on the floor and says,

"Bloody hell, Derek, what you doin down there?" She realises that he is obviously in a bad way and goes to ring for the ambulance. Whilst she's gone, me dad has turned himself around, gone back in his house and pulled himself up the stairs. He ended up lying at the bottom of Christine's bed, holding her hand while she is on the bed. We know this is a fact because the lady saw it happen.

She watched him pull himself up the last few stairs, and watched as he dragged himself to Christine's room to hold her hand. And would he let go? No! He wouldn't let go, not even when the paramedics came in and said, "Mr Smallman you're very poorly, you've got to let go of Christine's hand. You've got to come with us." And he wouldn't. Every time they tried to manhandle him off the floor he released Christine's hand and beat them away. Then he would grab Christine's hand again. Eventually the paramedics realised there was nothing they could do but ring the police.

Two nice policewomen came out and tried to pick him up. They said, "you've got to come, Mr Smallman, you're very, very poorly" and all he did, with his good hand, was beat them off. He would not go! He kept re-gripping Christine's hand. Even Christine was saying "go on, Dad, go", in her own little way.

After a while the next-door neighbour realised that all he was doing was making sure that Christine was alright. So the lady said, "Derek, go with the ambulance people and I'll look after Christine until Susan comes and everything will be fine." When she said that me dad let go of Christine's hand and went away with the ambulance people to Blackpool Victoria hospital. He stayed there for about five days until we had him moved. He went from Blackpool to North Tees Hospital, where he stayed for about six months until we found him a nice home opposite Kirklevington prison, where I was to end up.

So he was in his prison, over the road from me, a few years before I was there and he lived there in total paralysis apart from his arm and his grunt. The story goes on and I'll continue it in a minute, but just think about that, the dedication of a man to his child. Absolutely unsurpassed. I know that story is unbelievable, but it is absolute fact. We can piece that story together from what the next-door neighbour saw and what Christine said after it happened. She said, "me dad shouted at me" and then we talked to her and she said, "he went to sleep on the floor, but he shouted at me, so I went to bed". So we can piece the story together to be as true as it can be. My dad lived on for five years.

Me, my sister Susan and my brother Geoffrey — not the miserable one that I won't talk about — decided, with the advice of the doctors, not to have him treated if he got a cold or any sort of illness whatsoever, but just to let nature take its course. As it happens the will to live in my dad was so strong he got 30 or 40 colds and flus, bronchitis etc, and would never croak. He just would not let go. He wanted Christine to come to see him every day that my sister Susan was able to bring her to visit. After everything had happened, Christine had gone to live with my sister. Every day she visited, his face lit up and he knew she was fine. She was being looked after. She was actually developing and it was actually a good thing to get away from him, she was interacting with other people and life was a little bit different. So there was progression there.

I remember sitting with him one day and he was 'in'. Imagine a man who was 'in', he was fully aware of what was going on around him. He knows who he is, knows his life, knows he pisses and shits and someone comes to clean it up. He knows he can't express himself, he knows he can't move. A big independent man, he can't do nothing for himself, but he's in his head. He knows he's alive. How would you feel? However, he could still raise a smile in his contorted face. It was a lifeless face but he could still push a smile. I remember telling him a story of me and my friend Jimmy. It was a story that we had when we were ten or 11 years old, and we had our problems as the book has explained, but we were really good mates.

We used to build a little fire at the end of some council garages on a block of concrete about eight foot away from the garages. We hid on this concrete behind the bushes and built this little fire and one day this little fire just couldn't be lit. We wanted our jacket potatoes, we really did want some jacket potatoes. I hate them now, they're not for me. I'm not even sure I liked them then – they were always burnt to black and tasted like shit – but it was fun. We could build a little fire and be little men. We wanted our jacket potatoes but, on this occasion, it was too windy and we couldn't light the bloody fire. So what we did was move the fire to the concrete wall of the garages to get a bit of shelter. A little bit out of the wind so to speak, and it lit.

We had our little fire, and it wasn't big, no bigger than a laptop, and we had our baked potatoes. We burnt them to nothing really but we still ate them with a bit of manky butter that we had nicked from me mum's cupboard. We would stay there until 11 o'clock at night, some nights. On this occasion we only stayed there until about nine cos, unfortunately, there was a large explosion in the garage, on the other side of the wall. It was right by the fire we had lit and we shat ourselves. We legged it all the way to Jimmy's house, about quarter of a mile away, right across the park. We were thinking, 'my God what have we done?!' and I said to Jimmy, "you stay there, don't come out, wait for your mum to come home and I'm going home". It'd be about ten o'clock at night by then. Pitch black.

As I'm getting towards the house, I can see four fire engines and a lot of burnt-out council garages and I'm thinking, 'oh my God, what am I going to do?'! Anyway, me dad was stood on the doorstep which was only a hundred yards away from the garages, where the house was. He stood at the door with me mum and everybody else and as I arrived he looks me straight in the eye and says "is this anything to do with you?" and I went "no, Dad, it's not, nothing to do with me!" so he said "well you'd better get up those stairs and wash all that black off your face"! Obviously my face was covered in soot from our little fire, but he never said anything else.

Anyway, me dad's in his sick bed and I'm thirty-odd years late telling him the story that we didn't mean it. We were just making jacket potatoes and, luckily enough for us, there was nothing in the garages. All ten or 12 of them were empty.

We found out later that what started the fire was half a can of petrol right on the other side of the wall. There was some damage done to the buildings, but they were just concrete, crappy old garages. I said to me dad "it was me and Steven". Me dad just laughed through his contorted face. There were tears coming down it. He already knew. He laughed, and he laughed, and he laughed. His arm, the one that he could move, was flailing all over the place. It was like you do when you laugh so hard, and it really was flailing, he couldn't stop laughing! It obviously made me laugh with him, but it also made me very sad. It made me realise that he really, really, was 'in' there. Trapped with his total paralysis, his double incontinence, and all his pride gone through the window. But he was still there. He was still fighting. He was still wanting to make sure, at least, Christine was safe.

CHAPTER NINE – DOWNFALL PART ONE

T he National Distance Learning College was certainly the largest distance learning college in Europe and probably the largest in the world. We distributed 39 million leaflets every six months, purely and simply for advertising the college. Its success came through that leaflet. The leaflet itself went out, 1.6 million leaflets to every household every week on a six-week rotation. Mrs Jones or Mr Jones, or whoever it would be, who wanted to better themselves by getting some education, would fill a form in, or ring us up. Online wasn't used as such in 1997, when the NDLC was formed; although it existed, nobody bought anything online in those days, they just didn't trust it.

The college grew very, very fast and, at the peak, 2,500 people were being enrolled every week onto the courses. It took five to six hundred staff to administer the sales, the tutorials and all the supporting activities that went on around it.

Later on, in 2001, newspapers reported it was a bogus business. It was not a bogus business, it was a real business. Let me explain…a man comes up with an idea to educate adult individuals vocationally through distance learning. He puts his heart, his soul, a little bit of money, his banger of a car and his seven-months pregnant wife to work. The idea works and begins to flourish. The need to grow the service, the product and the staff base to implement the service, manifests itself into an outwardly growing spiral that takes hundreds of people out of unemployment. It gives hope and homes to those employees. It expands across ideas and genres to feed an ever-expanding vision of wanting to build something real, something to be proud of, something that would have an energy which would lead the way and for others to follow, and we did it. From my core idea to the day it all stopped, achievement was taking place and the 'want' to build something more special each day never stopped. Twenty-five years on, writing this book, it still hasn't.

The business wasn't a bogus business. It paid its taxes. It made money. As I said, it took people off unemployment and it trained them to a high standard. A bogus business on the other hand would be simply that — a non-existent entity with a couple of skullduggerous individuals, milking their victims and not providing anything. If you think about it, the 500 or so people that were employed carrying out a bogus intent would have been culpable of any alleged crime.

In the year 2000, the government introduced a scheme and that scheme was called the ILA — the Individual Learning Accounts. This was an educational granting scheme to help people in paying for their adult education in order that they could progress from a vocational point of view. What happened was that the government paid the large proportion of the educational bill and the student paid a smaller portion. That's the simplest way of explaining it. It is much more complicated than that, but effectively what the government was saying to the student was 'stop paying for your education and we will pay it for you, provided you pay £25 towards it'. So what I did was I tailor- made my courses, from a size, intensity and price point of view, to fit into the government scheme. So did another 8,500 learning organisations. That would be from a large organisation like London University right down to the one-man, one-woman band who taught IT on a Saturday afternoon once a week. Little companies, medium sized ones and great ginormous ones. Mine was one of those great ginormous ones.

We were embarrassing the government on many different levels. On one level was the level of education that we gave the individual for the amount of money that we charged, and also, on another level, the amount of people it took to educate those people. By way of example, an average university in the UK may have 15,000 people in it, 15,000 students that is. The ratio of student to tutor would be about 1:30. My ratio, with excellent results, was about 1:300. Normally learning takes place when you are sat listening to someone gibber jabber the information that is needed for the college course, mixed with research and mixed with your own thought processes. This has a particular name and it is 'notional learning hours'. It's how many hours it takes someone to get through a particular course. The way my courses were written was in paper form. These days you'd put them into a computer or download them from the internet but, at the time, all that hadn't taken off yet, so we wrote books, great books.

So there we are in my 'ivory tower', me as the chairman and Peter's administering as the managing director — I'd given that up and passed that on — of the largest and fastest growing distance learning colleges there ever was, and probably would ever be. Who knows what successes would have been reached had the business been left to grow organically. The individual learning accounts (ILAs) became available and it literally forced people, universities and colleges into buying into the scheme. How could any public or private university or college offer a course to an individual without offering them an ILA? Surely the person wanting the education would go to the organisation offering the ILA. It stands to reason; they would save a lot of money. No one was going to pay the full price for education anymore. To keep your college business alive, you had to work within the government's ILA scheme. So we did. By virtue of the number of people we were enrolling every week: as I say, 2,500 a week; an average of 110,000 year; not 15,000 a year like everywhere else. We automatically became the biggest company, college, contributing to the government's ILA scheme and therefore the one taking the most out of it. A lot of money out of it. But if you think about it, why not? The scheme is there to enhance the ability for me and my business to educate people. So we did. We filled in the forms, we took the people's £25s and we flew. Between 2000 and 2001, we enrolled 80,000 students to add to the 100,000 students that we already had. IT was Massive! Not all the people wanted or needed some form of qualification, but I wanted to offer, to those who did, something credible. We did that through City & Guilds, through Edexcel, which is the BTEC organization, and others. We had our own invigilation as well as external invigilation. This way we knew we were always maintaining the quality of delivery of the course. Our internal invigilators kept it right.

Anyway, we buy into the ILA scheme and everything goes right for quite some time. However, as time passed, we noticed a lot of other competitors springing up from nowhere. Colleges that hadn't previously existed. We found that some of these new colleges had discovered loopholes in the ILA's scheme and were offering the ILA grant to people on an illegal basis.

Foolishly, the legislation that Estelle Morris, as the Secretary of State for Education at the time, rushed to sign off, was so flawed and badly put together that anybody could put a few things on a disc or on a bit of paper and call it a course. The granting scheme that was written was so loose the course provider did not have to offer any learning outcomes – and that is insane! It was ripe for exploitation.

And someone wanting to exploit it could make up any old story. For example, a man could knock on your door and say, "would you like your hallway carpeted for free?" and you might say, "what's the catch?". He'd reply, "There's no catch. It's a new government scheme to entice you into education. If you fill in this form and sign it, and do this little course — it'll only take you ten minutes — you'll be entitled to £240. There is one little catch, you've got to contribute £25 to the course. You don't need to take any exams. You don't even need to complete the course. You just have to do your best. So when you've filled in the form, signed it, and given me £25, I'll process the form through the government. The government will then send you a card with a number on it. Now, here's my card. Just telephone me, give me the number on the government's card, and the next day I will come to lay your carpet." It was as simple as that. Could you be enticed and be a part of the con?

The bogus company would collect the £25, get the person having the carpet to fill in an ILA 1 form, and the bogus company would then send the ILA 1 form to an organisation called CAPITA, and receive the full £240 grant assigned to the individual. It was just as easy as that. That little course could be anything, how do you turn on the computer, here is how to do it, and that could be the limit of the course. It wasn't a course, it was a requirement in order to get the grant.

So for the con organisation that did this, they were selling an awful lot of carpet on the basis that the government was paying for it through the vocational scheme. That is just one example, and that on its own is difficult to understand, but it is one way of illustrating the corruption that went on behind the scheme.

The mistake Estelle Morris made was to sign the legislation off too quickly. She didn't develop the back-checking of the organisations claiming the grants. She didn't put any learning outcome requirements or any educational outcome as a prerequisite to obtain the grant. This made it easy for the grant system to be abused.

A senior lady within the ILA department asked us, the NDLC, for help because they knew they had got things wrong. They knew the legislation was weak, leaving the back door open to abusers. They didn't know the magnitude of the problem, or exactly what was happening, but they knew that what they had done was a gateway for potential disaster. My company, being the biggest of its type within the ILA granting scheme, was the obvious selection to help them.

After we'd alerted the government to the problem, my marketing director, Richard Bell, did the research and gave them the names and addresses of 17 organisations that were conning people in our town alone. As a consequence of that, they asked for more help. They said, 'you're the biggest one, you've the most experience with the granting scheme; we love you. We need your help to correct the legislation, to put things right, to close all the loopholes and to create processes'. To cut a long story short: we did.

We also found out, through my team of people doing investigations, and with the help of other education bodies and the people on the grant scheme, that Estelle Morris, who was instrumental in the ILA programme, had written the White Paper in such a way, such a lax way, that it allowed these aforementioned 17 scumbags to infiltrate it and get money for carpets, for anything, for nothing, which brought the scheme almost to a halt.

But not before we discovered that there was a huge overspend of many hundreds of millions of pounds, and much of that hundreds of millions of pounds had gone to the fraudulent traders, the people who were pretending to offer courses, not organisations like mine which were compliant. It was my responsibility to tell the government about this. Once I did this, and did it through a meeting with the government quango body, which I was previously invited to attend to give the government advice on about three billion pounds of adult education, surprise, surprise – my relationship with that quango body came to a sudden end.

Anyway, here's this ILA scheme with money falling out of the government's arse and I'm the man who's told them about it, and to protect a few people, not least me, they asked me to stay quiet. They were not trying to protect me, they were trying to protect themselves. They were trying to save face and avoid a huge scandal.

They said the story was 'not in the public interest' for all of this to come out and, if it did come out, it most certainly wouldn't have been in my interest. It was a concealed threat.

It was in my interest to be silent. But I wasn't going to be.

Had I chosen to be silent, maybe I'd still be the big businessman that I was. Maybe I wouldn't have gone to prison. Maybe they wouldn't have needed a scapegoat.

Let me explain something. People in the public eye, particularly politicians, judges and the like, use the phrase, 'not in the public interest'. Have you ever wondered why? You might take it literally, that a thing is not interesting to the public. But what it really means is, it is not in the interest of the person or body saying it because of what the public may think of them. That phrase, 'not in the public interest', like a Vivienne Westwood t-shirt, is the salvage edge of the fabric of the carpet that everything is brushed under.

I wasn't going to shush because there was more at stake than saving a few names and the embarrassment of the government. There were 5-600 jobs in my own business; there were tens of thousands of jobs within the industry; there were 8,500 compliant businesses within the scheme; huge amounts of taxpayers' money to consider. The country needed to know. The principles of the scheme were good and honourable. It would have been a sorry end of such great potential in adult education. And, not least, I did not want my moral compass compromised.

It was clear that I was not going to shush. I suppose I sort of pushed them into a position where they had to do something about me. At the time, the many hundreds of millions of pounds that they had let go through bad legislation was the biggest mistake financially that any government in the UK had ever made in history.

They needed me to shut up. And their way of doing this was to try to apportion the blame on me. Obviously, I couldn't be blamed for the bad legislation, the weak writing of the policies that surrounded the granting scheme. I wasn't involved in that. So, they had to try to find some dirt on me. This gave birth to the conspiracy. The conspiracy will be uncovered later on in the book. Let's carry on.

A parliamentary review was set up on the case. They organised a parliamentary report, which William Hague, the then Leader of the Opposition, my MP and, as it happens my next-door neighbour, sent to me later on. This showed them making investigations, and instead of inviting education providers and asking them about how the scheme was run, they talked amongst themselves, only inviting Vivienne Parry of the News of the World. The investigative committee's brief was to ask questions on why the mistakes had been made by Estelle and her team; to enquire about who was involved on the bogus college side; and to find out the feasibility of continuing the granting scheme. Vivienne Parry's knowledge was limited to an involvement with my NDLC business, and you'll see how much the News of the World and Vivienne 'had it in for me'.

How can you make an investigation into, and a worthy report about, a government mistake and the problems it caused without asking everybody concerned, or at least someone from each sector? It was clear, they admitted in this Parliamentary Report, that they had made a big mistake, but they hadn't quantified it into monetary value. It was their way of sweeping it under the carpet. 'Yes, we've made a mistake, let's carry on', that sort of thing. And why had Vivienne Parry been invited? What had she to do with anything? The only person the government's inquiry committee interviewed was the journalist from the News of the World, who wanted to bring me down. When you read on you will see how the government's remit to find a scapegoat fits in with the News of the World's remit to bring me down.

What the Parliamentary Report intimated was that there were some people who were responsible for a large hole in the scheme, and they wanted to find someone to lay the blame on. It intimated that they wanted 'a little man', 'a small man'. That was me.

They said there was a national company in the North that played a big part within the scheme, which the Report said Vivienne Parry was allowed to expand upon. To my mind, I suppose, and maybe you'll be of the same opinion, this was where the government and the News of the World were joining forces in order to begin discrediting me and my business for whatever ends they had. If I was a cynical man, you might say that they were using each other, nay conspiring, to ensure my silence and downfall. For me to be discredited would be the pseudo shush, cos nothing I could say after that would be believed.

The Parliamentary Report is too big, too deep to put into the book, but it exists. However, here is part of another document, which shows that the Department of Education were very, very aware of a problem within the ILA scheme. That problem, from a financial and reputational perspective, could maybe bring down the government, or certainly stop the re-election of Tony Blair, if it all came out.

Some time later, in October 2002, Estelle Morris resigned amid concerns, and this concern was rife at this time. It was at the peak of media attention but, in respect of the government, ILA schemes were not widely reported on, other than the alleged fraud that I was accused of and dragged through the hedge backwards over.

It becomes apparent from the document below, having read it a few times, that they were going to use me as a scapegoat.

SMITH, Sue-ILA

From: THICKITT, Sue
Sent: 27 APRIL 2001 15:34
To: SMITH, Sue-ILA
Cc: McGOLDRICK, Mike; DAWSON, Karen; HASLAM, Tina
Subject: FW:

Mike Sue

See John's reply

Tina Karen

ref only
----Original Message----
From: YOUDELL, John-LAD
Sent: 27 April 2001 15:26
To: THICKITT, Sue
Subject:

You consulted me about the current situation regarding a provider on the ILA list about whom the department now has reason to entertain concern.

In particular Derek Grover wishes to know whether one of the department's options is to suspend the provider, that is to take him off the list so that grants would be refused to those who wish to sign on for courses with that provider, until enquiries get to the bottom of the various causes for concern.

In my view the mere fact that there is no clear cut breach of the published rules for staying on the list is not decisive.

The Amraf case illustrates that it can successfully be argued that the "rules" are limited to what is administratively required for the operation of the scheme and that the SoS retains a wider discretion.

(As Amraf also illustrates we have not made it as easy to argue that as it might be because of the way the "rules" are drawn up and publicised.)

Taking the causes for concern in order, the involvement of the News of the World is irrelevant as far as legal considerations are concerned.

The 25 complaints received by the administrative agent are insufficient, by themselves, to justify a decision to suspend.

The MP's letter, by itself, is insufficient.

The concern of the DTI is insufficient (and may well be stimulated by no more than the actions of the News of the World.   *who + City +Guilds.*
Similarly the concern of the VAT authorities.

The question as to whether the provider can, in fact, deliver the City and Guilds qualification is a more directly relevant concern and you are more advanced in your enquiries. But you are not yet in a position to conclude that anything has, in fact, gone astray and you have not yet put your concern to the provider. It would be wrong to base a decision to suspend on that alone.

But, in my view you are entitled to aggregate these various matters to a degree.

Furthermore, while the press involvement might be irrelevant to a judge it is far from irrelevant from your point of view in advising ministers.

It seems to me that there is a risk involved in suspending but you will wish to balance that risk against the political risk of not suspending and thereby exposing ministers to criticism should the result of the N of the W article be for the provider subsequently to be shown to be ripping people off.

The risk of suspending is that the provider can meet most or all of the criticisms and subsequently makes a legal challenge to the decision to suspend.

There is a risk that such a challenge would succeed.

082

However, in my view the department can seek to justify a decision to suspend and, even if that justification failed I would expect a broadly sympathetic hearing. An adverse judgment might well be couched in terms that would not

1

...pose very great presentational difficulties.

We would say that the government has a legitimate interest in ILA money being applied so that people do promptly get the training that the grant helps to secure and that there is reason, aggregating all the above matters, to think that this is not happening in this case.

It will aid matters if, following a decision to suspend, the department acts promptly to get to the bottom of the actual situation. If resources allow it would help to interview those who are saying that they have parted with money but so far have had no learning materials.

If it turns out that the provider is kosher, it may improve the position if the department is willing then to offer modest compensation to the provider for business lost while the suspension was in effect.

The decision letter would need care and I stand ready to assist with it.

In summary, I advise that this is a judgment call with risk attendant on each of the alternative courses. It is perfectly reasonable, in my view, to give greater weight to the competing political risks than to the narrow legal risk.

John Youdell

You will probably be aware now, at the time of editing this book, that Donald Trump has been charged with criminal offences. I don't know if he's guilty or not. However, he made a statement in a television interview that his charges were fake and a sham. He went on to say the only way his opponents could 'keep him down' was to make things up and deflect attention away from their illegal activities. If you read the last paragraph of the above letter you will see that the UK government were trying to do the same with me. They said… "In summary, I advise this is a judgement call with risk attendant on each of the alternative courses. It is perfectly reasonable, in my view, to put greater weight to the competing political risks than to the narrow legal risk." I.e. the risk of me kicking up a legal battle about being a scapegoat!

As a result of the above letter, the Department of Education decided to commission two independent auditing bodies: one commissioned from the Scottish Executive and the other from the Department of Education. Each comprised auditors, an audit accountant, an educational auditor and a police person. What they wanted to find was that my organisation was administrating the ILA scheme incorrectly, and that I and my business was ripping everybody off, just like the carpet man that I explained earlier. This would have given them the hook to deflect the blame and attention onto me. So, I opened my doors to them, after they had turned off the funding and had stopped us being a provider. They came in and I let them have the run of my business on both occasions. They were investigating if the ILA scheme had been administered properly and if education was being provided. As you have seen from the earlier documents, no fraud was found and no non-compliance was found. They did everything in their power to try and use me as a scapegoat for the loss of hundreds of millions of pounds. They failed cos both reports, independently of each other, came back saying that same thing. "No fraud was found and no non-compliance was found." Ref. Documents on pages 58 and 59 of this book...

Conclusion

Fraud / Possible Fraud

- There were no issues that would suggest fraud/possible fraud

Non-compliance

- There were no issues that would suggest non compliance.

So phase one of trying to blame me for their problem had failed – they couldn't – and for a short while, a few weeks, they were obligated to reinstate the NDLC as an education provider, paying us about a £100,000, but owing the business many millions of pounds. In those few weeks we carried on with the courses.

One audit report did say that there was a complaint by a student who was unhappy – not that the course was shit, or that it didn't exist, or he wasn't getting what he wanted out of it. He was complaining that it ceased. Funny that. No other complaints from 180,000 students and the one complaint is, basically, a compliment. I'll tell you why it ceased. It was because, while we were suspended without payment, I had to cease the training for the students that the government hadn't yet paid us for. Legally, so as not to jeopardise the training of those students that had paid outside of the scheme.

In September 2001, they totally stopped the ILA scheme on the basis that they were unable to pin the problem on me. Phase two, following brushing the problem under the carpet, was then to shut the scheme down totally, leaving all 8,500 companies that were in the scheme delivering education, high and dry. Many, including my own, the National Distance Learning College, could not carry on. We had to shut down, we had to bring the receiver in cos the government stopped the money. I think it's fair to say that we were a business, not just a college, and therefore why should we continue to provide services to these many thousands of people if we're not getting paid for it? It was unquestionable to approach the disappointed students, left without their education, for the rest of the course fees, which were supposed to be paid by the government. And that's why we shut down.

It was the government's fault, it was their way of saying, 'this isn't our fault. It's not our mistake. It's just that there's so much fraud within it'. There *was* a lot of fraud in it, but not 8,500 companies committing fraud, and especially not mine, cos mine had been cleared of it. Anyway, that's why we don't have a National Distance Learning College now. I could talk about this for hundreds and hundreds and hundreds of pages, but I think you will now have got the gist.

Let me tell you, at the time of Estelle Morris and the people around her making the mistake to rush this granting programme through, they and she had no idea who I was. They had no idea of the possible consequences of what was to happen. They simply wanted to rush things through to score political brownie points with the voting public. When their mistake manifested itself and became public, they needed a scapegoat – someone to divert the attention away from them – and let me tell you, I smell of goat!

It was clear that I was not going to shush. Everyone is aware that the media – good or bad – bring out stories which relate to corruption of all sorts. From Watergate to Partygate. It doesn't matter about the severity of the corruption. Corruption in public office is endemic, and it is endemic because of opinion. Someone in the public eye, in a lofty position, has to make a decision. Sometimes that decision isn't the right one and some people might take umbrage with that decision. When this happens the media take a side and usually the side to discredit. As we know, huge organisations like the News of the World are no longer with us. With their phone hacking and deceit, and who knows whatever else. They certainly didn't do me any favours. From Prince Harry to little old me, the media have a history of deceit, deception and sensationalism just to get what they want. Hence the phrase 'print and be damned'.

CHAPTER TEN – DOWNFALL PART TWO

N ow... at the same time as all that ILA stuff was going on, the News of the World and the other 'red top' newspapers wanted me shut down. Why? you are asking yourself. Why would all those lovely, honest papers – that everybody knows are lovely and honest, don't they – want me shut down? It's simple. Earlier in the year, just after I'd got nominated for international entrepreneur of the year, I'd discovered that my leaflet – the 1.6 million a week leaflet that I'd put out from my college – didn't have to have just one business on it. It could have millions of businesses on it.

So, I approached the Royal Mail Chief Executive and says, "I want to use all your capacity for leaflet distribution." At the time the Royal Mail was bound by parliamentary law, or Acts of Parliament, to be more precise, that because they were a monopoly they could only put out three pieces of unaddressed mail – i.e leaflets or such – a week through one letterbox, which limited what they could do and who could use it. They had 26 million domestic letterboxes and 1.6 million business letterboxes that they could put a leaflet or a piece of unaddressed mail through. I thought to myself, let's up my purchase on the leaflets from 1.6 million a week to 26 million a week. That was a ginormous financial commitment from me. In short, when I asked this they said, "no, you can't have it". I said something along the lines of, "tough shit, I'm having it cos you cannot refuse me these contracts just because you say so". Parliamentary Acts impose certain restrictions on monopolies and when one is a monopoly – which the Royal Mail was in 2000 – they cannot make a decision who buys from them and who doesn't and to what quantity, provided it is a legal transaction. This is because there is nowhere else for the customer to go because of the monopoly. So, they didn't have a choice and they had to agree legally to the contracts, subject to only the availability. I remember one of my directors, a man called Alan Young, spending months simply signing pieces of paper for each postcode contract year upon year, upon year, as every postcode had an individual contract. Every route a postie takes – and there were 70,000 posties for every week of every year – had to have an individual contract, thousands and thousands and thousands of contracts.

This business strategy allowed me the ability to talk to people like Direct Line Insurance, the Book Club, and many other national companies in order to put their advertisements on my leaflets. I called this form of advertising Risk Free Marketing. It was created by me and placed into Thanx Marketing: a business created specifically to carry this service.

Risk Free Marketing in itself was a huge risk for me, cos I'd arranged a multi, multi, multi-million-pound contract to pay the Royal Mail to distribute 26 million leaflets every week. If my idea didn't work and generate business for my clients – and therefore I were not to receive the revenue for those leaflets – the whole of my group would have gone flat bust, owing millions to the Royal Mail. So, how do I get enough advertising revenue, enough advertisers to fill 26 million leaflets every week for 48 weeks of the year? I couldn't do that on my own, so I approached the third largest marketing agency in the country and that was a company called Brilliant. Mike Davis owned it and I approached him in his office in Leeds and explained to him that I wanted him to tell all his national companies that they could go on my leaflet for nothing, for free — risk free marketing.

He said to me "it sounds brilliant but how does it work? How can I guarantee anything works?" so I said to Mike at Brilliant "you tell all the organisations that commit money to you through their marketing budget that there is a new style of marketing and it's called Risk Free Marketing". Then I went on to explain how it was to work.

These big companies have a big marketing budget to generate a lead or an enquiry for their products or services. There were set budgets of large amounts of money and companies like Brilliant used the big companies' budget to purchase advertising. So, the big company would presumably say to Mike and his staff, "I want to spend £20m next year on newspaper advertising" – or whatever other form of marketing they were to do. What I was saying was "don't spend all of that budget, maybe only spend half of it, hold half of it back and send my business the copy of your advertisement. I'll put it into my leaflets and distribute the leaflets, 26 million a week, totally free of charge", therefore it was risk-free.

If no leads or enquiries came in response to the advertisement, there would be no charge and the big company would save millions. However, if a lead or an enquiry was to come, they'd pay me a fixed fee for that lead. How fantastic was that idea?

The biggest newspaper at the time was the News of the World, with a circulation of about six million. That's six million people, or thereabouts, of a fairly tight demographic – a demographic that buys the News of the World, The Sun, The Mirror, or The Whatever. Collectively the top five newspapers would have a distribution of about 12 million but now, for the first time, an advertiser could reach 26 million homes in the UK. That's every letter box in the UK for nothing.

At the time, even if you'd have paid multi-millions of pounds to ITV for a commercial to go out with Coronation Street every week, you would only hit 17 million at best. I was the man who put the fear of God into every form of media company. I could guarantee, without a shadow of a doubt, that at least one adult in every home, office, business, everywhere would see their advertisement because it was picked up with the post. Mr and Mrs Jones, who picked up the mail from their doormat would see the gas bill, the electric bill, their letter from Auntie Pauline, and my leaflet which contained the advertisements gained through Brilliant's client base. The difference being, with it being delivered with the post, it meant it had to be sorted through, to be looked at, not just put in the bin like a random distributed leaflet.

I advised that the companies should save half their advertising budget and only put half into the normal media route: newspapers, television, radio, magazines, or whatever – just to keep up some momentum. The other half they could keep back because they would get their leads through me. Many companies agreed to this, and they stopped spending very large amounts of money for advertising with the large 'red top' newspapers.

It all started to flow, everything worked fantastically. Mike from Brilliant approached his customers and explained the situation. They thought it was brilliant. If you think about it, the News of the World, for example, its maximum advertising capacity was to be in five and a half million houses per week. That was their distribution. At the peak of Coronation Street, 17 million people would see the commercials, but now, for free, you could get into every single house in the country every week if you wanted to. You just get your advertisement in one of Mike's leaflets. There was no risk, all that had to be done was to send a copy of the advertisement and I would place it in my leaflet. This is the clever bit... my leaflet was four grams in weight. It was an A4 piece of paper. All I did was take it to the maximum for the money. I was paying Royal Mail for 20 grams and so I added five more pieces of paper to the leaflet. This allowed me to put maybe another 100 advertisements in – all for free. I only needed some of them to work to make hundreds of millions of pounds.

The likes of Britannia Music and Direct Line Insurance said "how do we pay you?" so I opened a call centre in Sunderland where there were three to four hundred people working. They weren't my employees, another company paid them. I allowed them to take the calls for the leads. By way of example, one of my leaflets would go through someone's door, the lady or the man would see it and would, say, be interested in an insurance quote or a pension quote. They would ring the freephone number on it. A lady called Jane, who owned the call centre company, would get one of her operatives to read the screen as it popped up and say, "Hello, Thanx Marketing, how can I help you?" The lady or man would say they were interested in a car insurance quote from Direct Line or whoever. In some cases a coupon could be cut off the bottom of the leaflet and sent directly to my home address. The enquiries would be quantified, the leads filed and then we would invoice for the procurement of the lead to the company that it belonged to. It's as simple as that.

Now you can see why all these newspapers wanted to character assassinate me. Within a few weeks of this happening, Mike, from Brilliant, contacts me and says, "We've got a big problem." So, I go over to Leeds to see him. He told me he'd got a lot of angry advertising providers in the shape of the 'red top' newspapers. Their advertising revenue had gone down by 40% and they wanted to know why. He said, "They think it's us not selling it well enough!" It obviously wasn't that. He said, "It's happening because we're giving your risk-free marketing away in lieu of payment, in lieu of success of the marketing." The likes of the News of the World, The Mirror, The Sun and the other 'red-tops' were very angry. They were at the point of sheer fear that at some point they would have to shut down and close. Their advertising revenue was a large part of their business. What were they going to do about it?

At the time, the ILA problem, which I've previously explained, was going on. Everything was happening simultaneously. The newspapers knew that there was a problem with the ILA because they'd got complaints, not about my business, but about other businesses selling courses that didn't really exist. So, they were aware that there were problems within the ILA but they didn't know the full extent cos I'd not told them at that point.

They had found out that I was the chairman of the largest provider of education within the ILA programmes. So, the News of the World rings me up to ask me a few questions about the ILA programme, just general questions in the first place. I think they were just clarifying that I was the same person that was taking all their business away. Nothing really happens for a while. It all goes away, it all dies down and everything is fine and dandy, or so I thought. What was happening, behind the scenes and unknown to me, was that a conspiracy was beginning to grow. That conspiracy was the chiefs of the educational bodies and the newspapers, all with a reason to point the blame at me.

I'd taken myself off on a cruise around the Caribbean and was having a lovely time with my staff, Peter Kane, the managing director, and his family. We had a great time putting more weight on. I went over 18 stone. Yes, I was a big lad. A 'big fat cat'. Anyway, a member of staff on the boat came to see me. I was invited to come and talk to the captain about a telex message that had come across from the UK.

The telex message was basically saying that I was on the centre pages of the News of the World. It said, 'Mr Big steals £5.8m from Tony Blair'. They'd taken a chance on that, but it was easy for them. If I was able to sue them, they may have lost ten or 20 million pounds, but it wasn't going to be anywhere near their loss in revenue that they had already begun to lose through my Risk Free Marketing.

While I was on the boat, I instructed a few people to deal with it and to get the lawyers onto it. I went back to my holiday, but by the time I got off the plane in Manchester, the paparazzi and the TV cameras were everywhere. They all wanted to see the man who had taken £5.8m from Tony Blair! It's fair to say I'd never met Tony Blair and I still haven't to this day.

I raced back home and the press were outside my office, outside my home and they were out for my blood. They made up anything and everything for the best part of nine months in order to character assassinate me. Their character assassination was by printing as much shit as possible, as often as possible, and in any and every newspaper. Why would they want to do that?

Normally, when a businessman has been a bit naughty, they do an article and then leave him alone, that's it. I was their focus of attention week in, week out, every week for nine months. I pulled photographers out of bus shelters. I smashed a camera once cos I got so angry, and it's not like me to get angry to the stage of smashing something. Things got worse and worse and worse.

What had happened behind the scenes was that the News of the World and other newspapers had corresponded with the Department of Education. Vivienne Parry and a senior reporter from The News of the World – who was coincidentally the Treasurer of Princess Diana's charity after she'd died so I believe – had contacted the Department of Education and didn't get any joy. The Department of Education would have told them that I had passed the audits, that there was no fraud or non-compliance. They'd found out that I wasn't guilty of any skulduggery with the ILA because of the two reports that I've previously talked about. What could they do? What could the education authority do? What could the News of the World and others do but conspire to bring me down further? Obviously the News of the World didn't want to print that there was no fraudulent skulduggery found and that my business had been passed as 'clean and green'. So, they never did print that.

They'd realised that the way forward was to involve City & Guilds, cos all over my advertisements was the partnership my business had with City & Guilds to deliver the education and the qualifications at the end of it.

Now, City & Guilds had their own problems with me because of the time it was taking to develop the relationship. That time should have been weeks, but it had turned into years due to the incompetency of City & Guilds and the deliberate dragging of their feet for their own gain. I'll explain this further in a later chapter.

City & Guilds were simply asked by the News of The World if the National Distance Learning College was accredited to City & Guilds. Are they able to offer qualifications? City & Guilds write back and offer a one-line statement… "The National Distance Learning College is not accredited by City & Guilds and is not able to offer City & Guilds qualifications." That is all they said. That is the only thing that they said! Of all the things they could have said… like we have been working together for several years. We have approved their centre status to use our logo and we are happy that they are using mass leaflet distribution to every household in the UK and national television advertisements. Furthermore, we at City & Guilds have been slow to do our part with the accreditation of individual courses; however, this accreditation is now only a short time away.

Instead, they chose to avoid any future complications on their part or a risk to their reputation.

That was enough for the News of the World and the other 'red top' newspapers to carry on and absolutely pull my businesses to pieces like vultures, but little did they know that I would never lie down. They didn't need what they had been told by City & Guilds to be true because of the freedom of the press. They could simply use the excuse that it was in the public interest to be told that I was a crook and my business was bogus. Again, I can go on and on and fill this part of the book with hundreds and hundreds of pages. Just have a look at a few of the newspaper articles that I have included and you can see where they were going and what they were trying to do.

I'll point out something, however, that shows how ridiculous it all was, what they were trying to do and how distasteful they really were. On one small part of a news piece, Vivienne Parry says, "he said he was going to satisfy me, fat chance big boy!" and she put some sexual connotation on me satisfying her. What I'd said to her when she'd rung me up, was if she found that there was a complaint about any of my businesses, just to let me know and I'd make sure that she was satisfied, but she turned that on its head to be some sleazy, tasteless innuendo.

Vivienne Parry, later in court, ridiculed the people of Middlesbrough, inferring they were stupid. The prosecution barrister had asked her to read a letter of complaint that had been sent to her, but it was from a Welsh person. She said, "If I read it with a Welsh accent I don't think the jury will understand it" and, at other times, she openly said that a Middlesbrough jury couldn't understand something. To be honest, even though it was rude for her to say these things, this jury or any jury would have found it difficult to understand the pushing and the shoving of the barristers in my trial. And the innuendoes, which were very intentionally fabricated to make me seem to the court and the jury like I was an employee of the college, not the owner of a large limited company. The difference being, if an employee director of a college was spending the college's money for his own devices, this would quite rightly be a criminal offence. Implying this, and misleading the jury to believe this was what I had done, was only one example of many examples of the manipulation in the court.

I owned 100 percent of the shares in the NDLC. It was a private enterprise that sold and developed college courses for profit and I was fully and legally entitled to take a dividend at whatever level I wanted to. I was fully and legally entitled to spend it just like anybody reading this book would spend wages for the work they had done, or spend a dividend profit from their business. Mr Bottomley, of the aforementioned KPMG, the huge accounting firm, openly told the whole of the court that Mr Smallman could legally do whatever he wanted to do with the money — it was his. By way of example of the manipulation the jury, they were asked by the prosecution barrister, Andrew Wheeler, "Do you think it's right that Mr Smallman spent the college's money on a £70,000 racehorse and that he sponsored races, particularly at Wetherby Racecourse?" Well, Mr Bottomley said I could do what I wanted to do. It was my money and I was just indulging in my profits.

Many companies, including accountants' and solicitors' firms, market their business to heighten its profile by sponsoring a horse race or other event. If you think about it, most of my students were ladies between 25 and 50 years old, many of whom were on a course to better themselves. Lots of these ladies wanted some freedom from their partners or husbands, but the partner or husband didn't want them to do a distance learning course, or didn't even understand the needs of the individual. So, a part of my marketing strategy wasn't necessarily aimed at the user of one of my courses. It was aimed at the peripheral people in that person's life. This was in order that the peripheral person, who had a negative thought or feeling towards their partner bettering themselves, would have at least known that the NDLC existed and that it supported grass roots and urban activities.

Most people believe that horse racing is the sport of kings, and that may be so. However, at the time somewhere between five and seven million people normal people – you know the ones, you're probably one, average Joe, average Josephine – followed the sport. These people would therefore have a positive cognitive response to me advertising through horse racing sponsorship. So, therefore I ask you, is it unreasonable for a business such as the NDLC to advertise in this way?

I might say once or twice in this book that my barrister Peter Woodall, in summing up towards the end of the trial, tells the court that "there is no 'prima facie' evidence to convict Mr Smallman". The whole of the trial was a ruse, a continuation of the character assassination of myself. The prosecutor would say to the jury, "Do you think a normal person would act in this way?" Well, I'll answer that. I'm not a normal person. Your average Joe and Josephine wouldn't necessarily understand the highest business levels of decision needed to grow such a large company, nor would they be able to understand the level of finances needed to run a business of this nature. I'll add to that answer with a further question. Who established that not acting 'normal' was a prisonable offence? Should people go to prison for not being 'normal'? Who in this world gives barristers the right to act this way in court? Also, by way, what is 'normal' anyway? Is Richard Branson 'normal'? Is any leading entrepreneur 'normal'?

In court my barrister challenged Vivienne Parry for calling me a 'sleaze-ball' and she defended it by saying that City & Guilds had told her that my business wasn't accredited. She said she was glad that she had run the article and went on to say that if she hadn't run the article there would probably have been no case. In this instance I agree with her, she might just be right there! What sort of a mad world is this, that a 'red top' newspaper had this power and influence over the government systems? Not least because they make people who do have things to answer for want to hide and cover up what they can in whatever way they can: Estelle Morris, City & Guilds, am I ringing any bells here? Nevertheless, she wanted to take the credit for taking me down. Let me tell you, Ms Parry, if City & Guilds had told you the truth in the first place there would have been no story.

Parry chose to accept the word of City & Guilds as it worked in the newspaper's favour. I invited her into my business to see for herself that it was genuine and she declined the offer when, in the order of things, it would have been appropriate for her to visit me. She had the offer, she had the chance to prove for herself that we were a wonderful, legitimate business with hundreds of staff and with hundreds of communications with City & Guilds. If she had had a good honest journalistic intent, with a balanced perspective, she would have got an even bigger story. Professional journalism was never the intent here, the intent was simply to destroy me and my businesses. This was about grabbing any old straw to character assassinate me in order that my Thanx marketing business would fail and their advertising revenue would be rejuvenated.

Years on, we now know how corrupt the News of the World was with the phone hacking and other skulduggery they got up to.

Vivienne Parry and her article of lies gave the licence to every newspaper to follow her lead and character assassinate me en masse. That resulted in what accumulated to be a 23 year old nightmare.

Here is an article ran by Vivienne Parry in the News of the World.

College that will just never learn

WE'VE already urged you to keep your distance from the National Distance Learning College.

They told people who desperately wanted to better themselves that completing one of their courses would earn the City and Guilds diploma required by employers. It won't.

They also told students doing business ad-ministration that they would get a Btec qual-ification. *Not a chance.*

Now, as a result of our story two weeks ago, the government is to remove all reference to NDLC in their learn-ing provider databases.

The government has satisfied itself that our allegations are true, yet NDLC continues to lie. Readers who con-tacted them after our story appeared were told "not to believe eve-rything you read in the News of the World".

And they were still being told that they WOULD get C and G di-plomas. We suggest

WARNING: May 6 story that you check our story from the horse's mouth. Ring the spe-cial City and Guilds hotline on 0207 294 3357.

And when you calm down your next call should be to the trad-ing standards office.

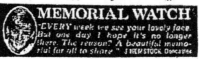

MEMORIAL WATCH
"EVERY week we see your lovely face. But one day I hope it's no longer there. The reason? A beautiful memo-rial for all to share." J NEW STOCK, Doncaster

The irony here is City & Guilds had said to Parry that my business wasn't accredited and Parry is prompting the readers of the News of the World to ring City & Guilds and ask about my college being accredited. Parry is printing this suggestion because City & Guilds told Parry that I wasn't accredited. However, from the next insert you will see what the top managers of City & Guilds were to tell their call centre to say if the public were to ask about my college accreditation...

From: RICHARD STOTT
To: ANDREW JOHNSTON, DI WALSTER
Date: 04 January 2000 12:04:34
Subject: National Distance Learning College - Tyne Tees Region TV ad 4 Jan

At the NDLC sales conference yesterday, it was confirmed that the 30 second ad will go out tonight in the Tyne Tees area at 20.22 during 'The Bill'.

In the ad, while the voiceover is saying that on completing one of the four courses available students will gain a City & Guilds qualification, the C&G logo is prominently shown.

Edexcel is not mentioned, although their logo still appears on the insert leaflets so as not to give concern to students who have already signed up for the BTech qualification. However, the new NDLC salesforce presentation pack refers to C&G.

Although we have yet not had any direct reponse to the NDLC leaflets, please brief your teams on the ad and possibility of inquiries. These should be dealt in same way, in confirming that NDLC are an approved C&G centre (041889) and offer City and Guilds qualificiations for their four courses; and refer the caller to NDLC for course details (freephone 08000 527439).

(The scheme number for suite of NDLC courses is 7236, but course details are not yet entered).

Other items from the meeting:
- NDLC salesforce (self employed, commission based) is expand from 50 to 80 over next 10 weeks
- each salesperson is given 6 confirmed appointments per day by NDLC
- current overall student retention rate is 50%
- continuing 1 million leaflets per week

Richard

I'd just like to reiterate that I was found guilty of illegally supplying City & Guilds' qualifications on the basis that my business was never accredited to City & Guilds. That is what I got found guilty of! I'll discuss more about that in a later chapter which covers my trial.

It was sometime in April 2001 that the News of the World had asked for a statement from City & Guilds and they made a statement that the NDLC was not accredited. Look at the date of this first document: January 2000! Anne Verdon, the call centre manager, had asked to be told what her team should say to the people in my call centre when somebody rang up about City & Guilds.

The senior management of City & Guilds basically say, "Tell anybody who rings up about The National Distance Learning College, that the National Distance Learning College is accredited to City & Guilds and on passing courses students will receive a City & Guilds qualification." Now why didn't City & Guilds tell Vivienne Parry that? That document's intention was still current at the point in time that Vivienne asked. We'd had a three-year relationship, a whole partnership, but more on that later, just look at this next document.

From:	RICHARD STOTT
To:	Cust Serv EXTERNAL EMAIL Anne Verdon
Date:	5/8/00 4:49pm
Subject:	Re: National Distance Learning College

Thanks for the copy of the email inquiry. We hope to finalise details of NDLC courses on Forward in the next few weeks. But the guidelines to answer enquiries continue to be:

- confirm NDLC is an accredited City & Guilds centre
- The courses are NDLC products.
- Candidates successfully completing the courses will a receive a City & Guilds certificate.
- The courses are not NVQs (and not funded).
- For course details candidates should contact NDLC direct

I hope this helps.

Richard

Sometime after my business has crumbled, when the police are investigating me, and this had all been shoved under the carpet as a big pile of shit so the truth wouldn't come out, the police go to City & Guilds and interview them. This is the result of that interview...

that this would be an agreement between them and City & Guilds to limit the purposes for which they could use the information supplied by us.

**** Katie believes that the police departed happily convinced that City & Guilds hadn't accredited NDLC courses, given permission to use its logo, or ever agreed that any of NDLC's assessments would lead to a City & Guilds qualification/certificate. However, she is concerned that detailed examination by the police of the documents received from the Official Receiver, will reveal that City & Guilds was slow in getting back to Smallman with feedback about the course materials NDLC had submitted. I gather from Andrew that documents had actually been lost by us. Our understanding of this is, that Smallman could therefore contend that he had submitted materials which he could legitimately expect at some future stage to be accredited by City & Guilds and he therefore produced his publicity accordingly.
Katie also feels that, since Andrew has been more immersed in the whole set-up than any of the staff still at City & Guilds, he is clearly the most appropriate person to be asked for witness testimony if this should be required. Customer Services have only been involved since the complaints started to come in.

Sue Berry 23/10/02

One person in City & Guilds has spoken to another person in City & Guilds and said how did the interview with the police go? The first lines tell it, "Katie believes that the police went away 'happily convinced' that the National Distance Learning College wasn't accredited by City & Guilds or able to offer City & Guilds' qualifications." Why didn't City & Guilds, at that time, tell the police what they had told their own call centre to use earlier?

Looking at these documents now, it just shows what big fat lies were told to the newspaper in order to make me look like the liar and push their inadequacy towards me and try to make me look like a criminal. These were handed to me as part of the evidence file that wasn't reviewed in court. Why weren't these shown in court? What did the police do with these? Those two documents could have undone my conviction. That conviction would never have been there if those two pieces of evidence, or the words behind them, had been told either to the News of the World, to Cleveland police, in the original investigation, or in my trial.

But hey, they didn't, and so I carried the burden of an awful long time in prison, the loss of my family, the loss of everything, and I'm here now writing this book to tell you all about it.

Here's one of the articles ran by The Northern Echo Group which is a report on the court activity.

Pair face jail for £16m college con

The News of The World's blindness to accept what the barrister was saying in court, reflecting the need for The News of The World to have me shut down.

I STAND BY MY ARTICLES
Writer defends her column

By GARETH LIGHTFOOT

A FORMER News of the World columnist has stood by her articles branding former Middlesbrough college chief Mike Smallman a "sleazeball".

Writer and broadcaster Vivienne Parry defended the stories in her consumer column "Cash and Parry" to Smallman's defence barrister Peter Woodall yesterday.

He claimed that Miss Parry was conned by leading education body City and Guilds.

"Madam, this man's life and company have been ruined, I suggest, because of your recklessness," he said.

Smallman and two other directors of the former National Distance Learning College (NDLC), based in Middlesbrough, are accused of making millions by misleading tens of thousands of students into believing they would obtain recognised qualifications.

Miss Parry said she received an "extraordinary" volume of complaints and information from a wide range of sources including NDLC students and staff and Trading Standards.

She stood by her "relentless" attack in the 11 million-copy-selling paper in 2001, which Mr Woodall described as "shock and awe journalism".

"It was a very shocking story," Miss Parry told the Teesside Crown Court jury.

"I thought that the language that was used to explain this particular story was entirely appropriate to the scale and extent of what I did indeed think was a scandal.

"It was outrage, indignation and fury, which was exactly what this particular story demanded in my view.

"I was so outraged by the level of criminality I thought had gone on in robbing people of their aspirations. I would not let my readers be bullied.

"I stand by this piece of journalism and I am inordinately proud of this piece of journalism because without it this case would not be run perhaps.

"I investigated so thoroughly that when I passed over my files the police started an investigation."

She said the use of the word "sleazeball" and her reported description of Smallman as "some scabby bloke from Middlesbrough" were appropriate. She denied prejudice.

She did not take up Smallman's invitation to visit the NDLC because "it would have been a lot of old flannel".

City and Guilds told her NDLC was not approved to offer any City and Guilds courses.

In an internal email, City and Guilds project manager Andrew Johnston described this press statement jokingly as "short and sweet like a chocolate-coated piranha".

They did not reveal that they had allowed NDLC to use their logo and approved NDLC advertising, including a TV ad wrongly claiming to offer City and Guilds qualifications, the court heard.

Teams were instructed to tell enquiring students that candidates would receive City and Guilds certificates, despite no courses being accredited.

And a City and Guilds lawyer told senior figures, including then Director General Christopher Humphries, of concerns they may face "criminal action... for aiding and abetting a fraud... in light of our inaction for nearly two years".

Mr Woodall claimed there was a suggested "agreement to deceive" and an attempt to pervert the course of justice in City and Guilds.

He alleged that City and Guilds permitted and encouraged the NDLC to market a product that wasn't ready then cut the NDLC adrift and scapegoated the college.

"That's a scandal isn't it, Captain Cash?" said Mr Woodall.

"I think that's entirely your gloss on the affair," she said.

"My view of Mr Smallman would not have been changed by this information."

Michael Smallman, 44, of Leeming Lane, Northallerton, Peter Kenyon, 42, of Roseberry Road, Great Ayton, and John Hornsby, 59, of East Close, Sadberge, Darlington, all deny fraudulent trading.

Proceeding

IN COURT: Vivienne Parry at Teesside Crown Court, and defendants, above from top, John Hornsby, Peter Kenyon and Michael Smallman   **Pictures by PETER REIMANN and ANDY STEVENSON**

CHAPTER ELEVEN
- SCORPIONS

Don't think for a minute that it's just News of the World to blame, but they did start it off. Almost all the national newspapers were to blame, all of them followed the lead and that became apparent. I'm guessing that, to them, it was worth following the lead of the News of the World in order to suppress me and suppress my marketing company: Thanx Marketing. It benefited all the newspapers to shut me up and to 'get rid' of me.

Just as the business was beginning to crumble, myself, Peter Kenyon and a director called Richard Bell were over in London. The business, literally that day, was written off by Deloitte Touche [the receivers], and it was shut down.

Another story that was going on in the press at the time, which many will remember, was about Michael Barrymore. Michael was obviously gay and was, let's just say, having a party at his house and a boy, a young man, was found dead in his swimming pool. The rumour was, the denigration from the press intimated, that he [Michael Barrymore] was responsible for this young man's death. The irony of it was that it was the death of my business, and me and Michael Barrrymore were walking across Leicester Square in London. The two people that were prominent in the newspapers on that day, and in fact that week, were Michael Barrymore and myself. We were walking across Leicester Square, who's there?

In a long, black, warm coat, Michael Barrymore. We passed the Square within two feet of each other and he looks at me and I look at him. Now I don't know if he knew who I was, but the look was knowing and I gave him back the same knowing look. It was as if to say, 'what the fuck are us two doing in these newspapers?' cos the stories that were being told about both of us were definitely not true.

I don't know what happened in Michael Barrymore's house that day. I don't really care, it's a sad story for him and the young man, but I do believe in my heart of hearts that he was as innocent as I am. I know that through the look that he gave me.

Before we went home that day, me and Richard Bell decided to wander about London. Peter Kenyon had disappeared and I didn't want to come out of London with nothing. I had this fanciful idea that although the Thanx Group was now dead on that day, I wasn't dead on that day. I walked into Discovery TV's European headquarters in London and asked to see a director, using my lovely business card as the chairman of the Thanx Group. It still had a bit of power and got me to see the person that I wanted to see. On that day, an idea hatched out in my mind. I proposed that my Please Publishing Company – that's the publishing company that did the Lampies magazines and other things, and was still 'alive' – did a magazine for Discovery Kids. They agreed. Over the coming months we created some fantastic documents, mock magazines. This enabled me to get the rights to 52 countries to create probably one of the world's largest distributions of children's magazines, all related to Discovery Kids, and what Discovery Kids TV programmes showed on Discovery TV. The only thing that ever came of it, because all my troubles escalated, was the mock magazines that my studio created. I'm not too sure, but I believe I actually still own the rights. No-one's ever said I don't, and there is still somewhere in the world a contract that says that I do. Nevertheless, it was just another catastrophe.

We went on from there, me and Richard, and took the digital audio tapes (DAT) of The Lampies' television programmes to America.

I think the date was 4th September 2001 when we went to see the number three in Viacom. We flew out to New York and went up the lift in a building next to the Twin Towers to about the 20th floor. We walked into this exceptionally posh office and saw Sumner Redstone's number three and discussed the selling of The Lampies series to Viacom. For those of you who don't know who Viacom are, they are the biggest, or certainly one of the biggest film makers and TV station owners in the world. I think they own CNN and other large news agencies. They own Paramount pictures and so on and so forth. They used to own Blockbuster Video, all over the world. They were ginormous.

We were in the early parts of negotiation that they would buy The Lampies, all 32 programmes, both series, for approximately £60m and the rights, of course, to do other things with them. To sum up and close the discussion I asked him, "Is that about right?" The last thing the gentleman said to us was, "It's not unreasonable." The only proof I've got of this is Richard – and he's out there somewhere. I'm sure he'd confirm that this is the truth, cos he was there in the room with me.

Anyway, we were laughing and joking on the way home, thinking the world had been saved, or at least our world had, cos we had £60m coming. The unfortunate thing for us – another part of our bad luck, but so much worse for other people – was that thousands of people were in the building when the 9/11 disaster happened. Several hundred people from Viacom were killed and we just did not have the heart after that to contact Viacom to ask about our deal.

This short little story is absolutely true. Another kick up the arse for Mike and his people – doing great, wonderful things, with fantastic ideas and not seeing them through because of events beyond their control.

Another thing, which was out of our control, was those nasty newspapers. As I say, it wasn't just the News of the World, there were others, particularly the Daily Mirror. There's a man there, and he's still there today, writing his garbage on all sorts of subjects. To give him his due, a lot, I'm sure, are justifiable. However, to come back to the point, if City & Guilds had told him the truth would he, like Vivienne, have had any story to tell about me? I invite you, Andrew, and Vivienne, if you're still in the world of media, to come and talk with me about the truth. Come and see the documents and work together to stop this sort of thing happening again. That's if you do really care about the truth.

One day, after the business had collapsed, I'm sat in my lovely house, trying to pull things together to move forward. Such as buying a lot of the students from the receiver. By doing that I could, with my own money, make sure that at least some of the people got the education that they had paid for, or at least had begun to pay for. We, myself and the staff I could afford to employ, under the business name Tutorial Services, we took on about 25,000 students. I couldn't afford to do it, but I did. It cost me 'an arm and a leg'.

I was able to purchase the students back from the receiver because they had found the NDLC to be a bona fide company and not a bogus company. So I did. Even with that intention Vivienne came at me without any desire to understand the truth, just a will to destroy me…

Another attempt to destroy my business through entirely biased reporting:

Back on course to lift your dosh

THE National Distance Learning College, purveyor of bogus educational courses, went into receivership on November 23—leaving nearly 60,000 people who paid upfront in the lurch.

Their tuition stops and they lose everything. But around 7,000 customers who pay monthly are now to get their tuition through a company called Tutorial Services Ltd. And

guess who's behind that—sleazeball Mike Smallman, owner of the NDLC, who bought these 'assets', also known as paying punters, from the receiver.

Since Tutorial Services now has only a handful of tutors, readers may experience problems getting tutored.

Another curious fact is that on the

very morning of the day NDLC went into receivership it received £77,000 from the government's Individual Learning Account scheme and banked it, even though they knew they could not provide those courses.

This is just one more scandalous aspect of this scheme which has rewarded shysters and penalised genuine learning providers.

DO YOU NEED HELP? Want anything investigated? Write to Cash & Carry, News 1 Virginia Street, London E98 1NW or e-mail Vienne.party@newsoftheworld.co.uk. Including a day in

Just a point: when a receiver takes over a business as Vivienne points out below, none of the existing directors have any power. The £70 000 would have been accepted and received by the new directors, which is the receiver. Another manipulation by the press.

Anyway, as I was organising the Tutorial Services one day, in order to salvage what I could, I was in my home office with my brother-in-law, my wife and a couple of others and we were having some building work done by my own company, Thanx Construction. We had four or five workmen flying about the place. I looked out of the window and I saw three fellas there in workmen's outfits. They just didn't look right. There was something about them. They weren't my workmen, and they weren't Steve's men. Steve was the director of Thanx Construction. I went outside and, as I opened the door, Penman, from the Daily Mirror, undid his coat and thrust into my hand a trophy of about a foot-ish tall. At the same time he says words to the effect that I was the most crooked businessman ever. Another man pulled out a big camera and started taking photographs while another was writing things down. For ten seconds of my life I was on the road to murder. I'd had enough. In my head – just in my head – I was thinking of using this thing, with its marble base, that he'd just thrust into my hand and sticking it through his head. Instead, I just stared at him and kept staring at him while I counted to ten. I'd advise everybody to do the same thing in similar circumstances: the murder rate would drop considerably! I dropped the thing on the floor. With my big arms I corralled the three of them together and said, "I'm arresting you for trespass."

One of them then ran to his car, hoping to drive off with his two mates. I stood myself in front of the car preventing them from moving. After saying a few choice words to them – which we won't go into, but they weren't very nice – I got my brother-in-law to call the police.

Some two hours later, after they'd contacted their legal department, they were considering ringing the police themselves. They were accusing me of kidnapping them, which was just ridiculous. I was arresting them cos they were trespassing on my land, and they were unwanted. Anyway, while we're waiting for the police – and it did take forever for them to come – I just, sort of, lost my temper. In the Daily Mirror article that ensued, every sentence was 12 words long, but six of the words were starred out. I had begun to tell them about what I thought about the government. I was explaining that it was a government conspiracy, but no-one was listening to me. The unfortunate thing for me was that I did use a choice phrase of words. Every time I said something positive for myself I still used the word 'fucking'. So, they just printed what I had said almost verbatim. They left all the fucking out of it and used f***.

They never printed anything about me after that, certainly not for a very long time until the trials came, years and years later. Simply because they'd read it themselves and realised there was more to Mr Smallman's problems, more to the truth that I was saying, more to the negatives of City & Guilds which I've previously explained. Interestingly enough, many of the online versions of the newspaper articles about my prison sentence have been retrospectively updated. That says a lot, doesn't it?

In this case though, it just shows you, even though The Mirror had printed something sort of positive, my side of it for the first time, they still pointed me out to be 'a foul-mouthed so and so'. I can't disagree with that though, considering what I said at the time!

The police came along two hours later and told me that they were going to arrest me for kidnapping. I thought that was really funny. If I didn't let them go – cos you can't arrest someone for trespass as it's not a criminal offence anymore – I would be arrested for kidnapping. So I chased them off my land instead and we all went our separate ways.

After months of all the cars and vans at the end of my drive, three or four days later a miracle happened. All the press had gone. I'm guessing it's because they read what had been put in the News of the World and they thought, 'Shit! This man's not going to lie down. This man does have a story. We've pushed him and pushed him and pushed him to the ends of the earth, where he's found it reasonable to kidnap three press people and tell them the f***ing truth about everything. Enough for the Daily Mirror to print it word for word anyway'. So they all left and they left me alone. All apart from one large black van.

I'd had enough. One day, on my way out in the car, I got out of the car, at the end of my drive, went up to the large black van and banged on the doors. Two of the biggest fellas I'd ever seen in my life got out. They were dressed in suits – like X-Men – and they invited me, very politely, to sit in the luxurious van. It really was luxurious – it had lovely seats inside. It wasn't anything like my van that I have now, Ste-van, I call it. I use Ste-van for any work I can do to keep a roof over my head. Anyway, they very politely told me that they'd got no grievances with me and that they didn't represent anyone in particular. They told me it would be good if I just shut up. If I stopped shouting about the government. If I stopped shouting about City & Guilds and the press and just left it to go away. Bearing in mind this is years and years before any policeman got involved – apart from my audits which I'd had six months earlier. They also intimated that it would not be good for me or my family to continue the fight. Somehow, they knew I was contemplating moving to Spain and they suggested it would be a good idea. I got out of the van, got in my car and drove away. I never saw them again,

I never saw anyone from the press, nor anyone from wherever the men in the black van were from, again on my drive. I thought it was over in some way. I thought it would be a good idea just to bugger off to Spain. I had a few horses over there, with some success, winning lots of races. The business was finished over here. I'd left Steve Caladine, one of my directors, and a few others, in charge of the bits that I'd bought back from the receiver.

So we sold up. Yorkshire Bank got half our money and we had a bit left – about £200,000 – and we disappeared into Sotogrande in Spain. Eventually we took Steve Caladine and his missus; Richard Bell, his wife and their two kids; and we all went to live together in a huge mansion that I was renting at the time. This cost me three to four thousand euros a month.

I tried all sorts of things to get business going, I'm not going to go into them, but the long and short of it was that, as my money disappeared, so did my 'best friends'. Caladine held me to ransom, with some of my horses that we took over to England in his name. Richard Bell just upped and went with his family. You really know at these times in your life, who your real friends are. I'd already lost all those lovely staff who I thought cared about me cos I took them off the dole, or whatever it would be. The one or two who were sticking by me were only sticking by for a reason. It's because they believed I would get through and come back and they would benefit from it. They didn't stick by me out of loyalty, that is a certainty.

So there we are, once those had gone, we were in Spain in our lovely house. The money was running out. I was doing little bits and bobs locally. I get a telephone call. We'd been in Spain for maybe 18 months now. The telephone call was from the police in Florida, in Orlando. They were saying, "Hi there, Mr Smallman, do you own a house in Claremont in Florida?" I said, "Yes I do." He says, "If you don't get over here right now the mortgage people are going to foreclose and repossess it. They've been looking for you for quite some time and the only way we identified you and where you were was from all the newspaper reports." The newspaper reports were hitting America.

I got on a plane on my own. I went over to America to find that our lovely three-bedroomed house had been ransacked. All the windows and roof tiles had been stolen. The pool heater and pumps had been stolen. The air conditioning had been stolen. The internal doors had been stolen. The light fittings and wall sockets had been stolen. The cooker and everything had been stolen. It was basically just a shadow of the house with nothing in it. I looked in my lovely pool and there was about nine inches of green slime at the bottom. There was everything but alligators living in it. There were snakes, scorpions and all sorts.

I thought, 'Hmmm, what's happened here?' That type of thing anyway. I went to see the police and told them that there was no mortgage on the property, simply because I'd paid for it. There was nothing on it. They said, "Well, there is and it's down to you," or words to that effect. But it wasn't me, it had nothing to do with me!

I went to see Gabby. Gabby was the estate agent who'd become a friend over the years. He was looking after the house for us and he'd rented it to his cousin. Even though it was not Gabby who did the 'naughties', his cousin had not paid any rent and he had re-mortgaged it in my name. He'd got several hundred thousand dollars from it.

Blown the lot. Done whatever he'd done and then stripped the house of all its shackles – if that's the right word.

Anyway, I couldn't do nothing about it. I couldn't prove it wasn't my mortgage – not without losing the house – cos it would have taken a long time to locate this man. He could have been anywhere in America. Gabby didn't know – or at least he wasn't letting me know if he did – where he was. He wasn't letting the police know.

I went down to Orlando and filed a Chapter Eleven bankruptcy to stop the repossession of the house. I sat on a long queue of chairs in front of a big, big judge. I say she was a big, big judge, she was a lovely lady – but she was big! She was a very big lady and she had a presence about her. She had several hundred people in line telling her their story about why they wanted this, that or the other. It came to my turn and I told her the story. She said, "I can't believe, Mr Smallman, that our American people have done this to you. So, I'm granting you Chapter Eleven bankruptcy, but we're not going to execute it. This will give you time to sort it out." So I did.

I flew back to England and told Angela all about it. We collected the kids, locked up shop – so to speak – in Spain and went to live in America. We went for six months at a time on the visa waiver programme. Whenever our time ran out, we would leave the country and then come back in. Anyway, my 40th birthday, what a great party I had! So, there was me, stood in nine inches of green slime, shovelling it out of my pool. It took hours and hours and hours. The germs that were in there, who knows how bad they were! The next few days I put new shingles on and installed the air conditioning. Shortly after that we put the house back into a state that we were able to sell it. We sold it very, very quickly 'for a song' and, effectively, stopped the foreclosure. We paid off the mortgage. The criminal was never found. We came out with about $25,000. We decided to stay in America and rent a house, but first what we needed was our full visa. We'd set up a business by that time and Angela had got a job in a top school in the United States. It was time to move our lives to America.

So we went back to England, with the blessing from Homeland Security in America, who said we could live there with a lovely job, a lovely business idea for me and lots of friends in America. I'm paraphrasing this cos it goes on and on and on. We land back in America and go to the Embassy, thinking all we've got to do is get the man from the embassy to sign our documents and we've got a seven-year visa entitling us to live and work in America, a lovely new life! However, after two hours waiting – with the little ticket we got and with all our documents ready – we went to the young man at the counter to get our visa. He took all our paperwork and disappeared. He came back 20 minutes later. He got my passport and Angela's passport and just stamped 'rejected' on them. I said to him, "What do you mean 'rejected'?" He says, 'You cannot go to America for ten years.' So, I asked, "Why not?" He says, "Because you're not domiciled in the UK." Now that was his excuse. He thought we had no intention to go back to the UK.

We go back to Durham, after buying a couple of McDonald's for £5. We go and live in Grandma's house and we find – two weeks later – a little rental property, a bungalow, in Leeming Bar in North Yorkshire. We're in there a couple of weeks, bearing in mind this was now 2004-ish. This was three years after the downfall of my business. Three years after City & Guilds lying to the press. Three-ish years after all that stuff with the press, all the governmental stuff from the Department of Education, with their big problem of three, four, five six-hundred million pounds, or whatever it was.

Sixteen policemen come through our door. They arrested me and Angela on the basis that I stole £16.8m. Where they got the number from, I really don't know. They took my kids and they searched them and then they sent them to stay with someone while we were in police custody for 16 hours being interviewed.

CHAPTER TWELVE – NAUGHTY POLICEMEN

Sometime in 2001, around about April time when the newspapers first started saying nasty things about me, a man discovered my email, mike@thenationaldistancelearningcollege.co.uk That man was called Stephen Liquorice; he worked for a firm of solicitors. He was one of their top solicitors, a fraud case specialist. He emailed me asking if I needed any help. I was all full of myself. I emailed back, basically, in a polite way, saying, 'Fuck off, I don't have a problem. I just don't have a problem.' Then all hell lets loose with one thing and another and all the newspaper things. Like I've said, we lose the business. The world turns upside down. I fly out to Spain and I fly out to America. We lose everything. We come back and the police come through the door in 2005.

Four-ish years later and luckily enough for me I'd kept that email. He knew, four years earlier, that for whatever reason, I would be needing him and, as I'm dictating this part of the book now, I'm thinking, well that was either a fantastic piece of marketing on his part to get the contract to be my solicitor in a big legal case, four years before there was any suggestion of a big legal case, or he was 'a plant' from somebody in order that in the future I would make him the first line of my defence team. So, it could well be that Stephen Liquorice was 'a plant' as a solicitor, knowing that I would appreciate his marketing prowess and actually think he was a good bloke to have on my side. Maybe not, maybe he was genuine, I don't know, but it makes you wonder. Why would a solicitor email a man four or five years before any trouble is going to hit the fan? Maybe because he knew the trouble was going to hit the fan and they needed, the government or whoever it was, whoever instigated my downfall, would need a man on the inside. It's a poignant thought.

Anyway, I emailed back Stephen, saying I've been arrested by the police, this was after I'd been interviewed for 16 hours. They did that without a solicitor being there cos I had no guilt in my mind whatsoever. I arranged to meet Stephen in his Manchester offices and he took the case on board on behalf of the company that he was working for. Within weeks the case had grown. I'd been interviewed a few times, and it kept growing and growing. He came to me and he says, "Mike, I want to start my own business." It was called Stephen Liquorice Solicitors. "And I want to take your case with me into my business." So I agreed because I trusted him. On the face of it, it really appeared that he was trying so hard. He'd come down to my house, in Catterick, and sit with me for two days a week, for several years helping to build my case.

He'd become a friend and it appeared that he really was dedicated and believed in my innocence. He is the man, who pointed out to the barristers that there was a conspiracy and he had a lot of pieces of paper to prove it, some of the ones I've got now, not all of them, but there was a definite conspiracy. I really believed in him.

Anyway, one funny time, he's come to my house and we were getting on great. We're having a laugh and a joke, we're pulling things together from hundreds of computers, thousands and thousands of documents and we are really putting a fantastic case together. He's sat at my kitchen table, typing away as I'm talking, and there's an irony here as there are people now typing away as I'm talking, for sort of the same reasons.

My dog, Alfie, who was the biggest black Labrador that you ever did see, and the nicest dog that I've ever met – bar one who's very close to me now and listening to what I'm saying, that's Merlin. I had to get him in the book somewhere, didn't I? Alfie sat there, watching Stephen Liquorice eating his sandwiches. My Alfie was the most drooly, drippy, slimy, slavering dog that you would ever wish to meet. The drools were cascading over his lips and not breaking until they hit the floor, they were ginormous drools. Anyway, I said to Stephen, don't give him none, cos he'll be getting fat, so Stephen just continued eating his sandwich and Alfie continued to drool and drool. Then all of a sudden Alfie must have got a little tickle in his ear and he shook his head violently. That drool went up the walls and up the side of Stephen Liquorice's suit, it was one of those 'Noooooooooooo!' moments! He had covered my friend, the solicitor, in dog slime. It was funny, I laughed and laughed and laughed. Stephen didn't though. He was covered in Alfie's slime.

Time goes on, backwards and forwards to London, backwards and forwards to the police station, backwards and forwards, backwards and forwards and backwards and forwards. Now one day, just before the trial, I have a meeting with Peter Woodhall. He's my number one barrister. We're there in London at a big, big table. It's one of those big board tables. I'm on one side and Stephen and Peter are on the other, and they've laid out about 40 pieces of paper to show that the Government and City & Guilds had been corrupt. They said, 'You are right, Mike, there is a conspiracy against you and we are going to prove this in court.' Every time I said something I used my Manchester colloquialism and said "yes, cock", "right, cock", "lovely, cock", "wonderful, thank you, cock," because 'cock' is this wonderful Manchester colloquialism. It's a term of endearment, it's like saying mate or pal. Peter Woodhall was a big, posh barrister, on the face of it again a very, very good man, and very much on my side. Through all of this I must have used the words, "Are you alright, cock?" many times and then I heard, at the end of the meeting, Peter Woodhall turn to Stephen Liquorice and whisper in his ear, 'Did Mr Smallman call me cock?' Cos he just didn't understand, or didn't appear to understand that I was just using terms of endearment, like us northerners do. Anyway, it's a funny little bit, about Peter Woodhall not understanding anything about anything really. I didn't realise it at the time, it was as if he had his head on a different plane, in the world of laughing and misunderstanding, he certainly misunderstood me.

Now, I don't really know what went on in the police investigation, apart from there were 17 or 18 police people involved and it was called Operation Anaconda. I only know what happened with myself and their dealings with me and my wife under caution, and that wasn't a very pretty thing. We'd gone backwards and forwards to the police station quite some time and we'd had lots of conversations outside the police station on an individual basis. The lead detective in it all was a man called Michael Bowman. He was just a policeman. I don't know whether he was corrupt, I don't know whether he was daft or whether he was just trying to do his best, but I do remember what happened the first time he arrested me. He delivered us back home after the 16 hours' worth of interrogation, and told me that he quite liked me and that he'd buy me a drink at the end of it. He told me that I'd sleep for weeks and weeks and that he had nothing on me. One thing was for certain, they weren't going to make any mistakes this time and they were going to get it right. I don't know what he meant by how many mistakes he'd made, but he'd made a lot, because Cleveland Police were always under some sort of investigation for doing daft things. Their leader, at the time, was under investigation and I think he was put on 'gardening leave' for a couple of years. He then became the mayor of a town after that. So they'd always been in and out of trouble, been rouge policemen so to speak and that doesn't mean by any means that they were all bent, or all corrupt, or whether Mick Bowman was bent or corrupt. I don't know, but what I do know, is when I was sat there being calm and cool and collected, simply answering the questions I was asked — about the probability of me stealing 16.8 million pounds, and all the inferences that were laid upon me – I said, "Investigate me as much as you want to, but please investigate City & Guilds properly. I had permission to use their logos. I had permission to give their qualifications out if people passed my courses. Please, please, please…" I said – and it will be on the tapes somewhere – "Please investigate properly, get the full account and you will see that City & Guilds are lying through their teeth." At the time, I didn't know what City & Guilds had said to him or whether he'd even been there. I'll only presume that he had been cos they'd been investigating for a number of years before this time, before they arrested me. It became apparent, that the reason we didn't get into America wasn't because we didn't have a house to live in in England, but was because the police had stopped us from going. They didn't want us to go back to America, so they'd told the Embassy, the American Embassy, to deny us access as it would have been very difficult to extradite us.

To cut the very, very long story short, there's a piece of paper I want you to look at, and this is a transcript of a document that City & Guilds people had created at the time, or shortly after the time the police had gone to ask them questions about me. No doubt the police asked a couple of the questions like 'Did you give this man permission to market City & Guilds' qualifications?' or words like that, and they effectively had said something to what amounts to the word 'no'. They've not mentioned the evidence above, nor all the documents I'm going to show you in the book when I talk about City & Guilds in more detail. This document that I want you to look at sums it up, about the police's attitude towards me and finding me guilty or innocent in the balance of the truth, and also City & Guilds' manipulation of the truth. It simply says, word for word, and read the whole thing in a minute, "Katie believes that the police departed happily convinced that City & Guilds hadn't accredited NDLC courses, given permission to use its logo, or ever agreed that any of NDLC's assessments would lead to a

City & Guilds qualification/certificate." Read it for yourself. It's a fact. So, why are City & Guilds saying they need to convince the police? What have they got to convince them about? So, the truth is the truth. They're saying, 'No we've not accredited him. No we've not had any dealings with him. No we've not done anything with him whatsoever.' But there's the evidence of what they've said.

> that this would be an agreement between them and City & Guilds to limit the purposes for which they could use the information supplied by us.
>
> **** Katie believes that the police departed happily convinced that City & Guilds hadn't accredited NDLC courses, given permission to use its logo, or ever agreed that any of NDLC's assessments would lead to a City & Guilds qualification/certificate. However, she is concerned that detailed examination by the police of the documents received from the Official Receiver, will reveal that City & Guilds was slow in getting back to Smallman with feedback about the course materials NDLC had submitted. I gather from Andrew that documents had actually been lost by us. Our understanding of this is, that Smallman could therefore contend that he had submitted materials which he could legitimately expect at some future stage to be accredited by City & Guilds and he therefore produced his publicity accordingly.
> Katie also feels that, since Andrew has been more immersed in the whole set-up than any of the staff still at City & Guilds, he is clearly the most appropriate person to be asked for witness testimony if this should be required. Customer Services have only been involved since the complaints started to come in.
>
> Sue Berry 23/10/02

Now if you look at this other documentation, it shows the police's inaction. That's what it says, 'we'll simply come back another day, or when we're passing for a coffee'.

> to be the signatory to the statement on behalf of City & Guilds, she suggested (tactfully) that maybe she should be dealing directly with Bob rather than with anyone else.
>
> • Most importantly, she wonders whether we should be telling the Police that, since Richard Stott started off the whole NDLC saga, they should be contacting him.
>
> • DS Murphy has e-mailed S B to say that he and DC J will be in London on Thursday 07 November and would like to call by for coffee. After first discussing this with Di, S B has agreed to this. Katie was not consulted about what really did look to Di and Sue as a ' We might call in if there's time ' type of arrangement ! Katie wondered whether she should be present but both Di and Sue are very clear that they mustn't provide any gratuitous information to the Police.

This is a very serious alleged offence they are investigating. Policemen that are offering to investigate a crime properly, don't 'call in' on someone who has been accused of being a potential suspect of doing wrong because I've said investigate them cos they are lying or could be a key witness in it. They do it on a professional basis, but these people were just 'calling in for a coffee'! I'm not sure that they ever went back and did anything. It clearly shows that it wasn't the police's perspective to find a balance of the truth – to find out who was lying. Was I lying? Was City & Guilds lying? It didn't matter to them, they only needed or wanted to collect evidence which was contradictory to what I was saying. They were looking for nothing that would support what I was saying. This goes on all through the police investigation and just these couple of documents that I'm putting in here prove my point. There is so much more, but hey, that's for another book.

Can I do anything about it? No. I've done the sentence, done the time and lived the life. All I can do now is put it in a book for you to have your opinion. Did the police do a balanced investigation? Ask this question to yourself: why wouldn't they do that? Cos the policeman, Mick Bowman, said to me, 'We don't want to make mistakes.' Why wouldn't you want to make mistakes? Has he been told not to make mistakes? Has it been said to him, 'Get this man screwed to the ground, do whatever you can'? I don't know, but it could seem that way, cos if you look at the broad-based evidence of everything, no one ever said that I did anything wrong. Not until the shit had hit the fan, but that will come out when I start talking about the City & Guilds evidence later.

So there we go, in and out of police stations, the wife and me. They hardly interviewed my wife. They just locked her in the cell. They were just putting pressure on me. They dropped all the investigations on her and stopped. Then I had a dilemma. I had a business account from one of my businesses that was still collecting money on people's standing orders, and it was collecting £15 a year but there were thousands of people paying into my association of professional development even though it had ceased to trade. That was because the bigger business had ceased to trade due to the shit going on and this went on for years. Now, because they were standing orders, I had no control over them and every time I went to Yorkshire Bank to try to close the account, they couldn't close the account because there was money in the account and they had no control over sending the money back. It just had to accumulate in the account. So I decided that I had to stop collecting from these people, withdraw all the money out of the account and, whilst the account was on zero, say on the Monday before more money came in on the Tuesday, close the account and that's what I did. I took about £15,000 out of the account to close it, to stop further collection, further loss from people who were sending their subscriptions to this business account. People who had just simply forgotten that they had a standing order set up for once a year and they wouldn't notice it. Anyway, the minute I did that, they re-arrested me on a new charge of taking money out of a bank account that didn't belong to me. The account did belong to me, it was my business. I had the legal responsibility to stop the collection of money from the people. So they just took the money off me, all £15,000 of it, and prevented me sending it back to the people it had come from in the first place. They just gave me another charge. They were rubbing their hands.

At that point in time, I'd gone home to my wife. We were very, very close, and I'd said to her, "Look if you want me to, to take any pressures off yourself, I'll go 'guilty'." It was the only time I ever considered going 'guilty'. I suggested it to mitigate the pressure on my wife. We talked about it for minutes, nothing more, and came to the conclusion between us that this shouldn't happen. She was not willing for me to fall on my sword and get maybe a couple of years in prison and for her to start back with everybody else fine and dandy. Too much water had gone under the bridge. She knew she wasn't guilty, so she thought she was not going to be found guilty, but she did. And she knew I wasn't guilty and believed I wasn't going to be found guilty either. We both believed in the criminal justice system. But little did we both know then, that a proper investigation was not going to take place. Things were going to be left out in the trial. Jurors were potentially going to be selected rather than just at random. So we agreed to carry on with our defence.

Is that a regret for me? Cos it would all have been over in a couple of years, a couple of years in jail maybe, gone short, investigation over, saved tens of millions of pounds in investigations and trials and all sorts of things. I wouldn't be here now telling this story because I'd have started a new business. I'd probably have become a millionaire again and everyone would have been fine and dandy, and it wouldn't have led to all the other things that were going to come. Who knows?

So the police do their investigation, they go and see City & Guilds, and City & Guilds lie through their teeth about our relationship. They go and see other people, here, there and everywhere and it was clear, clear to myself, that they were not doing a balanced investigation. They just simply wanted to collect evidence that would convict me. The first line of a police officer's contract, the Hippocratic oath, so to speak, is to be balanced. If everybody was arrested because somebody said somebody's done something, then we'd all be in prison, we'd all be arrested to some degree. So, to be a good police officer whether it's the 'bobby' on the beat, or the Chief Inspector, or any of the people between the two points. They have to be objective. They have to be balanced. There was no balance to their investigation. It was totally and utterly one-sided. 'We need to convict Mr Smallman.'

Let's just say, all the police that were involved in the investigation of me and the National Distance Learning College were good, honest, people. That they truly believed what City & Guilds had said to them, that we were not accredited to them and therefore advertising illegally and selling illegally – fraudulently. Let's say they believed that, their duty would still be the same … to investigate exactly the opposite to that. If a man, from City & Guilds or wherever, says someone has done something wrong. And the man who is accused of doing something wrong is pleading with the police to investigate the accuser more thoroughly to prove points. In failing to do so, it can be deduced that the investigation was biased and unbalanced. You can see from the documents that I have produced earlier in the chapter, that there was no intent of ever doing any thorough investigation on my accusations that City & Guilds were lying. They only wanted to get enough evidence, whatever that would be, and in whatever way that would be, to prove to the Criminal Prosecution Service (CPS) that there was enough evidence to charge this man and then therefore to convict him.

It's fair to say that I could have had many more witnesses – in favour of my side of events – available to me at the trial. However, during police investigations the police make it clear that when someone is being interviewed that they have a choice to be a crown witness or on the side of the defendant – the accused. It is common practice to explain if they choose the latter that they could be implicated and complicit. So, as a result, witnesses refuse to say anything or comply with what the police want them to say. Further, when the defence barristers or solicitors approach these witnesses they refuse to comment and say things like 'I don't want anything to do with it' and sometimes saying nothing is more damaging than saying something negative. The police commonly use these tactics to thin out the positive witnesses.

By way of example, where was my Marketing Director, Richard Bell? Surely he should have been on the stand with me or at least a witness for me as he formulated every piece of marketing? Why was Brian Dowd – as Educational Director – a prosecution witness and not on the stand with me? As Educational Director, Brian Dowd was responsible for every action relating to City & Guilds, and I could list many others, who stood back due to fearing the consequences.

Let's keep assuming that the police were innocent in all this, why would they believe City & Guilds, or a newspaper, or the Department of Education, or anybody for that matter? That is because they are noted, established organisations. You would think they had no reason to make a story up that a bloke from Manchester had built up this 'bogus' organisation into a huge organisation, for anything other than fraudulent purposes. Simply because they are establishments, City & Guilds is an establishment, why would it lie?

Well, it will come out at some point, within the book, of why they lied, it's not for now, but they did. The police believed them and their lies because they were establishment, and there was no real motivation to prove anything else. Even though I pleaded with them to look at City & Guilds' computers, to delve into them, not to accept their word as verbatim, they still did. This is me giving the police a little bit of an inch to say they were honest. Maybe they were, maybe they weren't. Maybe one of the police officers will read this book and come to see me and tell me the truth about it.

From the time of being arrested to going to court was the most unusual time. I set up a new business manufacturing clothing for people. Taking the ideas out of their head and turning them into reality. By way of example, Mrs Jones would come up to say, I want to start this clothing company, and all she had was an idea in her head. I would take it out of her head and get my designers to design the product that she wanted. To do all the aspects of sourcing all the products to make it and find the manufacturers for it. In some cases to manufacture it in my own factory that I'd built in Vietnam. I was flying backwards and forwards to Vietnam, India, to all places round the world and yet still having to come back, almost every single week to talk to my solicitor and barrister to build my defence case up. To see the police, to talk some more, to plead with them some more, to go on and on and on and on, begging the police, particularly Michael Bowman, or Mick as he prefers to be called. "Please investigate us properly, I don't mind you investigating me cos I've not done anything wrong." I kept on at them saying things like "I understand it's a difficult thing to understand, when you've got an establishment like City & Guilds saying that we were not accredited, and influenced by the newspapers back in 2001. Please don't you be influenced". But as I say, they only had one thing in their mind and that was to convict me, because maybe they were told by someone else to get the evidence to convict me, whether they lied about evidence, or could get real evidence, nobody really cared, just get me convicted!

These were very, very difficult times. Before the trial started, sometime in June 2008, one of my customers in the clothing business was the MET Police. The MET Police!! I think the guy was called Neil, he was a sergeant for the Greater London Transport Police which was a part of the MET Police. He rings me up and says, 'can I come and see you? I've seen your advertisement on the internet and I believe your company can help us'. He didn't know I was under investigation for the biggest education fraud that there ever was in the world. Anyway, he came up to North Yorkshire, Sergeant Neil, and says he's been given the task by the Chief Constable to bring the crime rate down on the Oyster card. Now the Oyster card is used by people who live and travel around London. Eight to ten million people every day. They put money on their card and they stick it on a gadget that's on the bus or on the train or wherever it will be to pay for their transportation. And every time they were taking it out of their pocket or wallet it was allowing — would-be — naughty people to rob them much more easily. So they'd come up with an idea of a glove, like a Michael Jackson glove, which the person would be able to buy and put on their left hand or their right hand and put their Oyster card in the back of the glove. That way they wouldn't need to put it in their wallet or their purse and expose their wallet or purse to the criminals. In principle it was a great idea, but I'd spoken to the sergeant and looked at the mock up that they had and says "it's not practical for you to make a glove. People have little hands, there's children's hands, there's big fat docker's hands and a glove, you would maybes have to have 20 or 30 different sizes in order to make it function properly. So they asked me to devise something anyway, and I devised a thing called the oyster sleeve, and here's a picture of one.

It's got the name of my company on it and Crime Stoppers numbers and the association with the MET Police all over it. Now the funny thing is, they loved the idea. The sleeve was made up of an elasticated fabric which you could make in one or two sizes to fit everybody and in the back of the little sleeve, when you pulled it on your arm was a little pocket which you could put your oyster card in so all you had to do was to keep your oyster card in there permanently. When you went on the bus it would connect and 'beep' without getting your money out, without getting your purse or undoing your handbag or whatever it would be. They loved the idea, they loved the idea so much that they ordered 5,000 of them to trial. We made some samples for them and they placed the order, five thousand of them at £1 each.

Anyway, here's the funny thing, it was up for awards, the idea — the Oyster Shell as I called it. They wanted to call it the Oyster Sleeve but I thought it was a much better idea calling it the Oyster Shell. I was invited with Neil the policeman, to be a keynote speaker at the Safer London transport Awards in 2008 because the idea was up for an award as were several other awards. The keynote speaking was to talk to somewhere in the region of 200 senior police officers all about the wonderments of the Oyster Sleeve, and there were other organisations talking about products that would cut crime on Greater London Transport.

Now the funny thing is here, let's call it Monday, I was up in the court in Middlesbrough in front of Judge Bonheartman, who was the head judge of the North East at the time and I was making my pleas, about a year before the trial. There's me on the 'Monday' saying "not guilty" and setting a date for the trial, there's me, the alleged biggest educational criminal in the world, on the stage, in the court, in the dock saying "I'm not guilty". Then on the Tuesday, travelling down to London to share a keynote conference, sharing the stage with the Mayor of London, Ken Livingstone and the Assistant Commissioner of the MET Police. The next day!! What an irony. One minute I'm the biggest criminal, only hours later I'm the flavour of the MET Police's month. Just think about it, there's me doing a keynote speech after the Assistant Commissioner of the MET Police and after Ken Livingstone. There I am talking about the crime prevention throughout the London area, through London Transport. Only the day before I was on stage in a different way, but it was a dock and there's me making an innocence plea for the largest crime of its time that the country had ever seen, I was allegedly the largest educational fraudster in the world, ever. Anyway, imagine my thoughts in my head, looking at 200 senior police officers in their uniforms, doing my keynote speech. I was thinking, if they only knew! To top it off one or two of them stood up giving me a standing ovation and all of them were clapping as loud as they could because they believed the idea for the oyster sleeve was fantastic. If they only knew that the day before I was in the court in Middlesbrough. What would they have done or said?

CHAPTER THIRTEEN
- THE SPLIT

I was back in Everthorpe waiting for the results of my appeal and I'd started getting myself back together. I'd gone back to the gym and was back with my pals. I call them pals, cos they are your pals at the time, but most of them I've never seen again. They are pals for the day, for the week, for the month, or the year. When they get out they promise to send you 20 quid but they don't. They promise to write but they don't. They promise lots of different things, but they don't. That doesn't matter really because I don't really want it, because they're 'criminals'... and criminals shouldn't really mix with criminals, should they? It gives them a bad reputation! It's a funny statement that — bad reputation. I've always had a bad reputation. I can't remember a time when I've had a good one.

Anyway, waiting in Everthorpe, going through daily life...going to bed, getting up, going to bed, getting up, going to bed, getting up, going to bed, getting up, eating shit and then eating more shit in the middle. There's stories to be told...God there's too many! One story, which is worth telling, was my addiction that really manifested itself in a terrible way whilst I was in Everthorpe. There was lads in Everthorpe — and I know there is in all jails everywhere — with heroin addictions, cocaine addictions and marijuana, alcohol, all sorts of substance abuse. I had one substance abuse. It was terrible, I just couldn't help myself. I'd had it for a long time...it was chocolate! I am the man who abused chocolate, cake and sweets of any description, it didn't matter what it was. And crisps, hmmm I love crisps.

One day I'd decided that because my body was now a temple cos I could lift 200 kilograms in a dead lift. That's more than double my body weight. I'd got really super fit. My daughter, when she visited, described me as a bull. There was very little fat and I was very fit but I was still eating lots of chocolate and I decided that I could not ever give up on chocolate and sweets and stuff. So, one day, for my canteen, I decided that I would order enough canteen chocolate, biscuits and stuff to last me two weeks. I got three bars of chocolate — big bars — not your little ones. Three packets of 150g bags of chews, caramels and others, four packets of chocolate Hobnobs, four packets of Custard Creams, four packets of Bourbons. I also got a jar of lemon cheese, or lemon curd as some people call it, and some plain biscuits to spread it on. Several large packets of crisps, and a Jamaican ginger cake. On the Friday afternoon at Everthorpe it was all delivered. I was going to be so good that it was going to last me the whole two weeks. It would have probably lasted a family of six a couple of months, but it was going to last me a whole two weeks. It was going to be my enjoyment, day in, day out, for a couple of weeks.

Bang up came on the night about five o'clock. I sat down, watched a bit of news and a bit of telly. I wrote a letter and then I started to twiddle my thumbs. Some blokes twiddle other things. Anyway, Coronation Street came on and I was thinking wouldn't it be nice to have three of my chocolate Hobnobs and a coffee. I got three chocolate Hobnobs out of the packet, put the rest away and watched the first part of Coronation Street. It was delicious. I was successful. I'd taken three chocolate Hobnobs out of the packet and didn't want any more once I'd eaten them and drunk me coffee. Then the advertisement break came on and I got a little bit loose and a bit bored and I thought well, if I have another coffee and just three more biscuits that would be OK. So I did. I had another three and then another three and then all the Hobnobs in the two packets had gone! So I thought, hmmm, maybe I could have just a few Bourbons and then all the Bourbons went, all the Custard Creams went, all the plain biscuits went, all the crisps went, all the packets of sweets went — all 450g out of all three packets. Everything went!

There was nothing left by the ten o'clock news an hour and a half later, they'd all gone! My cell was like... well it was like the bottom of a dustbin. All the wrappers were everywhere and I felt very satisfied on the tongue and very dissatisfied in my stomach. It was ginormous. I was becoming overdosed on sugar and chocolate. Anyway, I fell asleep after turning the light off and my stomach began to make noises. It was basically a rumbling noise but what it was really saying was go to the toilet quick! Go to the toilet quick! And I did quite often that night. I couldn't sleep at all cos I was shitting chocolate Hobnobs, shitting Bourbons and I swear down if you had taken one of my turds out of the bog and let it go hard you could slice it up and serve it to the lads and they wouldn't have known any difference; I swear I'd evacuated my bowels so often that night I couldn't sleep. They do say chilli gives you a ring of fire, but let me tell you there's nothing worse than shitting what I shat out that night. It was awful.

I decided to concentrate on the packets on the floor and pick them up one by one and noticed one of them had said the calorie content of the packet. It was something like 1400 calories. So, I decided to count all of the calories that I'd had that night by reading all of the labels on the packets. Unbelievable! The average man has about an average 2500 calorie requirement per day. Now bearing in mind that I'd had a breakfast and bearing in mind I'd had a lunch and bearing in mind I'd had a tea and a supper, on top of that my calorie count was nearly 29,000 calories! No wonder I was shitting for England. No wonder my toilet was blocked and no wonder I had to ring the bell to get some more toilet roll: 29,000 calories, my God! If that had been cocaine, or heroin, or anything really I'd have been dead! To be honest with you, I thought I was going to die, particularly at the back end of the shitting episode. My goodness the pain! Needless to say, by the next day coming back from the gardens about four o'clock I was looking for more sugar. More chocolate, more things to abuse myself with. You might think you might love chocolate, but nobody's eaten as much as me. These days I can resist chocolate very easily — I say this as I snap a piece of Dairy Milk off and pop it in my mouth. I know that if I wanted to, I could simply put it down and never have another piece of chocolate ever, but fuck it! I'll die young, won't I?

The next morning was Sunday, visits day. My wife, my two kids were due to come. They were to arrive about half past nine in the morning after driving an hour and a half from North Yorkshire into East Yorkshire. After arriving at the prison, queuing for ages and then being searched and humiliated, they were allowed in to see me. However, this day was to be a different day, a sad day. I sat there at the table waiting for my visitors to come through the door with all the other lads waiting for their family and friends to come. No-one came. Just as they were about to take me back to the cell I was asked to sit back down again because somebody had turned up. It was my wife, Angela, but no kids. She looked really upset. I was thinking the worst, where's me kids? I gave her a hug and she sat down. I says, "where's the kids? She smiled and she says, "I've something to tell you, so I've left them at home." She goes on to explain that if my appeal came through — because I didn't know at that time if it was going to come through or not, it took them ages to work it out, to write the bullshit in the reports — but if I was to come home, she didn't want me to. She said, "If I didn't tell you now, I never would do." I thought the worst. I thought she'd met somebody else and so I asked her had she met somebody else? Was there another fella? She said, "no, there's nobody else," and she told me that she loved me. She told me that I was her right arm, but unfortunately she knew that when I was to get out — whether it was on an appeal or in two years' time, cos I had two years left to serve — she knew that I would want to rebuild my big business, in whatever form it came in. She knew that I would want to fight my conviction. She knew I would want to prove the government guilty of some sort of conspiracy. That it was their fault, that they'd made bad decisions and they'd lost £650m — or whatever that figure was — of public money. She also knew that I'd want to prove that City & Guilds had lied to the press, the police and had lied in court. She knew the truth. She went on to explain to me that when she came out of prison she'd got a rental house with the kids, in Richmond, North Yorkshire. She'd found a safety bubble for herself and in that bubble the only thing that frightened her was me coming home. Deep down she wanted that to happen, but if I were to come home and to start the fight again, she knew that would bring the police back, the courts back and who knows what else back. Certainly her biggest fear would be back: The Sun, The Mirror, the News of The World, The Northern Echo. All the Gutter Press! They'd followed me about for so long. They'd destroyed our lives because it paid them to do so, and she didn't want any more of that. She couldn't cope with it. She'd had enough and was terrified of the repercussions. I said to her, "Are you sure there's nobody else?" She point blank reasserted that there was nobody else, that she loved me, but she just couldn't have all that disruption in her life. She just wanted to go on with a simple life, a nice easy going life without the mayhem of my forcefulness through it — my wanting everything back and wanting to be vindicated and to rebuild things. I believed her, that there wasn't anybody else and inside I was crying. Outside she was crying. There were tears and snot everywhere. The whole room had come to a standstill. There were several hundred prisoners — or it seemed like there was — there was certainly several hundred people. All the kids, all the family and friends of everybody, they'd all stopped dead to watch and listen to what was happening to me and Angela. It was silent and everybody was looking at us, listening to our conversation. They saw me grab her hand, holding it tight while she was crying. I told her that I believed her, that I believed there was not another man, that she loved me, but that I also understood that she had to go her own way, to find her own life. I told her she was probably right, that I would get out, whenever, and fight and fight and fight and fight. That's what I'd done all my life, when I was poorly as a baby, ill as a child, messed with, beaten up and so on. Fight. She knew I'd fight and she didn't have the stomach or the energy for it.

So while I'm holding her hand I said this to her: "If there's a man next week, next month, next year or whenever, and that man makes you happy, then that man is my best friend", and I let her go and she went. She went away that day with the understanding that we weren't going to tell the kids cos there was no point, I wasn't coming home for two years anyway, if my appeal didn't come through, and it didn't. That's another story.

Two and a half months later, after visiting every week with the kids we told the kids. "We've got something to tell ya." We told them that we were splitting up and we going to get a divorce. We told the kids that we still loved each other but because of what had gone on we'd kept it simple so we were splitting up. Christopher was probably a little too young to understand, but Grace, I'd never seen a girl's attitude to life change so much and it changed at that minute in time. She stood up, and I thought she was going to kill Angela. She shouted, "How could you do this to him, in here? How could you do it? How could you abandon him when you knew Dad was innocent? Everybody who knew him, who knew anything about it, knew he was innocent! How could you be so weak?"

Well, Grace didn't know much about the story, we never told them much about the story. She didn't know much about the battle cos we had shielded them as much as we could. She knew some things but not everything. We tried to explain to some extent, but it really affected Grace, in a terrible way.

I went back to my cell afterwards and was devastated. I didn't cry, mind. I was beyond that. Having to tell your kids that you're still in love but you can't be together. It's a terrible thing. That night Grace wrote a letter to me and you can read it now…

Dad, before I say anything else I want to say this I LOVE YOU. :')
I'm in complete shock like just I'm so angry, I just don't understand. She's just given up so early, she does still love you!!! After everything you've done it's just so ungreatful. You say you're to blame for all this well you're not she's just gone and fucking complicated things. I know you honestly did, and will continue to try your best! I love you so much dad. And I'm sick to death of life being soo hard on you! It's just not fair. It really isn't, you've done nothing wrong at all. I want you to get into your head that I know that please promise me you'll look after your self and keep your hope up. even if it seems like there's nothing left fighting for any more fight for me cause you know I love you. I don't want to sound ungreatful but I've just had enough... I really have. Like I'm 18 and just I've really had enough. Not that much to had has ha... but dad

you don't undastend how lost i some
times feel with out you. And mum now
doing this i feel even further away.
i just want you to hurry up &
get the fuck out of that place cause
i want my dad back before i get too
old! I LOVE YOU DAD. PLEASE undastend
i do.

Love your baby girl.

XX

P.S sorry that the letter's covered
in tears.

CHAPTER
FOURTEEN - BEIRUT

E verthorpe was a shit hole jail and I was there on B Wing, B for 'Beirut', as I've said, there was violence all around. Six months into me sentence, a couple of months into Everthorpe, I met a man who would be akin to Christopher Biggins, big, quite chunky and gay. He was called Martin, his first name was Martin. He was a nice enough fella and I became his friend and no, it's not what you're thinking — what happens in jail stays in jail type of thing — no he was just a friend. He was about 6'2" as I say, chunky, gay and very, very gay in his approach to his life. He came onto my wing and he got Cell 1 because he was an elderly man. He was also quite ill, diabetes and a few other things. He'd got three years for fraud with his boyfriend, his partner of 30 years or so. When they came in, the prison thought they were co-defendants and didn't know they had a marital-type relationship so they put them in the cell together. That was perfect for them, a three-year holiday together doing what gay men do and what we all do if we have the opportunity with our partners.

One night, after about six weeks, the night watchman was going round making his views through the slots in the doors of the cells. Have a guess what he saw in Martin and his partner's cell, yeah, they were doing it! They were having sex in their cell with each other. The very next day the Governor put them both on report and split them up. They were like chalk and cheese. Martin, as I say, was a big bloke and his partner, I can't remember his name, he was just a little dot of a man, 5' nowt and seven stone, he was just a skinny bloke. He got to be put on the enhanced wing because he was more vulnerable than Martin, and Martin was on my wing. Now, Martin was a character and he liked to make money, so all the pills he had for his illnesses, all sorts of tranquillisers, uppers, downers, he traded for Mars Bars and anything else he could trade with the pills. He wasn't a bad bloke though to be honest.

One afternoon I was locked in the cell with him, and that was the afternoon Angela and I had parted company with our relationship. I just needed someone to talk to and I did talk with him. Martin was quite a clever bloke, he'd understood the way you could get visitations and everyone has the right to visit. As his partner was in the same prison, just a different wing, between them they got double the amount of visiting anyone was allowed. One week his partner would invite him to a visit and the next week he would invite his partner to a visit so they were never out of the visit room together. They were having tea and biscuits and chats and keeping that communication together. Communication in the prison, not just my prison, with your family and your friends is very difficult, particularly in a closed prison as Everthorpe was. In high security you get the chance to make a ten-minute phone call once a day and a limited amount of time out of your cell to be able to make the call. Within that ten minutes you have to talk to your sons, daughters, mother, brothers, sisters, aunties and uncles and you've got to be able to pay for it. It's a tough time, it's exceptionally tough. Martin had it lucky, didn't he, as his one partner was in with him.

There was one occasion, when I was expecting a visit. This was before the date Angela had dumped us. They came to visit us every week without fail, my wife that was and my two kids. One day I'd rung Angela on the Friday and she'd told me that the prison visiting order hadn't come so they wouldn't be able to come on the Sunday. So I spoke to the SO, Mr Lang, and asked if he could put a copy of the visiting order on the gates, cos I knew he could. That way they could pick it up and come in, but he basically told me to fuck off. "Tough shit, you ain't getting your visit." Your visits are the most important thing to keep your sanity. Anyway, that evening, Friday evening, I was going to the gym and I had my head in my chest. Governor Bratley walked past and asked me what was wrong. So I told him that I wasn't going to get my visit, that the SO had said "fuck off". Now, Governor Bratley was a good bloke and I'd done him a few favours, saved his life — almost —once…

Let me explain: on each wing there was a wing rep, sort of like a union rep and on B wing it was me. My job as wing rep was to represent the one hundred or so men on the wing. I had to note their complaints, their problems and their needs and to liaise with the prison staff, the governors etc. to try to resolve issues, keep the peace so to speak. Every month all the wing reps from each wing would go off to a meeting room and air their views and wing issues to a governor. Generally speaking, these meetings would last an hour or so, the governor chairing the meeting would make some promises and subsequently never deliver on any of them. Anyway, at one particular wing rep meeting that myself and 12 other wing reps had been summoned to, on arrival at the meeting room we found Governor Bratley to be taking the meeting for the first time. Unfortunately, he was met with the wrath of the other 12 wing reps. The previous governor taking the meeting only ever gave lip service to their requests and the lads were pissed off. I sat there quietly watching the tension in the room, everyone was becoming more agitated. The lads were beginning to stand up and shout at Governor Bratley, stuff like, "what's the fucking point when you fucking governors don't do anything that you promise?"

and "We come here month in, month out and you lot just take the piss!". The pointing hands began to fly at Governor Bratley, violently gesturing that he was to blame. One lad suggested that a riot would get more results than these meetings and with that three or four men stood up shouting at Governor Bratley. I could see Mr Bratley becoming unsettled and nervous, edging towards ending the meeting and possibly towards ringing the emergency bell for assistance. These 12 wing reps were all long-term prisoners, some in for violence, some in for extreme violence, some in for murder. I felt I had to do something about it before tempers got out of control, so I jumped up and faced the lads. I shouted so I could be heard "listen, lads, just hang on a minute, it's not going to do us any good to shout and bawl, or worse… to get what we want…" I went on "…Especially with a man like Governor Bratley, because Governor Bratley is a fair man and I know he wants to do his best for us, so come on, lads, let's give Governor Bratley a chance to do his job properly." With that all the lads sat down. I turned my back on the lads and looked at Governor Bratley and he mouthed the words "thank you".

Not to give you the whole of the meeting, but one of the issues was that the bread served at meal times was disgusting. You couldn't make a sandwich with it, it was just like cardboard and it snapped when you folded it. It had no nutrition whatsoever, although you could eat as much of it as you wanted. So I proposed a trial just for B wing, that B wing was to be supplied with Hovis bread, but inmates were to be limited to two slices per meal. This way the lads got nutritious, lovely bread, without adding too much to the cost for the prison. Within one week the trial had started, within a month the whole prison was on Hovis. Within six months the prison had developed its own bakery which supplied high quality, delicious bread to all the inmates. It also provided a really high level training for inmates to have the experience to work in the bakery industry on release. Win, win, win, win. All without a riot.

Going back to what I was saying about my visiting order… Governor Bratley marched down to the wing and told me to have my gym and he'd send someone to talk to me. He then went down to the wing and ripped a new arsehole into the SO and told the SO he was to put a visiting order on the gates so my wife and kids could come in. The governor sent an officer to the gym to see me to say "don't worry about your visit, you're getting it, your wife and kids are going to come". He added, "If SO Lang gives you any problems in the future just to let me know." I know this seems a pretty, weak, loose story to tell, but it shows there are different characters in a prison; the officers, the governors, the prisoners and the staff, civilians you should call them. You'd think everybody would hate the prisoners because of why they're there and the type of people they seem to be, but the screws, in the most part, liked the prisoners. The governors liked the prisoners. The civilian staff liked the prisoners. However, all the staff hated each other, which made it very difficult. So, for example if they liked you, like Governor Bratley liked me, it would mean that I was getting favours off him. Then other officers who didn't necessarily dislike me but disliked Governor Bratley, would make my life hell; prisons are hard.

I was in a meeting once, cos I was a wing rep, and there were talks of riots and mayhem within the men. Governor Bratley pointed out that any prison only runs itself by the virtue and courtesy of the men. If you think about it on any wing at one point in time there might be two prison officers and one hundred men. The officers wouldn't have a chance, the men could pull them to pieces, could murder them quite easily or just pin them down, take their keys off them and walk out. So there is an etiquette within the prison that you are in. Very, very few people do try to escape because they are in and it works itself on the virtue of the men by the grace of the men in there, cos it's the men that run a prison.

On the wing that I was in there were various gangs, various people who would fight each other, pull each other to pieces. They would trade with each other, but they all seemed to revolve around one common denominator, a fulcrum point and that was me. I had the ear of the staff, the ear of the governors, the ear of the civilian staff and the ear of the men. On one occasion I came back from the gardens and Mr Lang was arguing. He was arguing with all the servery staff who were all prisoners and it looked like there was going to be mayhem, not least a big fight between Mr Lang, the officers and the servery staff. Apparently, a loaf of bread had gone missing and Mr Lang was accusing the men. The men were obviously not admitting it. Even if they had nicked something they would never admit it. The big lad who was running the servery, the hatch where they slop you the food, and was the main prisoner in the servery, saw me come in. He shouted me over and asked me to arbitrate between the officers and the servery lads. They were all arguing loudly and I asked them just to shut up and let Mr Lang speak. Mr Lang just simply said "one of these bastards has nicked a loaf of bread, we want to know who it is or we are going to sack the lot of you and just stick you all behind the doors". So I said "that's fair enough," and turned round to them and said "have one of you nicked the loaf of bread, it's simple isn't it, have you or haven't you?" At that point in time the big bruiser of a lad who was running the servery got angry with me and called me a screwboy and said to me, "you're just one of them, aren't you, fucking screwboy, you're as bad as a screw. You come on and off this fucking wing just as you fucking want to, you do what you want, when you want. You come and go and think you're fucking marvellous, you think you're fucking it, you're just a dirty fucking grassing screwboy". Now, I wasn't known for my temper at all but I lost my temper. This man is probably a good six inches taller than me, a real hard man. I went over and just looked him straight in the eye, nose to nose so to speak, maybe nose to neck, and I said, "let me tell you, I'm not one of them, I'm certainly not fucking one of them, but let me tell you summat' else, I ain't fucking one of your lot either, I'm just me". I marched off with my legs wide apart, walking like a gorilla because I was so angry! I stomped up the three flights of stairs on my way to the top landing. On the middle landing there was another screw overlooking it. He was a nice fella and as I walked past in my anger he says, "Mike, you're not one of us and you're definitely not one of them." This was a realisation, a third of the way through my sentence, that I'd kept 'me' together. That I was an individual who didn't buy into the criminality that was there, but also didn't buy into the compliance of what the prison officers and society and regime the prison wanted me to do.

Many things went on in the prison at Everthorpe, hundreds of them, big, big stories. Some nasty ones. One of the nasty ones happened one night time. It was about nine o'clock and it sounded like the lad in the next cell to me was smashing his cell up. It was as if he was throwing his telly and bits of furniture about, absolutely smashing it up! I could hear the two night watchmen, who were just screws, talking, saying "just leave him to it, let him smash it up, let the morning staff deal with it". No doubt cos the lad did have a bit of a reputation for being a bit of a scallywag and he probably would have gone and smashed his cell up at some other time instead. Anyway, it all went quiet after about 20 minutes. I thought thank God for that, I can get some sleep! I smiled to myself…daft git, he'll have no telly and he'll be bored out of his head now cos he's smashed it. I could actually hear it smashed. Anyway, eight o'clock came in the morning. They started unlocking the cells, then all of a sudden they told everyone to get back in their cells. All that just as they opened the door of the cell next door to me.

Well, the lad *had* smashed his cell up, but it transpired that he hadn't smashed his cell up in a rage or to make a point; he'd had an epileptic fit! He'd fell all around his room and that's what the smashing noises were. Then he'd choked on his vomit and died. He'd be about 22 years old. All for the sake of a couple of prison officers thinking he's smashing his cell up and not checking on the lad. Cos if they had, he'd probably still be alive today. They'd have noticed he was choking on his vomit. They could have done something about it. Even just checking on someone. That will have been someone's brother or sister, maybe someone's dad, who knows? Certainly, someone's son, but he was dead simply because he'd choked on his own sick.

It does show, to some extent, that prison officers, although a lot of them are good people, have a disregard for what could be happening, a disregard to their duties. Once they are in the system they don't always follow the rules. A person joining the prison service for the first time, I have no doubt, they join with good, positive intent. I'm sure they have an attitude that is one of wanting to help to make a difference, but after a month all their positive views and good intentions will get broken down by the regimes in the prison. By way of example, a young lad about 24, who'd been in the army for a few years, came on my wing as a new recruit prison officer. He was a really nice lad. When bang-up came and he's locking people up behind the doors, he was saying things like "come on, lads, get behind your doors please". He was ever so polite showing respect for other human beings. Within weeks of being told by more experienced officers — and no doubt being influenced by the way some inmates behave — he was saying things like "if you don't get in your fucking pad now I'll break your fucking necks, you scum bag bastards"! This is just a small example how the regime changes the prison officers. Only the best hold onto their humanity. I met a few. Ryan, the man I met on the landing, and others — they know who they are. Some really great blokes. Others just had the attitude that "all inmates should be kept behind their door, that it should be welded shut and not opened again until you're either dead or your sentence is over". Isn't that right, Mr Lang? That's exactly what he said to me.

Another time in the same prison, in the cell next door to me there was a friend of mine with another fella, or that's how I've liked to tell the story in the past. He wasn't really next door, he was in my cell, the 'other fella' was me. I like to say it was next door sometimes as it takes it away from my mind. It allows me to detach a little. It was quite horrible for me. It was pitch black, it was about 11 o'clock. Colin was young. Well, he was about half my age at the time, 25, something like that. I'd be about 46 or maybe 47 then. I said to him, "Colin would you turn that fucking tap off?" Cos I could hear it dripping and I know he'd been running the tap. It was dripping and dripping and dripping and it went on and on and on all the night. I was just falling in and out of sleep. Every time I woke up it was dripping and dripping. It was getting annoying... and then more annoying and the more I shouted at him to turn the tap off the more it annoyed me. Anyway, after some time I decided to get off my bed and turn it off myself. As I put my feet on the floor I noticed it was wet. As I stood up both my feet were wet. There was like a viscous slipperiness to the floor. I turned the light on and it wasn't the tap dripping, it was his blood. He was slumped over the toilet, dead. He'd cut his carotid artery and he was dead and there was blood. There was nothing I could do about it. It took nearly two and a half hours of me banging on the door to attract the two night watchmen to come and give it some attention. The story goes bigger and deeper than that, but that's enough of it really.

The amount of people who commit suicide inside prison is only a fraction of the people who commit suicide because of prison. I have a friend called Giles, who was released at a later date from a different prison with three other men. So, four of them got released on the same day. Within a week three of them were dead, three of them had committed suicide. One of them, I remember him coming to me and begging me to ask the Governor if he could not release him as he couldn't cope on the outside. I did speak to the Governor, but what can they do? If your time's up, your time's up and you're out the door, that's that. So, he killed himself.

Prison is a place to go if you've been convicted of an offence. Time inside supposed to be fixing you, putting you right, helping you if you need help... and they all need help. Every single one in there, for some reason needs help, but unfortunately the regimes in prison — the way you're talked to, the way you're fed, the way you're clothed, the way you're marched about — takes everything away from you. If you have very little to start off with, you're certainly going to have a lot less and that's not just in your possessions. It's in your mind, your heart, your soul or what you really believe you want to live for, cos you don't believe you can any more.

A fair few people, bigger than the percentages admitted to, either commit suicide in prison or go on to commit suicide after prison. The longer you've been in prison, the more you know about. The more you meet and the more you come across it. Terrible, isn't it? You're put in there to make you better and you come out ten times worse, certainly from a mental capacity.

In prison you go to the gym if you want to keep fit. I was there all the time. You see things in the gym which you wouldn't see anywhere else in the prison. By way of example, if someone has a very big lump of metal in their hand, you're likely to get hit with it. You're likely to get your brain smashed in, unless you're one of the boys and then you won't. Going to the showers after the gym...20 to 30 naked men all in the showers together. Most of them have got some prison disease like scabies and so on and so forth, so you're likely to catch something while you're there. They are dirty, disgusting places, prisons.

I did another eighteen-ish months at Everthorpe before going to an open prison at Kirklevington. So I'd done two years in closed conditions in extreme circumstances. During which time I took on everyone's problems and dealt with them all on my own. In the first three days at Kirklevington, I was numb. I could hardly talk to anybody. I couldn't think for myself. To be honest, even though I had the freedom of an open prison, I could walk about, go in the garden, do whatever I wanted to — apart from walk outside the prison — but I just wanted to go back to the closed prison to be locked behind my door. After about two days one of the governors noticed I was not being me because she knew who I was. She came up to me and she said, "Michael, I need a word with you," and she took me into a side room. She says, "The two years you've been in Everthorpe and the other prisons, you did [this], and you did [that], you helped [this person] out, you helped everybody out, you helped the Governors out." She looked at me and carried on, "But you did nothing for yourself." She told me if I was to do something else for someone in Kirklevington, she would send me back. She said, "You won't get the home visits, you won't get nothing, you'd just go back." She carried on to explain herself by saying "because this is the time for you to work on you". I nearly said to her there and then, just send me back, put me behind the door, let me be everybody's crutch, everybody's friend. Let me help everybody. I wanted to. I really wanted to, because it meant I didn't have to deal with my problems. What was I going to do when I got out? What about my family? I'd lost my wife, what could I do?

The things that happened within that first time at Kirklevington were really finding out about myself. Who I was and where I was going in life. It was pretty uneventful really, apart from the fact that when I was able to go outside the prison and get paid employment — get a job — I'd got to meet a man called John. John Hamilton, he was the owner of a small dye sublimation printing factory in York. When I first met him he was mentally falling to piece. He was having a nervous breakdown. A friend of his, whom I'd met whilst doing some charity work with people with multiple sclerosis, had arranged that

I'd have an interview with him through the prison and he gave me a job. As far as prison was concerned it was to mop the floor, make the tea and stack boxes, but on my first day with John he told me that he just couldn't cope with it any more. He gave me his laptop, business cheque book, credit cards and bank account and asked me to be the managing director of it. Albeit, not in name but in the duties that I did. After a while we won business with ASDA and other large organisations for printing things like your dog or your granny on a cushion. They're still going today as a business.

I wasn't allowed to drive the van but John, one day, says "can you go and pick up some cushions?". We were in the van and driving down the road on the way back from Oldham. I was working there for John but I shouldn't have been there. I shouldn't have been going to Oldham but I did. On the way back at 70 to 80 miles an hour, John decided to get out of the van to try and kill himself. Luckily enough I was able to grab his jeans and pull him back in and then he just locked the door. It was a moment of madness when he just wanted to end his life. We get back to the factory and I say, "Let's ring an organisation that buys cushions and prints off us to sell them the working part of this business." I was talking about the bit that was making money, and he did. He sold it for about £160,000. The naughty thing that I did was that I emailed the prison, pretending to be him as it was his computer. On the email I said that when we come back after the Christmas the factory was moving to Newton Aycliffe. I explained this made it easier for me to get there. The prison said great. ☒ John went to live on the south coast and I had the remainder of his business. It was called 'The Photographic Memory' and I ran 'The Photographic Memory' from a factory that he was renting in Newton Aycliffe. I ran it as my own factory cos John had sold his part to the company down south.

Every time I emailed the prison, as if I was John, I got myself extra days out. I did a million different things. When everyone else was in the prison on bank holidays — when no one was working — I would send a request to the prison: "Dear prison, can Mr Smallman please work the bank holiday?" On one particular bank holiday I went into work and my son came round. We had pizza all day and I had eight hours with my son. The things you get up to, trying to pull the wool over the prison's eyes so you can have some sort of life! On this particular occasion when my son was there, and he genuinely shouldn't have been there, an officer came to check up that I was actually at work. Luckily for me I'd spied the car coming into the car park and realised it was a prison vehicle. I'd said to my son, "Go and hide in the basement." I was tidying away and putting cushions into bags when the screw came in. He said to me, "I knew you'd be in work, I knew you wouldn't be up to any mischief" and I just smiled. He smiled back at me and went away. Really what I was into was not just running John's business, which was now my business, I was securing other businesses. The main one was my "Your Own Label" business. It was manufacturing garments for individuals who had an idea to set up a business. They had an idea for clothing, and thought they could take over the world by selling clothes, but they didn't know how to do it so they'd come to me. I would take their idea out of their mind, show them how to design it and show them how to procure the fabrics. I'd do the critical path development which showed them how to price it and how to sell it and how to do all the things that were necessary.

I helped an awful lot of businesses, even before I got out of prison! Well, that continued when I got out.

The other thing I did was work with John's friend, a guy called Darren. Little did I know then that I was an exceptionally arty person, cos I'd not started painting or anything then. This was years before I found that out. Darren had a company called Click for Art and it wasn't doing particularly well. It was doing rubbish in fact. He had a few contacts in the art world and wanted to use their art to put onto cushions and fabrics and so-on. Whilst all this was taking place I re-wrote his business plan, sorted out his VAT problem — as he owed tens of thousands of pounds to the VAT man — and developed a business called Click for Art. It's still there now, but under a different name. It's called Limited Edition and you'll see it on the internet, hosting around about 100 of the world's top artists at different times. All this from a prison cell room! All exceptionally cheeky!

Anyway, months later, June 2012, I got out of prison. I was up and running. I'd already done about £40,000 worth of business in my own Newton Aycliffe business before I got out. The prison never knew; it didn't really matter, did it? That year, 2012 to 2013 was a fantastic year. The business turned over about a million pounds and I employed about 20 people. I helped people develop their products, some of which are now household names. I'd made a real good life for myself and then I met a lady who was from Ukraine called Uliia. We began to live together and we were happy, for a while, but I'm not writing about this here because that is a big story that will appear in my next book.

By the middle of 2013 I'd started to try to exonerate myself. I was still fighting the fact that I'd lost my business and I began to move forward with it. Angela, my wife, was right. She knew I'd battle on and fight my corner, fight my conviction and would fight everything. She was right to go her own way simply cos I just brought it right back on myself! September 2013, I was right on top on the world and then one of my staff says have you seen what it says on Twitter? One of my customers had just gone on Twitter saying she wasn't going to get her horse rugs cos' she'd just found out I was a criminal. That was even though her horse rugs were directly in front of me. Anyway, that led to another sentence — another five years in prison — and another book to follow this one.

CHAPTER FIFTEEN – HEAD ON A STICK

Y ou might be thinking why have I done business? Although I've not talked about this for so long, I will do now. Some people might say it's for hedonistic reasons, others would say it's because I'm quite unselfish and I want to help people. I suppose it depends on which way you look at things. Throughout this book you'll find lots of different reasons why. Also, while the book is being told in this way, you will realise who I am – the person I am now, and how I was in the past, with only the subtle differences of change through experience.

My childhood wasn't particularly nice and, when going through that, I wanted so much for everybody about me. I have carried that 'want' all my life. I 'wanted' for the people around me, all through the past, now, and the people that are to come in my future life. My family and my friends, the people I love, the people that I meet and even the people for whom I should hold I hate. Everybody. I want something out of my passion, it suits me and I know who I am with that. If I were to ask you the question: 'what is the most important thing in the world?', I would want you to answer 'me... me... me... me...', and I'll tell you why. It isn't a hedonistic point of view, it's a more important point of view. If you cannot indulge yourself in the things that you want: the things that make you laugh, make you cry, make you smile; then you cannot do them for anybody else.

Nobody else can appreciate the things that you do and you can't appreciate the things that other people do. I got married for me, cos I wanted a lovely wife. I had children for me, cos I wanted lovely kids. I bought a bar of chocolate for me, cos chocolate [and, as I'm talking the crazies are listening, and one's pulling a face because she wants the chocolate as well!], then, yeah, because I got it for me, I have the ability to share the things I wanted for me.

People, particularly psychiatrists and psychologists, would say, 'Oh, there is something negative about this man, or that person. It's all about them. They are hedonistic.' They'd say that and they'd write it in their books and their reports – particularly prison reports or psychological reports if you were in 'the nuthouse'. Hedonism, narcissism, and all those "isms" that we can attribute to ourselves, live in the word 'me' and, from 'my' perspective, they live in the word 'you'. The characteristics that build us up as human beings are all there, and it's not them that are important, it's what we do with them that's important.

Just to fit into the psychiatrist/psychologist's opinion that it's all about me, this book *is* all about me. Yes, everything I've done, everything bar nothing, I did it for me.

For example, I wanted to get out of the shithole that I lived in. That doesn't mean the house. It means the area of violence, drugs, bullies and paedophiles. I wanted to get out of that area for me, because I didn't want my children to grow up in the same way. What I really wanted was the perfect environment. Wouldn't anyone want such hedonistic things? Wanting, wanting, wanting, wanting things for you, all of the time, in every direction. This triggers the thought 'keep your head on when you are head-on-a-stick' and want more and more, and more of the good things in life.

When you have a big house, and big everything, it's good to be able to share it. If the things I wanted made people euphoric, if it made them laugh at my jokes, if it made them smile, if it made them feel fantastic [because they live in the great big house I used to have, that I wanted for me], if it made them cruise down life's highways or Yarm High Street [blaring the music out of my £90,000 car, with the sunroof down – because it was mega for my two kids – blasting the music out on a sunny day]…then great!

The things I did for me, I did for them, and it's the same with everything that we do as individuals. When someone says it's all about 'you', that's a good thing because when you are building 'you' up 'you' cannot help but share those things. You may have a husband, or a wife, or a brother, or a sister, or mother, or father, an auntie, or uncle, a friend, or an acquaintance. If you've done well in your life – whatever that means to you as an individual – you cannot help but share it.

Everybody should want the world on their plate. If someone cooked you a meal, and let's say the meal was grown out of the ground by the hard-working farmers and put on a plate by a nice friend and you've stuck it in your belly and you've thought hmmm, the salty taste… so nice. Well you ate it for 'you'. I ate it for me. It was all mine and if someone had touched my plate, I'd show I wasn't happy. They cannot take my food off my plate, cos it was made for me. The enjoyment of me now talking about it is being shared to others.

So, when you look at narcissism or hedonism and all those 'isms' that psychologists and psychiatrists label us with, in order to say that our behaviour is out of the 'norm', I'd say, 'thank you!'. Thank you for noticing that I am bothering about me, and the things I do, with the things I want, and what I do with them, and how I behave. The fact is, for the most part, they are fantastic and let's all share them.

Now, an 'app' on my computer, which is now listening to my voice, is oversharing, cos it's writing things down wrong. Very much like people's first perceptions when they see/meet someone.

For example, you walk into a court room and you've got a suit on. The jury and the judge have what people would call psychological cognitive thoughts. A pre-conception of who you are. If you go in there looking like a punk, they have a cognitive thought, a pre-conception, of who you are. When you've got tattoos all over your face, up your arm and half an ear bitten off, they have a cognitive opinion of who you are. When you read a book like you're reading my book now, you will have a cognitive opinion of who I am. You may get it right, you may get it awfully wrong. It don't matter. I don't care. What I do care about is the sharing, the sharing of my life by reading it, and you will get something out of that.

That something that you will get out, I guarantee, will, in some way, be positive in your life. You will see the hedonistic person in yourself and it could be because you're an alcoholic and you want all the alcohol, you want all the money, you want all the this and all the that, whatever it may be. If you're chunky you want all the food and, like the 'crazy' sat listening to this, she wants all the chocolate. Well, if we do go and buy a bar of chocolate, I'll guarantee I get most of it cos I want it all – but I don't mind sharing the flavour.

CHAPTER SIXTEEN – THE COLOUR PINK

W ell of course, as I've just said, 'me, me, me, me'. I didn't want much for myself, but I did occasionally self-indulge, and my first self-indulgence came in the very early months of the business. The business was doing alright, but it was in the early stages and I didn't have much money. Now, I always wanted a racehorse, but I couldn't afford a racehorse then…

I went to a meeting in London. I drove all the way to London in my XJ6, which was about 23 years old and it got me there, but that's just about all you could say about it. I'd bought it for about £400. It had no air conditioning in it. It was broken. But it was OK. It got me there. I parked it up and went to me meeting. Nobody turned up for it. Never mind. I then noticed a text on my brick. It said: "The meeting's cancelled, can we leave it until another day?" I hadn't looked. Those were the days of not being 'phonified'. We are all 'phonified' now. We go to bed with them. We sleep with them. We love them. It's the first thing we talk to in the morning. Anyway, I hadn't looked at the phone and the meeting was cancelled. I didn't want to just drive all the way back, so I had a wander around.

I was in a London suburb, called Wimbledon, and there was this huge building to my left hand side, and I could hear noises coming out of it. Really, I thought, "What's all that about?", and it drew me in. It drew me into the Greyhound Stadium. It must be about 11 o'clock in the morning. Anyway, I go in. There was no greyhound racing on but I could smell chips and that drew me further in. I could see a coffee machine type thing, a vendo – coffee, chips – and I could see what was going on.

I was in an auction… hundreds, and I mean hundreds, of greyhounds were being sold. You might be thinking, 'What's this gotta do with anything?' Well, it has to do with various things, but most importantly it's to do with never, ever giving up on something.

So, it goes like this. I get a bag of chips. I get myself a plastic cup of coffee, which was disgusting. I might add, if the vendor at Wimbledon stadium is there, 'your coffee is disgusting'. The chips were edible. Then I listened and watched the auction with no intention of buying a greyhound. I was just killing time and found it interesting. Some dogs were going for £500 or £1,000. Some were going for £15,000 and £20,000 and some, one or two, were going for £30,000 or £40,000.

On about lot 298, with just a couple of lots to go, one dog went for £15,000. It had never run before. Obviously it was a trained greyhound but it had never run in a race. The next lot had a story to be told. The auctioneer stands on his stand and says, "this little dog," and he wasn't so little, "is the brother, the full brother, out of the same litter, as the dog that's just been sold for £15,000…" The auctioneer continued to tell the audience that the dog had a story. The story goes that the trainer, the man who was selling it that day, was walking the dog on the Mountains of Mourne. Something had spooked the dog and he slipped his lead and ran off into the woods on the mountains. The owner couldn't catch it. So, the Irishman said to himself, in his deep Irish voice, "fuck the dog, it'll come back when it's hungry". But it didn't. For several weeks the dog was loose in the woods in the Mountains of Mourne. Eventually he caught the dog. It had lost half its body weight. Even though it was a very fast racing greyhound, it couldn't catch a bite. It couldn't look after itself and it had lost an awful lot of body weight. It was quite ill. Nevertheless, the owner had faith in it, not least because he wanted to sell it for as many thousands of pounds as his brother sold greyhounds for. He was living in hope. He built the dog back up. He trained it on his race track, without it racing. He then took it for another walk, in the same place and déjà vu happened. The dog got spooked and, yet again, it runs off into the Mountains of Mourne. A few days later, the dog does come back, a little bit thinner, but not too bad.

So the trainer decides to send it to the sales to see what he could get for it. And, as we know, his brother has just sold one for £15,000. The auctioneer went on, "...and if you take a look at this dog, he isn't a little dog, he's a big strong dog. This dog is going to have ability, but because he's a little bit nervous, and because he keeps slipping his lead, and because he's had a traumatic time in the mountains of Mourne, who will give me £5000 for him?" The room was silent. "£4000? £3000? Who will give me £1500? Who will give me £500?" And then some 'knobhead' shouted, "I'll give you £100 for it!" The 'knobhead' was me. The auctioneer says, "Very brave of you, sir, to offer £100 for a dog with such potential, but not even this Irishman is mad enough to accept your £100. It's worth much, much more than that." With that, the Irishman stood up and says, verbatim, "Let him have the fucking dog. I'm sick of it!" The hammer dropped and I had bought a greyhound.

I paid my £100 plus the £20 commission and bought a lead off somebody else for about £22. So, £142 down and I'd got an 18-month-old greyhound.

My God, what was my wife gonna say when I brought this thing home! What was I gonna do with it? I had two labradors who were lovely, but, now, what was I was gonna do with this one? Well, I've got another dog. It was lovely. It was very quiet. Mind you, he did try and pull a little bit as we put him into the Jaguar. He'd seen something and wanted to be off. So, I thought, "Oh, that's a good thing. He wanted to be off!" I put him on the back seat of the Jag and we began to drive home. We were going to drive home in the 90 degrees Fahrenheit heat. It was the middle of August and, with no air-conditioning, mile by mile this dog was beginning to dehydrate. He just wouldn't drink nothing. I gave him everything. I even bought him an ice-cream. The truth of the matter is I did eat half of it first because I had to encourage the old fella to eat it. He didn't want that. It just melted all over me seats.

Six or seven hours later the dog was so dehydrated he could hardly stand up. He just wouldn't drink, he couldn't do nothing. Evening had come and we were five or six miles from home. I thought, 'Well, I've gotta do something with this dog. I can't just land home with it, not with me other two dogs there! I'm not telephoning nobody now and saying I've got a greyhound.' Luckily enough for me, on the roundabout of the A1 services, there is set of dog kennels, a livery for dogs. I pulled up there and knocked on the door. I explained the situation – how I'd come across this dog – and I asked her if she would put it up for the night. I gave her £20 – or whatever the fee was – and she took it off me. I explained the dog just wouldn't eat or drink or do nothing and she said, "Yeah, he does look very dehydrated." She took him in anyway.

I went home and told my lovely wife that I'd bought a greyhound and she said to me, "You're a knobhead. What are you gonna do with it? Because it's not a pet, it's a racing greyhound!" She also reminded me that we had a pet rabbit! It just didn't all fit together.

So, in the very early days of Google, I googled a trainer – a greyhound trainer – who lived between Thirsk and Northallerton, and still does to this day. We were living in Northallerton at the time. The next morning, I collected the dog and took the dog to Shirley Linley, the greyhound racing trainer. She said to me, "Don't leave that thing here. I've heard about it. I don't want that dog. Look at it, it's scrawny, it's half friggin' dead!" He was still suffering. Anyway, I talked her into it. I think it was £32 a week plus racing fees, if he ever raced. I left him there and six or eight weeks later, Shirley says, "We're going to try him out, in a trials race at Sunderland."

Sunderland was a low-grade Greyhound track in the north-east of England. You could see it on the telly occasionally and you could see it on the telly in the bookies. So I let it go. I drive up to Sunderland to watch him in his first trials race. It wasn't a real race, it was just to see if he could make the time. The time that had to be achieved to go in the lowest grade, at the time, was 29.18 seconds.

He went round the track and he went round alright with two other dogs. He went round the bends fine, but he went round in about 32 seconds. If you think a greyhound can run about 40 ft/s that means he was 80 foot behind the very worst dog that there ever was to run at Sunderland. Bearing in mind Sunderland was one of the worst greyhound tracks in the country, he was rubbish! He couldn't do nothing. He was a waste of time.

"Take him as a pet," Shirley said, "this is not a racing greyhound."

I've learnt over time never to give up on my life. In a previous chapter we were talking about sharing, about having things that you want for yourself and one of things I wanted for myself was success. I wanted success in everything that I did and I was going to have success out of this dog, no matter what. Even though it would've been an absolute miracle. I talked Shirley into having a few more trials and he did get a little better, he got off the mark at one point of doing about 29.6, so he was about 20 feet behind the slowest dog and couldn't qualify for a race. Now, I don't want to drop anybody in it, but somebody paid the handicapper £100 to change the figures they had marked in the book to 29.18 seconds which meant it would qualify for a race. An A11. The bottom grade race for a greyhound is grade A10. He was in the grade A11, which was a supplementary race for the ones that can't make it. He couldn't make it, but he was in it, even though it took a little bribe to get him in the race. I called this dog – his racing name that is – 'My Son Christopher' which has a poignancy in its own right, cos who knows what my son Christopher, my real son Christopher, is gonna grow into? He's a nice lad, got a lot going for him, but I suppose he's got time to make his mark, as I'm writing now.

Anyway, Wednesday night, it's raining. He's in trap one, which is the inside trap, on his first race. The excitement for me was watching a no-hope dog go into a race. I related that to myself because I'm in a race and I say that because you don't know when you're gonna pop your clogs. So I'm gonna have to do as much as I can, as fast as I can, and as well as I can, before there is no more racing. He breaks out quite well, in line with the others. I thought "He might have a chance!" Then it all went 'tits up' because instead of going around the corner he went straight across and knocked three of the other dogs over. He jumped the three-foot rail and started running round in the crowd.

I don't think he was looking for me. He was just wagging his tail and looking at all the people. He was a total and utter embarrassment. Racing that day was suspended for maybe two hours whilst they put everything back together and caught him because they couldn't have a greyhound running around on the course, and he just wouldn't come back for nobody. Eventually he was caught and he went home with Shirley to the training yard and I went home laughing my head off all the way.

CHAPTER SIXTEEN - THE COLOUR PINK

A couple of days later Shirley rang me and says, "Come get the dog. He's been warned off", which was an official term to say he can't race anymore. I was not having that, somebody saying 'can't' to me! He can't do that, with anything that's associated with me; dog, camel, man, woman. If someone says 'can't' to them, I will rebel, because they can and they're gonna! My commitment to those people is as much as it was to this dog. It sounds derogatory or dogatry, if you like that play on words.

Anyway, I was able to convince them to let it run again and paid the handicapper and the person that did the draw, to make sure that he was drawn on the outside so he wouldn't knock any other dogs over. He got another race. The bottom end race, again, and another Wednesday night, for all the dogs that couldn't run fast.

He's in trap six. The dogs come out, they run around and believe it or not he ran around, he went all the way round. He finished about a week after the others, but he ran round. He went around, he did, he genuinely went around! That year he had something like 14 races and, believe it or not, he didn't come last all the time. There was one time he came fifth because one of the others was knocked over. He was constantly last apart from that one time. He was no good. He was useless. He had nothing going for him, other than he could be someone's pet. Or, I don't know what they do with them, if they're nobody's pet – put them down, put them in the ground. But I wasn't going to give up and never would give up, not even when Shirley Linley rings me and says, "This dog can't run again, don't do it no more, Mike"... blah blah blah... "you're just wasting your money. I've got a nice dog for ya." I wasn't interested in no 'nice dog'. I wanted this dog and I wanted this dog to be successful. I just didn't know how it was going to happen. They let him have one last race. I'd become a laughing stock, in a nice way, cos every time I went to watch him run he was always like 500 to one, in the worst race in the world, and, as a bit of fun, I'd always put some money on, £20 here, £10 there. It was just to show my support.

Now, on this particular day he was 500-1 and in a dog race that meant impossible. Everybody knows he was going to come last. For some reason, I think I might've had a couple of hundred pounds in my pocket, so I went down to the rails knowing that this was going to be his last race. I put £20 with every single bookmaker in the place. They're just happy to take the money off me and give me any price that I wanted. Anyway, the race comes up and everyone's pointing. Everybody who goes there regularly knows who I am, I'm the man that owns 'that' dog, the worst dog, the worst racing greyhound that ever lived. Stupid me, I'd named him after my son, 'My Son Christopher'! Anyway, the race comes up, the hare comes out. He's in trap six – and you have never seen anything like it in your life – he doesn't knock any dogs over, he doesn't run straight and jump over the rails and run round into the crowd. He comes out first, goes from the outside to the inside as if he was glued to the inside rails. He went round the first bend in the lead. The crowd was silent, totally and utterly silent. Anyway, the back-straight comes up and he just goes further and further away in front of these dogs, at least five dogs, coming down the home straight. Normally, you hear lots of cheering but there was no person on this earth had put any money on him, so there was nobody cheering him apart from me. And he won. He won by 11 greyhound lengths, which for those who don't know, that's about a grade 5 not a grade A10 or 11. The stadium was silent. It was the most strangest thing you would ever see at a greyhound track, where it's normal that people are cheering. There was just nothing, absolutely nothing there! I was gobsmacked.

Anyway, I didn't know what to do. They took him away, as they do, cos they go for a blood test for drugs. I thought, "Well, I'd better collect me money." I turned around and half the bookmakers had disappeared, cos each one of them owed me about £10,000 and they didn't have it. I got the money eventually. I fought them all.

A few days later, Shirley Linley gets a letter summoning us to the greyhound track to discuss why this dog had just done a time which was six or seven grades better than the grade he was running in. The drug tests had come back fine, no drugs in him, no nothing and they could not understand it. Luckily, on this day, there was a visiting vet, from a better greyhound stadium, on the track, and the stewards had called him into the room to examine the dog. The vet couldn't find anything wrong with him. A fine healthy dog, well looked after. There were no explanations why. He'd just dramatically changed the way he'd run. The vet asked to talk to the groundsman and he asked the groundsman, when he appeared, if there was any changes done on the ground on that day? The groundsman said, "The only change we'd made was that we'd changed the hare from a white hare to a summer hare." Now a summer hare is pink. The vet thought 'hmmm', got his pen out with a light on the end and he shined it in the dog's eyes. He said, "This dog's colourblind. I'm confident he's colourblind and the change of the hare meant he could see it. He couldn't see it before. He was just following the dogs around. He wasn't chasing the hare."

That year, out of his 32 races, he won 19 of them. He went up nine or ten grades. He was never the best dog in the world, but was a very good dog in his own right. He was nominated 'greyhound of the year'. Now, if that isn't a reason to stick by anything and anybody... The worst of us or the ones of us with... I don't know...no legs, no arms, no tongue, eye missing...or whatever it is...or maybe an attitude in life, or an addiction of some description, alcoholism, there's millions of them... people that would seem a waste of time...then what is! That could be yourself saying that to yourself...but I'm pretty certain that my doggy, 'My Son Christopher' – who went on to win another

12 races the next year before he retired – he knew he could run fast. He had belief in himself. He just needed someone to stand by him, to understand his potential and for the time to be right for him to show his potential.

If anybody doubts this story, ring up Sunderland dog track and ask them about 'My Son Christopher'. It's a fact. The moral of the story is that you can be going down the streets in life and the roads, and all the areas around in London, going nowhere, and then you can find something that inspires you. Maybe it doesn't inspire you to start with but you latch onto it and you live in the hope and the belief that something good is going to come out of it. That could be a relationship, couldn't it? It could be a business. It could be an idea. It could be anything. In my case it was this daft dog. Buying something I didn't really want. I certainly wasn't ready for all the things that went wrong with it, and there were more things that went wrong. But, as I say, the moral of the story is that when you say you're going to do something, do it! Believe in it. See it through to the end and make it your word to see absolutely everything that you promised through until you can be released from that promise because you've achieved the goal.

My son Christopher, my real son Christopher has the same – or if not more – good intent from his dad to make sure that he gets where he wants. At the moment he's doing his own thing, but it may be sometime in the future that he'll need his dad or other people about him really to believe in him. To take a chance on him, to drive him in a direction that everybody else may think it's a nutty thing to do, it's the wrong thing to do.

As a publishing company that I know says, "there are no mistakes" and there aren't any mistakes. Even if it had never won a race, even it had never seen a pink hare, even if it had never been realised that year that it was colourblind, it doesn't matter. The intent to get him to where he needed to be as a racing greyhound, to have success in the thing that he was bred to do was the real success. It was achieved. The success in his races was one thing, and it was pleasurable, and he was inspiring; but the special point was the 'Never, ever stop. Never give up attitude' to try anything to make it happen… That is the real success.

CHAPTER
SEVENTEEN - DARWIN

---

ave you heard of a man called John Darwin? Many of
you will have done. John Darwin was a fraudster. What
he'd done was he'd planned with his wife to fake his own
suicide. He'd got a canoe and rowed out into the North Sea. Then
he abandoned the canoe and made his escape to Panama, leaving,
supposedly, his wife and his adult children to believe he was dead.
He did this so he could claim the insurance money.

There's a TV programme about him, five or six episodes and there's a
book, there's all sorts out there. He's probably one of the most famous
criminals of the modern day. Well, I have a couple of stories to tell
you about John Darwin, 'the canoe man'.

Halfway through my trial in 2008, John Darwin's trial was taking place
in the same Courthouse. I was in Court One and mine was a big deal.
He was, I think, in Court Eight. Although it was a serious offence, it was
no big deal. Anyway, all the jury, all the press, everybody, is listening to
my trial and all the shite that the prosecution want to put out before I go
on the stand.

The day I go on the stand to shout out all the positives that I had, the
crux of my defence, the John Darwin jury had come to a decision

and it had been announced in the court. His jury was coming back to announce the verdict. So, what happened to all the press people? The local press, all the national press and the international press, the radio and the TV all upped and left me with an empty court room and went to listen to the 'canoe man's' verdict!!

None of them heard the evidence that I was giving. They didn't get to hear what I was trying to say to everybody because John Darwin stole my thunder. Whether it would have made any difference to my case or not, to my trial, I don't know. I certainly believe it may have made a difference to the reports that came out of the Court. Every negative thing that could have been said was reported. None of the positive things were ever reported on. Quite simply, they were listening to John Darwin's verdict. Anyway, he gets sentenced to prison and he goes off to prison, to Holme House. The same prison where I was to go when a few months later, I get found guilty. I get a couple of months' bail to sort out my affairs, then I got seven years shoved up me arse.

You've read about some of the antics that was going on, but when I got moved to Everthorpe [after I'd settled into Everthorpe for quite some time], I found that John Darwin was apparently in the same prison as me. He was on a different wing. Because he was an ex-prison officer, he was always getting a punch and a kick, or beaten up by some of the lads who wanted to get some retribution, somehow, on prison officers. He was an easy target.

Anyway, on a few occasions, I was asked to keep an eye on him. I was to make sure, sort of, that I befriended him, in order that he would get a little bit of kudos with me being with him. The lads, if he was with me, wouldn't have beaten him up. To cut a very long story short, we're sat there in the library at Everthorpe and we're chatting away. We were just talking about general things and books and whatever else. Some lads had come in to chat with us, others are looking at John as if to say, 'If Mike weren't there, I'd beat the shit out of you'.

One lad, big lad, 50 years old he was. He was built like a brick shit house and was a good friend of mine. Tex, a black lad, with dreadlocks all over the place. He comes over to him and says to him, "You fucking disgrace", or words to that effect, and walks away. He put his bit of terror into John Darwin. John turns and says to me, "No I'm not." So I says to him, "John, why are you not a disgrace?" He says, "Well all I've done is committed fraud against an insurance company. No big deal. People do it all the time." He carried on, "I got far too much time and, really, I shouldn't be guilty of anything cos they're ripping people off all the time." I said, "John, do you not realise what you've done? You've stolen the identity of a dead baby." He says, "I know, but the baby was dead, it didn't need its identity. I did, and I got my passport in the dead baby's name." I believe it was a baby called John Smith, who died about the same time as John was born so their ages correlated perfectly.

It was a perfect way to pick up a passport so he could leave the country for Panama. He seemed to be able to justify that, in his own way, he thought it was a clever action – a way of getting out of the country. No doubt it was, but it was certainly quite despicable of him. I said to him, "You also lied to your wife. You lied to your wife on many occasions about how easy it was going to be." Even though she was party to the fraud, he led her along the way, telling her that he loved her and telling her that everything would be fine and dandy, and really enhancing her culpability by using his relationship with her and her willingness to maintain it. We carried on discussing it all but I told him that what was more despicable, was that he had lied to his children, making them believe he was dead. I says, "How do you think that made them feel?" John Darwin just simply turned round to me and said, "No I didn't, they knew all the time."

I'm not trying to say anything, but the connotations of this are obvious.

CHAPTER EIGHTEEN
– "WAKE UP!"

I'm not going to go into the trial too much. I want to write a whole book on it. But, it's fair to say my barrister summed up my innocence in his closing statement. He said to the jury, to the judge and to the court, that there was "no prima facie evidence that would convict Mr Smallman". None.

Sometime in June or July, I can't remember the date, but it was 2008, we were going into the courtroom for the very first day of the trial. I went in an exceptionally confident mood, knowing that City & Guilds representatives had been lying. I was confident that this, when it came out, would stop the trial and we could get our lives back.

We knew it was going to be a three or four month long trial. The opening speech from the prosecution barrister goes a little bit like this, "Ladies and gentlemen of the jury, this is going to be a very long trial, probably taking some three or four months." He went on, "So you need to make notes, you need to have your wits about you, and you need to ask questions, questions like the name of things, what does something mean? Because the law that we are going to talk about covers educational law, accountancy, business law, commercial law, civil law, all sorts of different laws. So you need to ask questions. You'll be hearing words like 'gross' and 'net' and so on."

He then goes on to say how naughty I, and the other defendants, have been and then it was adjourned for lunch. Me and me wife go outside, through the doors of Middlesbrough crown court and right there in front of us is a ginormous television screen: 45 foot or something like that. It was showing the World News and there was something on it – I could see it from a mile away – the red line that travels underneath was all about me. It was saying that the trial had started and that it was going to last a long time. At the time I was trying to run a business and trying to get my life back together again.

I was believing it was all just a waste of time as I was going to get found not guilty. However, when we went back in, the jury went back in and says, "We need some clarification about the opening statement." They passed a note to the Clerk of the Court who passed it to the judge. The judge said, "It seems, Mr Prosecutor, that the jury already has a problem understanding two of the words that you used. Would you be kind enough to explain to them what the word 'net' and the word 'gross' mean." I turned to my wife and says, "We're fucked!"

This was a very, very complex case from anybody's point of view, not least because the evidence was manipulated by the powers-that-be. This jury was selected from general members of the public without adequate knowledge of business law.

It's fair to say that this was a perfect example why, for many cases, the jury system doesn't work and where a panel of qualified professionals should be used at the very least. They couldn't even understand what 'gross' or 'net' meant. How the hell could they understand, or even remember, any part of my very complex 91-day trial? One of the jurors was a young lad, I'm presuming 18 to 20 years old. I'm guessing that because you could never see his face, he had his hoodie up throughout the full 91 days. I also believe the chairwoman of the jury was a police 'plant', who was there to manipulate everybody on the jury. Why was this woman brought to my attention? Simply by watching her mannerisms and her body language. It was just a feeling.

We were going to prison, I knew it. I knew there was a conspiracy. I didn't want to believe it, but I knew it was there. In 2001, years before the police even got involved, I said to anybody and everybody who would listen to me that there was a conspiracy going on to use me as a scapegoat.

Preface

Life is like a sh*t sandwich-the more bread you want, the more sh*t you have to eat!

The book you are about to read is true in all but some of the names have been changed to give these people anonymity. Not that some of them deserve it because they don't! They know who they really are and their shame and guilt will live with them until the day they die.

For my part, I am who I say I am, (Mike Smallman) and proud of it. This autobiography of the first forty years of my life will take you through every emotion possible as you follow me through some of the ups and downs in my life. Although I, just like you are ordinary, in every way it seems that my first forty years have been a roller coaster of intrigue, passion, desire, betrayal, conspiracy and the ruthless determination to succeed. From total character assassination from some U.K. national newspapers to the loss of a £40 million company due to a government mistake that has turned out to be the most expensive government cock up ever. From my rags to riches and back to rags and my never-ending fight for success. From the terrible bullying and abuse I was subjected to as a child to the strong, never give up attitude I now have as an adult.

For those who know me, love or hate me, you will never forget me for my aim in life has always been to make an impression. I hope, through this book that I continue to make an impression. I mentioned all the emotions I am going to take you through. Whilst you read my story let it get into your heart and I will make you cry, feel sad and lonely and then lift your spirit to a level of hope and inspiration that will stay with you for the rest of your life. Anger will run riot through your mind, sorrow will overcome you, and even hate will consume your soul. In contrast, you will find love, passion and laughter and hopefully direction in your life. No matter what your life brings, good or bad, it's your life and you have to make the most of it.

One thing you will find, I will never let ANYONE grind me down. I will always remain true to myself and the only thing that will ever stop me getting where I'm going and getting what I want for me and mine, is death.

I hope you enjoy my first forty years and I hope you will be able to relate to parts of it.

REMEMBER Direction in life is not the way you are going. It's the way you point yourself.

Some years earlier, on my 40th birthday, after cleaning my slimy green pool, I started writing a book: 'Life is Like a Shit Sandwich'. This was before policemen or prisons or anything had come along. I'm talking in the preface of the book about a conspiracy in 2003, five years before the trial and two and a half years before the police arrived at the door.

I wrote this, and if this isn't foresight I don't know what is. When I was 45 it came to fruition in the courts. Five years earlier I'd known there was a conspiracy, even though I couldn't prove it at the time. It appeared later that there was more than just a conspiracy, it had turned into people's personal vendettas to put me down, to keep me shut up.

Think about this. I, a man, finds a problem about a few individuals. The few individuals then conspire between themselves to shut this man up. Ergo, a conspiracy, but then the actions of the conspiracy are passed down to individuals and groups of people as 'false truth'. These groups and individuals take the 'false truth' seriously. They believe it to be true, so it becomes their truth. They really believe that someone rips off the government and people and, quite rightly so, thinks it disgusting. More so when Vivienne Parry is calling the man a 'scumbag'.

Of course he's a 'scumbag' and, of course, Vivienne Parry and others, such as Andrew Penman and Mick Bowman, a detective in the – paid for – investigation, are in their right minds. When it's printed around the world time after time after time, that 'false truth', created out of the conspiracy, becomes the truth to the world. It goes on through Chinese whispers. Personal loss and vendetta manifesting itself in hatred. How could a man cheat the government? It's disgraceful! How could a man cheat all those poor people just wanting to better themselves in their education? How could he?!

The thoughts that manifest themselves out of the 'false truth' develop into a belief that the world is truly flat. For hundreds of years, people believed the world was flat and feared falling off the edge. What if Mick Bowman, or one of the other investigating officers, had acted like one of the great explorers who proved the world wasn't flat? What if the investigating officers had pushed the boundaries of belief? They may well have found the truth. What if a suspecting employee of City & Guilds, who thought that something wasn't quite right with the City & Guilds statements, had looked over the edge? What would they have said? Or perhaps a suspecting employee of the Department of Education? Maybe people were just scared of falling off the edge, or being pushed off? At least now we know, through proof, the world is, at least, slightly misshapen. Ball-shaped in fact.

As things fell into place the trial went on and on, with no evidence that was clearly against me. Time and time again people got on the stand and said these are not 'false certificates' they are just 'certificates of merit'. All supporting my case. Time and time again it was masked by character assassination and suggestions to the jury that what I was saying was unbelievable and that the conspirators were telling the truth. There was no evidence against me, certainly nothing that you could take seriously.

British justice says 'beyond any reasonable doubt' and everybody I met, including Ian Reeves of the BBC [who was the local business editor who was following the trial], heard everything that went on and they all said to me, "You're going to get a 'not guilty' verdict." Ian Reeves, at a later date, before I'd been sent to prison but after the conviction had been given, had emailed me and, basically, said, "I cannot believe you have been found guilty!"

The court, the trial, was one lie after another including the judge. At one point I shouted at him to wake up. He'd fallen asleep! I don't think he liked that. It's probably why he'd given me seven years instead of five. The evidence that was presented wasn't all the evidence. The evidence of my innocence was held back. I could go on and on about it but what really is the point? At the end of it I got the seven years and my wife got the 15 months and the two that had run the business for me got off scot-free. I'm not at all inferring here they were guilty of anything. I'm just asking, if there was real belief I was guilty, why didn't they receive any conviction? They were running the business. It was simply just a one-man hunt with poisoned spears and my wife got hit on the way just to make sure we were silenced.

The prosecutors were saying it was a big bogus business. Think about it this way. There were many hundred members of staff. Am I such a clever, manipulative man with such great powers that I can order around 600 people to develop a cunning ruse, and then post that cunning ruse on the television and through every single letter box via leaflet? Not only for a short space of time, but for years, with not one person asking a question or raising any concerns or suspicions? Surely that speaks volumes in itself? Nothing was brought up from the inside out, but only from the outside in, when the conspiracy is developed years later. Not until the News of the World went to print based on the lies of City & Guilds.

On the administration side of the business, the tutorial side and the directorial side there were many people that were all dealing with City & Guilds in some way. My wife, who was our internal invigilator, Brian Dowd, my Educational Director, who signed every certificate, and his team of about ten people, who created the conditions to work within the City & Guilds parameters. They dealt directly with City & Guilds for accreditation. On the stand, my Financial Director John Hornsby and my Managing Director Peter Kenyon were also on trial with me.

These people, as you would be able to see from many letters that I could have put into this book, had a great level of contact with City & Guilds. In particular, Peter Kenyon, who wrote to City & Guilds saying, in a much more polite way than this, but, "W... the f...you playing at, City & Guilds?" Why weren't they convicted? The people who ran the business? Again, I am not inferring guilt here in any way at all. I'm just asking how does one man get found guilty, who has little to do with the day-to-day running of the business anymore, and the people who ran it get off scot-free? It's weird, but it happened.

This is difficult to understand because there are many facets to my story. Initially the focus upon me was a deflection of a governmental mistake. It was prescribed that I was guilty of fraudulently handling government grants. I've explained already that no fraud was found and, in fact, there was not even any non-compliance found in the initial, very detailed, investigations. Everything was fantastic. We were given a clean bill of health. We were reinstated as an educational provider, but then, about a month later, they shut the whole of the ILA scheme down to hide their embarrassment, leaving 8,500 educational establishments high and dry. Thousands of people losing their livelihoods.

Now, imagine this, the government authorities digging a hole in the pursuance of me and finding themselves at the bottom of that hole. What do they do? Then, just as realisation of that and the consequences of that are apparent to them, up pops an opportunity for them to continue to keep me under wraps and divert their investigative attention to the possible fraudulent behaviour that was alleged against me. That is the City & Guilds saga.

All 'the powers that be' needed to do was to influence the powers at City & Guilds, either directly, or indirectly through the police investigations that they paid for. I'm guessing that the Department of Education bigwigs – after failing to pin the ILA catastrophe on me – worked with City & Guilds chiefs to cajole City & Guilds into distorting the truth about our relationship. This would explain why City & Guilds didn't simply say, 'We've had a relationship that has lasted several years' and go on to say that the relationship was good. I've shown from the documents that I'm presenting that the relationship was good, and there are many more documents to that effect. It explains why City & Guilds didn't say that they were slow and that they had problems in delivering the desired outcomes. It explains why they didn't show to the press, the police, and so on, the documents I'm showing in this book.

As I have said, there are one or two reasons. Either they were influenced by superior forces, or they wanted to deflect their inadequacies. Possibly both.

There is a document in existence which is a record of a meeting between governmental leading players in the Department of Education and the Treasury. This meeting is said, by the Department of Education, never to have taken place because the many millions of pounds overspend at the Department of Education meant that the ILA granting scheme needed to be suppressed and hidden.

The general conversation in this meeting was two-fold. The Treasury saying words, possibly along the lines of, "What the hell is going on? You have overspent many millions?" It goes on and says the legislation was written very laxly and in a set of words, which in general terms states, "We need to find someone who will take the brunt of this problem. Someone 'small', a 'small man' (Smallman!) who can't fight back." Now these aren't the exact words but this is the context of it. There are many people who have seen this document. I wish I had it to put in the book.

Soon after my barrister – disappointingly from my perspective – summed up by saying, "This is the lacuna of a fraud." Why didn't he just say, 'The fraud was absent' or perhaps, 'There was no fraud', instead of expecting the jury to understand Latin?

If you think about it, the trial was 91 days long. It had taken years to get there. It had involved tens of thousands – if not, hundreds of thousands – of documents, hundreds of prosecution witnesses and hundreds of witnesses in my defence. In fact, if you were ever bothered to read the official trial transcripts you would find that approximately 98 percent of the prosecution witnesses, in their statements in court, were unable to support the prosecution's allegations, and in many ways, supported my case.

To give you one example of what a debacle the trial was and how the police had their own agenda, I'm going to tell you about one particular prosecution witness who had taken the stand. She was there to confirm to the prosecution/jury what a terrible man I was. This lady had been my personal assistant (PA) for quite some time. Her name is Caroline Mohan, or was, because she is married now and has changed her surname. She was party to the things I did on a day-to-day basis. So the police hoped she would come on the stand and say things like, 'I saw him do this!' or 'I heard him do that!', and, 'What a terrible, terrible man he was!'. However, when Caroline got on the stand, it was with some trepidation. Before getting on the stand she was asked to read the statement that she had made to the police five years earlier. This was in order to refresh her memory. On doing so she told the authorities that this was not her statement and that this had been hand-written originally by a police officer. She told the official that changes had been made after she had given her statement and the changes that had been made changed the inference of her statement from one of being positive, to one that was negative.

Caroline gets on the stand as a prosecution witness and offers nothing to the prosecuting barrister that he could hang his hat on. My junior barrister, Mark Harris, began to cross-examine her. He had an ulterior motive cos he had just seen the prosecution barrister fail to pull out any derogatory facts from this lady. He begins by asking her – and I paraphrase, "Can I ask you a few questions on behalf of Michael Smallman who I represent? It was with, was it not, regret that he told you about your redundancy? Did you get that impression?" She says, "Very much so." The barrister says, "Because he spent – and you will have known this from your close contact with him – a great deal of time, and a great deal of effort, trying to preserve the employment status of the staff." She says "definitely". Mr Harris continues, "And, certainly insofar as the college is concerned, you can tell us – can you not – that he spent a great deal of effort trying to preserve the interest of the students?" Her reply: "Yes." He goes on, "And is it fair for me to sum up his evidence in this way: that he was a man who put his heart and soul into trying to make these businesses a success, as far as you could tell?" "Definitely," is the reply. "And it was with some bitter regret that he had eventually to concede defeat, was it not?" "Absolutely," she says.

What Mr Harris, my barrister, is trying to do is to prove, using this lady, that I'm not the conman people perceived me to be. Needless to say, she would know, spending so much time with me. He is setting a foundation in place to show that I did my utmost with all aspects of the contrived downfall of myself and my organisation.

Mr Harris explains that I was a 'larger than life' character. My enthusiasm was boundless and infectious and I did not hide my light under a bushel. He shares that I had amazing ideas and wanted to make every single one of them work. Caroline continues to confirm what he is narrating. He questions her by saying, "Again, that was all part and parcel of this man, who aside from that kind of persona, was also at the heart of every sincere hard worker?" "Yes. Definitely," she replies. "You of all people, being his PA, would have been someone who could understand that. You were at close quarters and had first hand contact with him?" She says: "Yes."

"And consequently, when it came to everything beginning to go wrong with the City & Guilds situation," Mark is saying, "he took that as a very heavy blow?"

"Yes," she replies.

"Was it your experience that he tried to do everything he could to resolve the City & Guilds situation?"

"Yes."

"...and he was on the phone, non-stop, to everyone he could, shouting to be heard?"

"Yes."

"...and the City & Guilds situation was plainly at the forefront of everybody's thoughts and knowledge within the college?"

"Absolutely," she says.

This all goes on, question after question, giving her the opportunity to say something derogatory, if there was anything at all there. All she did was continue to confirm a positive after a positive about me and how I dealt with forward-thinking in all the negatives that had hit the business.

Let's just jump a little bit forward into the evidence that she is giving, under oath, on the stand. Mr Harris brings to light, to the court, that she told the court official that her police statement had been changed. He says, "Miss Mohan, you quite rightly brought to the attention of the court staff that your statement has been changed by the policeman who typed it up and that the policeman had put negatives in it." He asked her, "In the 19 pages, how many instances have you highlighted that do not represent what you wanted to say... where your words have been twisted and words actually being added to the statement that you did not use at all?"

She says, "Eighteen different instances — absolutely."

Mr Harris says, "I suppose, for completeness' sake, I ought to say that the evidence that you've given to me, when I have been asking you questions today about Mr Smallman, is absolutely genuine?"

Caroline says, "Yes."

"...and the utter truth is it not?"

"Yes," she says.

In the transcript that I'm quoting from, Mark Harris, my barrister, he has clearly pointed out, using this lady, that the police had manipulated her evidence from positive to negative. All that she had said were positive things. Now, before my barrister could deliver a 'coup de grâce', Judge Moorhouse shouts, "I do not want to interrupt. I'm sorry, but I think one of the defendants is a little poorly – not feeling very well – and it might be appropriate to adjourn for five minutes."

What a time to make an adjournment! He's obviously interrupting the flow of my barrister and the impact of this witness's evidence!

How did the judge know someone wasn't feeling well? Obviously a very perceptive judge? Where was the judge's focus of attention? He had just been informed that a key witness's police statement had been illegally changed and he said nothing! But he interrupted the court about something totally unrelated. What a debacle!

Later on, the court comes back in. My barrister thanks the judge – for what, I don't know. He turns to Miss Mohan again and talks to her about this statement. He mentions that it was written by a policemen called John Duff and says, "You've been speaking with John Duff over the last couple of days on the telephone?"

She says, "Yes."

"Is this because John was the original police person that took the statement?"

"Yes," she replies.

My barrister quantifies that John Duff took her statement and wrote two pages of notes which were later typed up by another policeman. My barrister says, "Don't worry about the notes for a minute, I just want to establish how all this came about. You telephoned him yesterday and highlighted the negative changes, the concerns that you have?"

Caroline replies, "Yes."

"…Now we've mentioned that there are 18 instances in the 19 pages of the statement and we are not going to go through them all. I just want to select a couple." He asks her to turn to her statement that had been changed by the police and time after time he points out words that have been added by the policeman that typed up the statement.

"... and is it true, that as you went through these deliberate changes to your statement with the policeman, you were horrified as to the different connotations?"

She says, "Absolutely."

"...and you thought those different connotations were unfair, so you corrected your statement?"

She says, "Yes."

It's fair to say that as my barrister questioned Miss Mohan, she resolutely confirmed that her statement had been changed deliberately by the police to put a negative spin. He goes on, referring to line 32 of the transcript from the court. He says, "Because you thought that those words were plainly not your words?"

She says, "Yes."

He continues, "That these words added sort of suggested some cloak and dagger situation going on?"

Caroline again replies, "Yes."

He says, "Something sinister or untoward?"

"Yes," she says.

The interesting juxtaposition here is that the inference added to the statement that something very wrong was happening within the NDLC, was actually, in contrast, happening by depiction within the police. Evidently so, through their actions here and elsewhere as I have discussed earlier in the book.

Mr Harris then tries to identify which police persons were involved in Caroline's police statement and confirms, through her, that a second man called Mick Bowman was involved. He goes on to suggest that the policeman called Bowman, quote "has twisted the words that you have used and appears to have given a negative connotation that you were not happy with, is that right?"

Miss Mohan replies, "Yes, yes."

My barrister continues and points out the words, and reader, to give you some idea of the words here's one of them: "con". Mr Harris points out that Caroline never used the word "con" in her statement. He asked her did she use the word "con" in her statement to the police officer and she says "no".

"So the introduction of the word "con" was made by the police officer?"

"Yes," she says.

"…and you would agree that you never used the word 'con'?" asking her to repeat it over and over.

Caroline agrees.

"…and this plainly was inserted, for whatever reason it is, and it changed the entire connotation of what you were trying to get across?"

She replies, "Yes."

The transcript ends by Mr Harris saying, "Thank you very much, Miss Mohan."

Harris looked at the judge, as if to say, 'what are you going to do about this?'. He, the judge, did nothing. and that's that! If you read all the transcript, it's even more damning than I have paraphrased it here. And this was a prosecution witness!

So, just to go back to the judge; it has been revealed right in front of him that the police have committed deception during their investigations and he didn't bat an eye! The next witness came on the stand and it's all forgotten about.

The underlying connotations, that this witness had just testified to, shows – and is reflected in other documents in this book – shows that the police were happy to manipulate statements in order to fulfil their goal. Whether that be not interviewing or investigating City & Guilds properly, or alienating positive witnesses in order that they don't come on the stand, or dragging things out for year upon year, or allowing City & Guilds' statement to be manipulated by a legal firm. This just shows, without any doubt, that their investigation was not balanced and had an agenda. I refer again to the term... 'beyond any reasonable doubt'!

Something profoundly ironic that also occurred in this Kangaroo Court was that one of the counts that I was found guilty of was not collecting money from the students. To explain, the Department of Education states that in order for a student to receive their grant, the college had to take from them a £25 contribution. Therefore, if I didn't collect £25 as a contribution from the student, I'd obtained their grant fraudulently.

The prosecution put a man called Mr Lorna on the stand. Mr Lorna was a very senior civil servant in charge of the whole ILA project. He had helped Estelle Morris write the legislation. So you would think he would know the rules! Now, Mr Lorna was asked by the prosecution if Mr Smallman had organised his staff not to collect the £25 contribution from a selection of 42,000 students, would Mr Smallman have broken the rules?

Mr Lorna says, "Yes he would." Thereby incriminating me.

My barrister, Mr Woodhall, goes on the stand and says to Mr Lorna something along the lines of, "I've been on the website of Capita this morning to pull the Individual Learning Accounts' rules and regulations that you are in charge of." [Please note this is not verbatim.] "You just told my learned friend that, regarding this section of 42,000 people, if Mr Smallman's business hadn't collected the £25 – which they clearly hadn't – he would be guilty of breaking the rules, and that would clearly make him guilty of the offence?"

Mr Lorna agreed.

Mr Woodhall then shows Mr Lorna various paragraphs in the legislation that he had helped create and runs this analogy by him — again not verbatim... "An individual is entitled to a £200 ILA grant, is that right, Mr Lorna?"

Mr Lorna agreed.

Mr Woodhall continued "...and in order for the individual learner to receive that £200 grant they had to pay £25 of their own money towards it to qualify for the grant?"

Mr Woodhall continues (not verbatim), "We know that for all the students that Mr Smallman's business took on board for their first period of learning, Mr Smallman's business collected the £25." He goes on to explain, "...but Mr Smallman only collected £150 of the £200 available grant, leaving £50 of the grant unallocated. So, Mr

Smallman [being a clever businessman] offered all his students a short course in something else in order that he could collect the remaining £50 and the student would benefit by having an extra course with nothing to pay themselves. They had nothing to pay themselves for the second short course that their grant was to pay for, because they had already paid £25 for the first amount, which covered their legal liability. Mr Lorna, can I ask you, is that ok?"

If I was to show the transcript in the book (but it's too big), you would see from the transcript document, Mr Lorna answered like this...

"Err, yeah, I'm sorry I forgot about that."

This is one of the things I got found guilty of. This alone carried a one-year sentence... for not taking £25 off the public.

I have to ask you, was anybody listening?

Mr Lorna's statement, "Oh – I forgot about that", proves I was very entitled to do what I did. It was perfectly legal for me not to take a second contribution from a student. Was the judge even listening? I still got an additional year for this crime that also never existed.

CHAPTER NINETEEN - YOU DECIDE

T his is the last chapter. Well, it is the last one for this book, but there's still another 15 years to tell you about in the next book.

Some documents in this chapter were withheld by the prosecution and they help show my innocence. They were strategically withheld until the end of the trial and after the jury had left the room to make their decision. The judge said it was too late to include them, but because they were submitted, I could no longer use them in my appeal. Interesting, isn't it?

In 2001, before the shit hit the fan and before City & Guilds lied to the press about my company's accreditation to them, I was on target to become one of the UK's leading entrepreneurs. Their lies fuelled my downfall which helped the Department of Education to use me as a scapegoat for their huge financial mistakes. Their lies allowed the press to jump on the bandwagon and character assassinate me in order to stop the progression of my Thanx Marketing business. If they hadn't lied I'd now be the huge philanthropic businessman I always wanted to be.

A small reminder of my Thanx Marketing business cards

As you have read before, The Department of Education found no fraud and no non-compliance during investigations which had left them nowhere to go. So, they abolished the ILA scheme and left many, many companies high and dry, mine included. However, City & Guilds, the newspapers and The Department of Education needed a second bite at the 'Mike downfall cherry' after the investigations. So City & Guilds continued their stance because they didn't want their shortcomings to be exposed publicly. They continued to profess that I was not accredited and no permissions had been given.

This chapter is finally to bring together the various lines of corruption that independently took place within the national newspapers, the

Department of Education and City & Guilds. To quantify things, I point out the three bullet points below, that singularly identify the three protagonists' agenda.

The national newspapers, particularly the News of the World, wanted me shut down because my Thanx Marketing business was taking a lot of advertising revenue from them and character assassination was their game.

The Department of Education wanted a scapegoat to blame for their multimillion-pound legislation mistake. I – my business – was the leading education provider within the granting scheme that they had made a mess of.

City & Guilds needed to blame their inactions and inadequacies in dealing with my National Distance Learning College on somebody else. Therefore, to protect themselves from prosecution, they lied and said that the problem was created by me.

I'm not saying all three colluded, it's just that the timing of all three sequences gave each organisation a hook that they could hang their agenda on in order to remove me, and my business, from their world and from society in general. Thereby alleviating themselves of consequences, blame and scandal.

The focus of this chapter is purposefully placed upon what I got found guilty of and the underpinning actions by City & Guilds that made this happen. I ask the reader, in these following explanations that I offer you, as I tried to offer in the court, did City & Guilds lie? Did they lie to the newspapers, which set the ball rolling? Did they lie to the police during the investigations? And did they subsequently lie in court? All of which founded the conviction, my life being removed and a prison sentence being served.

An online news article by The Guardian about my conviction

This online news article shows what I got found guilty of: a £16.8m fraud that was based on myself lying to the public that the National Distance Learning College was accredited to City & Guilds and that I had permission to use their logos. I'd like to ask you more questions, reader…if City & Guilds hadn't lied to the press would there be any negative stories about me?

Would there have been a police investigation costing millions of pounds? Would there have been a trial costing many more millions of pounds? Furthermore, if they hadn't lied to the police, would the investigation have stopped and would there even have been a trial? Would the trial have been stopped if they had told the truth in court? Imagine this: "No, sorry, officers, we lied to the newspapers."

Or: "No, sorry, Your Honour, we lied to the newspapers and the police."

Once the ball was rolling they couldn't get off. So they stood up in court and told their concocted, hugely misleading story there as well.

As I've said in a previous chapter, I believe that the Department of Education wanted to use me as a scapegoat for their multimillion-pound cockup. After their cockup had been brought to their attention by me and my staff, they wanted to sweep their problems under the carpet. That carpet was woven with the threads of City & Guilds, the press and the illegal payment to a police force. As you will be able to see from the following documents and from the following explanations of those documents, City & Guilds gave me permission to market and approval to offer accredited qualifications. They then go on, not mentioning these permissions to the press, but also lying to the press and denying that they existed. A few years later, they lied again to the police and withheld the relevant documentation to the police, preventing the police conducting a balanced investigation and subsequently lying to the court.

All the documents that are provided are genuine, mostly obtained from City & Guilds' own computers and other involved organisations. In general, these documents represent internal conversations between City & Guilds' members of staff and other City & Guilds' members of staff. I'm sorry if I repeat myself with these explanations of who is involved, and what things are. It is a complex deception that City & Guilds hang their hat on in order to bring about my downfall, to save their skin and the skins of the individuals from City & Guilds who had made mistakes and subsequently colluded. I repeat myself in order to get my point across in different ways.

In court, when the case started, I was charged with several things. The main charge, count one, was that I had defrauded the public into believing that if they bought one of my courses and passed an examination, they would get a recognised qualification, such as a BTEC or City & Guilds. This was the main focus of the trial and it is this that I was found guilty of.

In the words of the press, my National Distance Learning College was a fake, dodgy, bogus college. The first set of documents I'm going to show you illustrates why they believed that. It's simple: on 26th April 2001, as you will see from the document below, City & Guilds have made this as a press release to Vivienne Parry of the News of the World, *"We have not approved NDLC to offer any City & Guilds courses."* This was their first lie.

City & Guilds statement to Vivienne Parry of the News of The World, Dated 26 Apr 2001 at 13:41(pm)

ANDREW JOHNSTON - NDLC   Page 1

From: MICHAEL OSBALDESTON
To: TFS:"v@vparry.co.uk"
Date: 26 April 2001 13:41:13
Subject: NDLC

Vivienne

I have had a chance to speak wth my colleagues and we have approved the following statement with regard to NDLC:

"We have not approved NDLC to offer any City & Guilds courses"

Best wishes

Michael Osbaldeston
direct line 020 7294 2550

Now, to show you how skulduggerous that statement was to the press by City & Guilds, just a few hours later, a member of City & Guilds had asked another member of City & Guilds, how did the press release go? You can see from the document below, what they said... *"Short and sweet, like a chocolate coated piranha."* I ask you, reader, before I show you some damning evidence, is that the way a professional institution would talk? Is that how you would expect them to behave?

Internal email within City & Guilds Dated 26 Apr 2001 at 17:00 (pm)

From: MICHAEL OSBALDESTON
To: ANDREW JOHNSTON
Date: 26 April 2001 17:09:39
Subject: Re: Fwd: NDLC

nice one Andrew......see the next one.....

>>> ANDREW JOHNSTON 04/26/01 04:23pm >>>
Short and sweet, like a chocolate coated piranha.

>>> MICHAEL OSBALDESTON 26/04/2001 15:06:30 >>>
Andrew - for info - having agreed with Keith and Shani

Vivienne is News of World consumer lady

regards

Michael

Now let me take you back to 1999. There my business is, a growing empire. It's already accredited to EDEXCEL for BTEC qualifications. See below.

Document showing the NDLC has approval to offer BTEC qualifications. Dated 22 Feb 1999.

As a side note here, one of the newspaper cuttings that I have shown earlier, shows Vivienne Parry goading the public by saying, "They [NDLC] told people who desperately wanted to better themselves that completing one of their courses would earn them the City and Guilds diploma required by employers. *It won't.* They also told students doing business administration that they would get a BTEC qualification. *Not a chance.*" She goes on to suggest that people ring the 'horse's mouth' to find out for themselves.

Later that year, it became apparent that my modern-styled Distance Learning College was fast and reactive to students' needs, but EDEXCEL was slow and bureaucratic. The typical student of my college was an adult, someone over the age of 18, who wanted to progress their adult learning spectrum and I genuinely wanted to provide the very best. I'd lost my patience with EDEXCEL and instructed a board meeting in my offices in Middlesbrough. There present were all my directors; too many to list here. I expressed to them that my goal to offer the best possible package of education and qualifications to our student customers was not being met. I wanted all our current and future courses to be accredited by City & Guilds, and set them the task of making this happen. So, my Human Resources Director, Dr Roy Grimwood, and my Director of Education, Mr Brian Dowd, elected to take up the mantle of making this happen, under the leadership of my friend, my Managing Director, Mr Peter Kenyon.

Roy and Brian went off to an educational conference that City & Guilds were attending and approached City & Guilds regarding the possibility of them accrediting my college and its courses.

In November 1999, City & Guilds came to visit the NDLC to investigate the possibility of working with us. On 19th November 1999, City & Guilds sent this letter to my employee, Dr Roy Grimwood. It shows their conclusion from that visit. They were "very impressed by our operations and quality assurance systems" and they were "delighted to be associated with NDLC", on the basis of this visit. They wanted us to visit them to show us their operations. This letter, amongst other prime documents, never saw the court.

Tell me, looking at this letter, does my business sound bogus to you? Or did they clearly give me permission to use their logos?

City & Guilds

103

19 November 1999

Dr Roy Grimmond
The National Distance Learning College
102-103 Borough Road
York House
Middlesborough
TS1 2HJ

Dear Roy

NDLC & City & Guilds

Firstly, I would like to take the opportunity to thank you and your colleagues for the time taken in showing Linda Steel and myself the NDLC operations on Tuesday. We were very impressed by your operational and quality assurance systems, and City & Guilds is delighted to be associated with NDLC. We are confident that our wide ranging services will proactively support you in achieving your ambitions and challenging business plan.

Following our visit and subsequent telephone conversations, I trust this note will summarise the ongoing actions:

1. National Press Advert & Leaflet Campaign

   We confirm the use of the City & Guilds name and logo as in the draft design supplied. Our only design suggestion is that, as with other City & Guilds adverts, the "ampersand and lion" symbol is used in the bottom right corner of each relevant course description box.

   On a formal point, the phrase "We Guarantee to Get You Through Your Course" refers to NDLC only, and there is no liability for City & Guilds to guarantee that a student completes a course.

   Please let us know when the advert will be run, so we can brief our staff accordingly.

2. Visit to City & Guilds

   We would like to show Mike, Brian and yourself the range and scale of our operations, and talk in detail with some of people who will deliver the services in support of your national and international objectives. And also progress the commercial discussions.

   We would suggest Thursday 25 November from 11.00am to 4.00pm, and please can you confirm if this is convenient. We will forward a detailed schedule next week.

1 Giltspur Street London EC1A 9DD Telephone 0171 294 2468 Facsimile 0171 294 2400
http://www.city-and-guilds.co.uk

The City and Guilds of London Institute Incorporated by Royal Charter Founded 1878 Registered Charity 312832
Founded 1878 Plans Mary Lane of Edinburgh KBKT

265

City & Guilds' two-page letter to the NDLC dated 19 Nov 99.

MAY.2001 17:21   CITY AND GUILDS 0171 294 2408   NO.786   P.10
8268 4442453 51   FROM to 020 7294 2411   TO at 01705/01 14:12   P9.

) Verification Visit

We have provisionally asked our regional lead verifier, Lesley Hebron, to visit NDLC on Monday 29 November at 11.00am. Please can you also confirm if this is convenient, and in particular Lesley would like to meet Angela Smallman.

The purpose of the visit is two-fold. Firstly, our quality assurance system requires a visit to a new centre from a verifier. However, this is usually not until later when certification is in progress, and the main purpose is begin our support in looking at any assessment issues which could impact on future funding requirements and international certification.

Please do not hesitate to contact me if you have any questions, and hopefully we can look forward to welcoming you to City & Guilds offices next week.

Yours sincerely

Richard Stott
Business Development Key Account Manager

Direct line 0171 294 2700

So, in November, as a result of that meeting, City & Guilds asked to be able to preview our marketing material. The next document is the front of the proposed advertising leaflet and represents the overall general message that we were going to put out – with their permission – through all our various marketing media. As you can see, we have placed the City & Guilds logo in the bottom right hand corner, as instructed by City & Guilds in the document above.

Front page of the proposed advertising leaflet with the City & Guilds logo on it – as agreed by them.

The day before, on 18th November 1999, Richard Stott of City & Guilds sent an email document to his big boss, Bob Coates, a Director at City & Guilds. You will be able to see in detail, but I'll summarise what it says in the letter. They confirm that they had got the leaflet and confirmed their knowledge that I intended also using the national press. They confirm that they can see that each course advertised would carry the phrase, *'On passing the final examination, you will receive a City & Guilds' qualification'*. This is not just for one course, but for all my four courses, and it goes on to say that they had checked us out financially and we were low risk. Furthermore, it says that we provided our proof of accreditation to the Edexcel organisation and our course modules for them to review.

Internal Email within City & Guilds discussing the leaflet for the national press – 18 November 1999.

SARAH DHANDA - Re: NDLC - City & Guilds brands use   Page

145

From:	RICHARD STOTT
To:	BOB COATES
Date:	Thu, Nov 18, 1999 12:40 pm
Subject:	Re: NDLC - City & Guilds brands use

To confirm telecons re your email, and summary progress following 16/11 visit to NDLC with Linda Steel.

1. NDLC Leaflet/National Advert

1.1 Draft of leaflet by separate copy (to BC, DM, SM, SD). This will be now used not only for the end year leaflet campaign, but NDLC have also advised it is also looking at a national ad (The Express?) next week, with copy deadline 19/11.

Over a summary box for each of three NDLC courses (Business Administration, Computerised Accounting [Sage], & Book-Keeping) there would be the phrase:

They New

"Upon passing the final examination you will receive a City & Guilds qualification".

From this stage what

1.2 For the fourth NDLC course in Practical Computing, which is currently from Edexcel, the wording is:

was out on the leaflet

"Upon passing the final examination you will receive a B.T.E.C. Diploma in Computer Skills (at Higher Level)".

During the visit to NDLC, it was noted that this is sold as being equivalent to NVQ level 3.

1.3 Although there are no City & Guilds contact details, the national ad will generate some enquiries direct to City & Guilds. We would need to brief inquiries unit to redirect to NDLC.

2. Financial Check

The credit check reported NDLC as a low risk. The best financial reference would probably come from the Yorkshire Bank.

3. Centre/Course Accreditation

NDLC has provided the Edexcel accreditation papers and EV reports. Although our own requirements may be expressed differently and other confirmations required, no significant problems are anticipated.

NDLC have also provided course modules.

Action: SM/SD/LS/RS meeting 18/11 to progress action points.

Richard

>>> Bob Coates 11/11 8:08 pm >>>
Richard

Can we see (by fax) the leaflet that is going to carry our logo please? Just a precaution! Otherwise this is good news. What did the financial checks say?

Regards

Bob

268

The next document shows, just a few weeks later, Mr Richard Stott explaining to two other City & Guilds employees that he had attended my National Sales Conference, with many of my employees there. He wrote that he had seen the TV commercial, that lasted 30 seconds, and that would go out at a prime time during the airing of the popular TV programme, 'The Bill' [how ironic!]. He comments on what he sees in the commercial, *"Students will gain a City & Guilds qualification, the C & G Logo is prominently shown."* He goes on to tell these two members of City & Guilds to expect enquiries from the public and gives them this instruction, *'These enquiries should be dealt with in the same way in confirming NDLC are an approved City & Guilds Centre, centre number 041889, and offer City & Guilds qualifications for their four courses.'*

Internal City & Guilds Email discussing City & Guilds' position upon the NDLC advertising campaign.

From:	RICHARD STOTT
To:	ANDREW JOHNSTON, DI WALSTER
Date:	04 January 2000 12:04:34
Subject:	National Distance Learning College - Tyne Tees Region TV ad 4 Jan

At the NDLC sales conference yesterday, it was confirmed that the 30 second ad will go out tonight in the Tyne Tees area at 20.22 during 'The Bill'.

In the ad, while the voiceover is saying that on completing one of the four courses available students will gain a City & Guilds qualification, the C&G logo is prominently shown.

Edexcel is not mentioned, although their logo still appears on the insert leaflets so as not to give concern to students who have already signed up for the BTech qualification. However, the new NDLC salesforce presentation pack refers to C&G.

Although we have yet not had any direct reponse to the NDLC leaflets, please brief your teams on the ad and possibility of inquiries. These should be dealt in same way, in confirming that NDLC are an approved C&G centre (041889) and offer City and Guilds qualificiations for their four courses; and refer the caller to NDLC for course details (freephone 08000 527439).

(The scheme number for suite of NDLC courses is 7236, but course details are not yet entered).

Other items from the meeting:
- NDLC salesforce (self employed, commission based) is expand from 50 to 80 over next 10 weeks
- each salesperson is given 6 confirmed appointments per day by NDLC
- current overall student retention rate is 50%
- continuing 1 million leaflets per week

Richard

CC: BOB COATES, CAROLYN ROBERTS, CHANDRA MORAR, DAV...

Well, reader, I suppose I could stop here and ask you, do you think it was right for City & Guilds, in April 2001, to lie to the press that we were not accredited? Or should they have said, we've been working with them for 18 months or more? Don't answer it yet, wait a little bit and answer it later. I'll carry on with some more documents. The next document shows communication from Andrew Johnston, Richard Stott's boss. He's stating that our television commercial has been on the TV a few times and, I quote, *"Very good free publicity"*.

Internal Email within City and Guilds, 13 Jan 2000 discussing the television advertising campaign

From:	ANDREW JOHNSTON
To:	RICHARD STOTT
Date:	13 January 2000 09:30:45
Subject:	NDLC

Apparently the ad has been on several times now, including daytime TV. Very good free publicity!

I need to be clear about the quality assurance aspects of the NDLC project. I understand that the programmes we are likely to accredit are to be developments of ones they already have in operation. We will need to go through an approval process for the individual awards once they are properly developed. It is possible that this would be a fairly quick process (could be desktop) but it till needs to happen.

Also, there is usually a running in period of 6 months between approval and first monitoring visit, and only after that can candidates be accredited. Whether this needs to be as long as six months is open to negotiation, but there does have to be a period of implamantation and monitoring before we certificate.

I wouldn't want to get to a position where there is an expectation that we would certificate candidates without proper monitoring. Given that many of the candidates are probably already working on NDLC programmes, this could happen. Can you keep us advised of the actual development of the awards - and in particular what kind of quality assurance is going to be incorporated?

CC: CAROLYN ROBERTS; Newcastle

The next document is the first page of a memo, dated in July 2000, which shows the intent and preparation to approve our scheme by City & Guilds. It confirms why I approached City & Guilds, as I said earlier. It shows what they were expecting in the numbers of candidates. It confirms that they knew and accepted we were putting a million leaflets out each week, had videos and TV advertising, what we were charging for the courses, and so on.

As a side note here, it also says, in point 1, paragraph four, "Distance learning courses can have a relatively high fall-out rate (50%+), usually soon after commitment; NDLC current rate is 35%." ....and we were referred to in the national press, and throughout the court hearing, as a 'bogus business'.

First page of a memo in July 2000 which shows the intent of approval of the NDLC scheme by City & Guilds.

RICHARD STOTT - NDLC SA1&SA2 Cover Note.doc

Memo DRAFT
DRAFT

To All Signatories

Cc [Click here and type name(s)]

From Richard Stott

Date 25 July 2000

Subject SA2 Approval to Offer - 7236 National Distance Learning College Accredited Courses

1. Approval to offer this scheme (number provisionally identified on Forward) is requested for an award which accredits the distance learning courses (four to date) developed and marketed by the National Distance Learning College.

NDLC has accreditation with Edexcel, but the low level of flexibility and service together with high level of bureaucracy led NDLC to initiate contact with City & Guilds at the IPD exhibition in October last year.

The current courses, and 'registrations' are:
Practical Computing (from Edexcel) 12,184 students
Business Administration 1,234
Book-Keeping 1,400
Computerised Accounting 868

NDLC are planning for total of 30,000 students in 2001/02. Distance learning courses can have a relatively high fall out rate (50%+), usually soon after initial commitment; NDLC Current rate is 35%. With this in mind, our agreement with NDLC would have an up-front total registration/certification fee (see point 5 below).

2. NDLC is a privately owned company. It has 130 staff, of which 100 are the direct self-employed sales force). NDLC are looking to expand in UK, and start business in the USA, South Africa, Malaysia and Australia (either by direct or franchised operations).

NDLC markets its products by direct mail/leaflets (1m leaflets per week), videos and recently TV advertising (pilot in Tyne Tees area) to generate appointments for the sales force. The net cost of a course to a student is approx. £550, which students pay mainly by direct debit on a monthly basis. This is inclusive of all materials, support, tutoring and examination costs.

NDLC do not operate an APL system, and candidates must undertake all the relevant modules. There is no time limit on students to complete a course, but after five years NDLC charge a re-registration fee. The company also operates a computer leasing system for students.

3. The courses are divided into Foundation, Intermediate and Advanced levels, with a series of modules (approx. 12-25 depending on the course) with assessments to be completed and returned to NDLC (written or electronic).

Support to students is by written or electronic responses and by on-line/phone tutors, with personal visits in special circumstances. Module work is assessed to set criteria giving a

A month later in August 2000, an email was sent from Richard Stott to the Customer Services Manager, Anne Verdon. She was the Manager at the City & Guilds call centre. The email is confirming that she is to continue to tell the public that 'NDLC is an accredited City & Guilds Centre, candidates completing the courses will receive a City & Guilds certificate'. We are now about two years into our relationship.

An internal email within City & Guilds regarding answering calls with respect to the NDLC

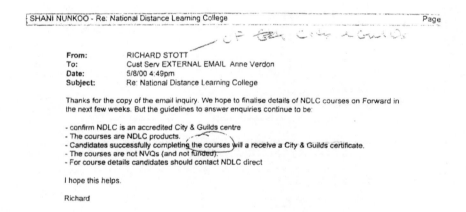

SHANI NUNKOO - Re: National Distance Learning College   Page

From:	RICHARD STOTT
To:	Cust Serv EXTERNAL EMAIL Anne Verdon
Date:	5/8/00 4:49pm
Subject:	Re: National Distance Learning College

Thanks for the copy of the email inquiry. We hope to finalise details of NDLC courses on Forward in the next few weeks. But the guidelines to answer enquiries continue to be:

- confirm NDLC is an accredited City & Guilds centre
- The courses are NDLC products.
- Candidates successfully completing the courses will a receive a City & Guilds certificate.
- The courses are not NVQs (and not funded).
- For course details candidates should contact NDLC direct

I hope this helps.

Richard

The next document in October 2000 shows emails between Andrew Johnston to another City & Guilds employee, Eleanor Ross. Eleanor Ross had asked Andrew Johnston, 'Does anyone know of the National Distance Learning College?' This was because she was getting enquiries about the NDLC. Johnston replies, *"This is the National Distance Learning College, an ongoing key account."* He explains what we do and goes on to say this centre was unusually approved by this office in order to allow their advertising to be valid. We were viewed as a key account, meaning our relationship was important to them. Andrew Johnston goes on to state *'This process has taken longer than expected, but is definitely in hand'*. This is possibly the first instance that shows the signs that City & Guilds are inadequate and expresses the extended time being taken.

Just as a side note – and I'm being cynical here – the document doesn't inform her to tell people that we've been with the NDLC for two years now and we've told them many, many times to stop saying that they are accredited and you can't offer City & Guilds qualifications. The reason for this is because that didn't happen! We were encouraged by them to do more marketing, it was good publicity for them and all at our cost of millions of pounds.

Internal City and Guilds Email October 2000

From:	ANDREW JOHNSTON
To:	ELEANOR ROSS
Date:	05 October 2000 15:43:25
Subject:	Re: Distance Learning College

It is the "National Distance Learning College", based in Middlesbrough. This is an ongoing devlepment and Richard Stott of Key Accounts can give the most detailed background to the negotiations to date.

They are a distance learning organisation who specialise in business programmes. They advertise (usually by leaflet drop) nationally and their advertising carries the City & Guilds logo, with the statement to the effect that on completing the course you will receive a City & Guilds award. The programmes are tutor supported distance learning through materials and assignments, typically take a year to complete are will in due course finish with a formal examination.

The centre was - unusually - approved by this office in principle some time last year, in order to allow their advertising to be valid. The approval was CAP only and the intention was to get specific learning programmes accepted by City & Guilds (ie product agreed and then SAP process) so that final examinations could lead to a C&G certificate. This process has taken longer than expected but is definitely in hand. Sarah Dhanda's team are dealing with this side of things, especially the specific titles that are under consideration. There are also a number of pre-existing courses run by NDLC that are not linked to C&G awards.

Give me a ring if this is not clear.

>>> ELEANOR ROSS 05/10/2000 15:02:11 >>>
Dear all
Does anyone know of The Disatance Learning College and the arrangements with us for C&G accreditation.? We are having a number of enquiries from prospective students who have concerns re their direct sell approach and also the nature of the C&G qualification.
Any info greatly appreciated as I cannot locate them via F&T or Evita.
Eleanor

CC: CAROLYN ROBERTS; GLENDA HORNE; HEATHER JOHNSON; ...

Meeting minutes (two page document) taken by City & Guilds during a meeting held at the NDLC November 2000

Minutes

Confidential

Meeting: National Distance Learning College
Date: 22 November 00
Place: NDLC, Middlesborough
Members: Mike Smallman (Chairman) Peter Kenyon (MD), Syd Hutchinson (Group
             Sales Director), Brian Dowd (Education Director), Andy Egan, Heather
             Ainsley (Practical Computing course), Jeff Cotton (M&BS course)
City & Guilds: Richard Stott

1. General

NDLC is the main subsidiary of the Thanx Group (270 staff in total). Accounts, audited by KPMG, show profit growth of:

1996   (£140k)
1998   £0k
1999   £400k
2000   £1,000k
2001   £4,000k projected

Main other businesses in the group:

Fiche & Chips – NDLC previously leased computers to students, but with purchase of their supplier has formed this company which sells basic hardware and software package to students and general public. The company is receiving hardware 'decommissioning' license. Cost of package is £199.00 inclusive of VAT, and projected 2001/2002 profits of £2,000k.

Brookes – Fashion jewelry marketing and sales. Pilot phase.

Lead Machine – NDLC is the largest DM leaflet account for the Royal Mail. In moving from a 2-page to 4-page leaflet, it will also sell insert space. Projected 2001/2002 profit of £1,000k.

2. City & Guilds Fee Income

i) initial proposal to NDLC is based on £45 per candidate fee to include:
-       verification/development
-       registration at completion of Foundation module
-       CUC Foundation module
-       CUC Intermediate module
-       Certificate for Advanced module

Transactions to be via the Walled Garden. There is a possibility that there could be only two key transactions (registration and final certificate).

Minutes

NDLC figures on candidate numbers currently at each level in the courses:

Course/Level	Foundation	Intermediate	Advanced	00/01 Fee Income
Practical Computing				Est. £900k
Management & Business Studies				Est. £270k

Based on the above, on accreditation we should expect xxxxx candidates to register (£xx,xxx).

With the development in ii) below, although these full courses will be available, it is expected that most new business will be from the bite-sized course route. To this effect, NDLC will reduce/eliminate their sales force to concentrate corporate sales for full or bespoke course. Companies such as Jaguar cars, Teeside NHS Trust and Inland Revenue are clients.

Heather Ainsley has completed assessment format for modules 1 to 8 of the Practical Computing course, and is forwarding to Paul McCloskey. If format satisfactory, she can rapidly complete the same for remaining four modules. Heather will then do the assessment format for the Management & Business Studies course (estimate 2 weeks).

Actions a) Response on receipt of assessment format to Heather – Paul McCloskey

ii) NDLC will change their business approach to market bite sized courses using the existing modules to create eight combinations of modules. The courses will be sold from direct response to the DM pieces, not through a sales force. NDLC brochure attached.

Market testing has shown a significant interest with a 15% response rate to DM pieces. NDLC budget to increase DM campaign from 1 million to 4 million leaflets per week. NDLC are planning on a 0.1% response with conversion to 264,000 sales in 2001.

NDLC will market the courses at £175, with DfEE VTR grant of £150 and candidate to pay £25. This has been agreed with DfEE. The problem may be in over response to use most of VTR budget. The change to ILAs is not expected to change these estimates.

NDLC proposal is to offer candidates the opportunity for a City & Guilds certificate at an additional cost to the candidate, for example £10. Also discussed possible license/registration fee for brand and development/verification costs, for example £5 per candidate. NDLC had some resistance to this amount, but recognised possible license amount for verification costs.

Actions b) Certification of shorter courses – Paul McCloskey
c) Costing, pricing model & contract proposals – Richard Stott

3. International

NDLC are setting up office in Holland and proceeding towards DM campaign there. The Practical Computing course will be offered at first, using City & Guilds International logo. Next European country will probably be Portugal. Further work is being carried out in Florida.

Richard

Letter from City & Guilds to the NDLC regarding a meeting held at Wetherby Racecourse.

AC-1| 35
203

City &⁂ Guilds

28 November 2000

Mr Peter Kenyon
Managing Director
thanx Group
York House
102-108 Borough Road
Middlesborough
TS1 2HJ

Dear Peter

thanx Race Day

I would like to thank you for a most informative and enjoyable day at the thanx Race Day at Wetherby last week. Sadly it was not as profitable for me as for those who had remained faithful to the National Distance Learning College 'stable' in anticipation of a pay-back day!

The morning presentation on the growth and plans for the thanx Group reinforced my understanding of the exciting development of the National distance Learning College courses in the UK and beyond. If a hard copy or e-mail version of the presentation is available, please could you send one to me.

At our meeting the preceding day, we outlined the issues which City & Guilds need to expedite to support the current students and your future business plan. And following my meeting with Heather Ainsley, we now hope to rapidly finalise the format for the accreditation of the Practical Computing and Management & Business Studies courses. We will also respond with our proposals regarding the new shorter courses within the next two weeks.

We also discussed the letters from Mr Mooney to City & Guilds and the recent judgement from the Inland Revenue on another company in this market - please could you also forward the copies to me. Regarding the latter, you may wish to also bring this directly to the attention of Bob Coates, Director Marketing & Sales Director, at City & Guilds.

Yours sincerely

Richard Stott

Ideas to join us.

Richard Stott
Business Development Key Accounts Manager

Direct line 020 7294 2700
e-mail   richards@city-and-guilds.co.uk

236

1 Giltspur Street London EC1A 9DD *Telephone* 020 7294 2468 *Facsimile* 020 7294 2400
http://www.city-and-guilds.co.uk

The City and Guilds of London Institute *Incorporated by* Royal Charter *Founded* 1878 *Registered Charity* 312832
President HRH The Prince Philip Duke of Edinburgh KG KT

From these two documents above you can see that the level of communication between my business and City & Guilds was extensive. The document above was in November 2000 and it's interesting to point out that the letter is not addressed to me but to a member of my staff. Namely my managing director. Surely this letter – amongst many others addressed to my managing directors, and others not on the stand as defendants – and the resulting 'not guilty' of Peter Kenyon, shows that these communications with City & Guilds were accepted by the jury as legitimate communications, between City & Guilds and the NDLC? Was there a second relationship between myself and City & Guilds in which, for some reason, I was found guilty? Of course not!

It just shows how the court was only interested in convicting me. Peter Kenyon only worked under my instructions and, if Heather Ainsley and the others are having cordial positive communications with City & Guilds, this alone shows doubt upon my conviction?

Now let's move on to the next document, some three months further on. It's February 2001, not long before the shit hits the fan. The highlighted points in this document show many inadequacies within City & Guilds. It shows me pointing out that I am not happy with them. In the first paragraph of this document, they mention my name and that of the Chairman and say, in effect "this is a real nightmare of bad management of the customer account by the account manager". Read the rest for yourself. They confirm, in paragraph two, their account manager is lax. In paragraph three they say they [the NDLC] do have a case to some extent. Paragraph four says the accreditation process has been going on forever, but they should be able to accredit soon. Paragraph five states they confirm that their Account Manager seems to have given them approval to go ahead with promotions of it all. Paragraph seven says their Product Manager seems incapable of recognising the basics of account management — never mind sales. In the last paragraph they say that they have made such a mess.

Internal Email at City & Guilds regarding a committee meeting discussing the NDLC as a key customer account. Dated 12 Feb 2001

From:	CAROLYN ROBERTS
To:	CHRISTINE JOHNSON
Date:	12 February 2001 16:29:58
Subject:	Your Fax - 9th Feb

With regard to notes for the Exec committee, I have nothing to add/delete

NDLC - Mr Smallman is the Chairman I am advised. In event, this is a real nightmare of bad management of the customer account by the Account Manager, little regard to getting it sorted out from the Account Manger, the usual delays in getting anything through Product Management and a bit of the customer - mostly exasperated but also not playing the game.

It is a can of worms and not easily answered in a few lines. The last meeting had Richard involve Keith Brooker. Product Management have some serious concerns, I have had one of my more active Account Mangers visit the customer to give me a view on their credibility. What we have is a lot of fall down by us mixed with their commercialism and play upon our lax account management.

I suspect the reasoning behind some of this will be the press interest and also the interest of the Trading Standards body. It looks to me as if they are now using our inadequacies against us when in fact they are not totally innocent bystanders in this. This said, they do have a case to some extent.

The issue is two fold, the original request for accreditation which has been going on for-ever. This is currently with Product Management, Paul McClouskey is dealing with it and is apparently due to meet up and should be able to accredit. However, I know Sara Dhanda has concerns.

The second issue is that they have now promoted a partnership with us in print for bit sized training. They should never have done this, it was this issue that Keith got involved in, and despite the advice of myself and Keith, the Account Manger seems to have given them approval to go ahead with their promotion on it all. We are not at present looking at any accreditation for bit sized learning that I am aware of.

Then finally there is the fact they they have used our name for over a year now, and we have received no income, which has raised questions from candidates who thought they were getting a C & G qualification. This is where Trading Standards came in. Despite advising the Account Manger in August to stop NDLC from continuing to promote until we could get something sorted out, the Account Manager did not, and then we had the current situation explained above.

In a conversation today, the Account Manager just advises that he has left it with Product Management - he seems incapable of recognising the basics of account management never mind sales. All this despite having had conversations through line management and direct on a number of occassions.

I have no where else to put this, it is a Key Account and not one that I had wanted to hand over to the region in such a mess - even though I do not doubt that the region would do a better job. However, I cannot simply keep giving the work of Key Accounts to others whilst Key Accounts sit and do what? This said, the region is fully aware of the situation, actually takes the calls for most of the complaints of candidates and the Trading Standards and could pick it up and run with it - if Product Mangement could make a decison as to whether to run with it or not.

Carolyn

The above takes us up to February 2001. Up until that time they have never said anything but positive things about us leading towards accreditation, other than we might be a bit too commercial for them. However, they loved the potential of what we could bring them; with the volume of candidates that we could generate, and, in recognition of that, the money that we could bring to City & Guilds.

You can see from the letter, Trading Standards were involved and there are a number of complaints, but my business, the NDLC, at this point had no contact from the press and no contact from Trading Standards. These two organisations were contacting City & Guilds who were being asked questions along the lines of the one from Vivienne Parry. Is the NDLC accredited? Similarly, Trading Standards were talking to City & Guilds, asking the same thing. There were some people in the public ready to go to examinations, and, quite rightly so, were concerned that we couldn't give a finite date of their examination.

You can see from the trail of these letters from 1999 all the way to February 2001, and later, which I'll continue to show, City & Guilds had accredited us as a Centre. They had been working with us and had approved the courses, but for some reason they just couldn't get the signatures from the upper management. All of a sudden, Trading Standards said to them, 'What's going on?' The News of The World were saying, 'What's going on?' And they had to make a decision. Now the choice they had to make was, do they admit their lax performance and get the four dozy officials of City & Guilds to sign the document? Or do they negate three years' worth of hard work, development and good honest intent and tell the News of The World that we are not accredited and tell Trading Standards that we are not accredited? You can see this is the point of ignition. Lighting the blue touch paper that sent my life and a lot of other people's lives into absolute chaos. And they did this to cover their inadequacies.

Below you see Andrew Johnston, of City & Guilds, advising his colleagues not to say anything. He was in fear of him, his colleagues and City & Guilds appearing on 'Watchdog'. This is an indictment of their fears and bolsters my conclusion that their denial of our accreditation process was to cover their inadequacies. Should City & Guilds have been in court as a defendant as opposed to me?

Internal Email at City & Guilds showing their fear of what they had done and what was happening.

JOHNSTON - NDLC

From:	ANDREW JOHNSTON
To:	newcastle
Date:	05 April 2001 17:53:28
Subject:	NDLC

I'd advise referring any NDLC questions to the press officer (Henri Forde x2556), but in case of emergency break glass and read the fluorescent pink statement on my desk!

Nothing new has happened, but I'd hate to see any of you on Watchdog tomorrow night.

You can see from all the above that we, the NDLC, had a very close, in-depth relationship with City & Guilds. It's clear that City & Guilds were worried for themselves because of their inadequacies. They had lied to the press about our accreditation status and lied, or more poignantly, said nothing, about our long-standing relationship. Now, imagine, a huge, huge newspaper like the News of the World, and another like The Daily Mirror, and all the others, are read by tens of millions of people: the general public. Within the general public there are officers in the police force, employees in the DTI (Department of Trade and Industry), in the Department of Education, the VAT departments, Customs and Excise...all the departments related in the above letter are seeing this newspaper report of the so-called 'cheating, lying conman' – Michael Smallman. They all want to get to the bottom of things. Particularly the Department of Education, which is funding us. They, in some way, communicate with each other, club together and this results in the following letter, driven by Sue Thickitt, from the Department of Education.

Email between City & Guilds Sue Thickitt and Sue Smith of the Department of Education ILA scheme. 27 April 2000

SMITH, Sue-ILA

Legal

From: THICKITT, Sue
Sent: 27 April 2001 15:34
To: SMITH, Sue-ILA
Cc: McGOLDRICK, Mike; DAWSON, Karen; HASLAM, Tina
Subject: FW:

Mike Sue

See john's reply

Tina Karen

ref only
-----Original Message-----
From: YOUDELL, John-LAO
Sent: 27 April 2001 15:26
To: THICKITT, Sue
Subject:

You consulted me about the current situation regarding a provider on the ILA list about whom the department now has reason to entertain concern.

In particular Derek Grover wishes to know whether one of the department's options is to suspend the provider, that is to take him off the list so that grants would be refused to those who wish to sign on for courses with that provider, until enquiries get to the bottom of the various causes for concern.

In my view the mere fact that there is no clear cut breach of the published rules for staying on the list is not decisive.

The Amraf case illustrates that it can successfully be argued that the "rules" are limited to what is administratively required for the operation of the scheme and that the SoS retains a wider discretion.

(As Amraf also illustrates we have not made it as easy to argue that as it might be because of the way the "rules" are drawn up and publicised.)

Taking the causes for concern in order, the involvement of the News of the World is irrelevant as far as legal considerations are concerned.

The 25 complaints received by the administrative agent are insufficient, by themselves, to justify a decision to suspend.

The MP's letter, by itself, is insufficient.

The concern of the DTI is insufficient (and may well be stimulated by no more than the actions of the News of the World.   *who   + City + Guilds.*

Similarly the concern of the VAT authorities.

The question as to whether the provider can, in fact, deliver the City and Guilds qualification is a more directly relevant concern and you are more advanced in your enquiries. But you are not yet in a position to conclude that anything has, in fact, gone astray and you have not yet put your concern to the provider. It would be wrong to base a decision to suspend on that alone.

But, in my view you are entitled to aggregate these various matters to a degree.

Furthermore, while the press involvement might be irrelevant to a judge it is far from irrelevant from your point of view in advising ministers.

It seems to me that there is a risk involved in suspending but you will wish to balance that risk against the political risk of not suspending and thereby exposing ministers to criticism should the result of the N of the W article be for the provider subsequently to be shown to be ripping people off.

The risk of suspending is that the provider can meet most or all of the criticisms and subsequently makes a legal challenge to the decision to suspend.

There is a risk that such a challenge would succeed.

However, in my view the department can seek to justify a decision to suspend and, even if that justification failed I would expect a broadly sympathetic hearing. An adverse judgment might well be couched in terms that would not

1

pose very great presentational difficulties.

We would say that the government has a legitimate interest in ILA money being applied so that people do promptly get the training
that the grant helps to secure and that there is reason, aggregating all the above matters, to think that this is not happening in this case.

It will aid matters if, following a decision to suspend, the department acts promptly to get to the bottom of the actual situation. If resources allow it would help to interview those who are saying that they have parted with money but so far have had no learning materials.

If it turns out that the provider is kosher, it may improve the position if the department is willing then to offer modest compensation to the provider for business lost while the suspension was in effect.

The decision letter would need care and I stand ready to assist with it.

In summary, I advise that this is a judgment call with risk attendant on each of the alternative courses. It is perfectly reasonable, in my view, to give greater weight to the competing political risks than to the narrow legal risk.

John Youdell

You'll find some very poignant parts which really show how City & Guilds' lies affected my good standing. Make your own conclusions, but I want to point out this... as you know, aside from the City & Guilds problem, I'd found a large financial problem within the Government. Because of this they had wanted me to be closed down but had found no fraud and no non-compliance in their audits. This letter is the prequel to their actions, and the last line of this letter sums up the reasons for their actions, and the reason why they were willing to use me as a scapegoat.

I'd like to strike out a few comments in this letter, one being about interest from the VAT people. It's true that the VAT people invited me to a tribunal. That was because I had claimed back £2.1m worth of VAT over a period of time. It was found at that tribunal that my ability to reclaim this money was justified for two reasons: one, ostensibly my product was a book and books are zero rated with respect to VAT and, secondly, in the weeks that I'd started the business HMRC had misdirected me regarding my VAT status. Ergo I, my business, could keep the £2.1m. That is a story for another book. Regarding another point in the letter, it is clear, even from their perspective, that City & Guilds had never mentioned any negatives to us and this document was dated after the press statement.

Regarding the involvement of Trading Standards. They had visited me, asked the questions – such as, 'Can you give us proof that you are accredited to City & Guilds?' and subsequently we gave the proof to Trading Standards which resulted in a letter to City & Guilds mentioning these letters and putting them on the spot. Basically, Trading Standards were saying to City & Guilds, what's your problem? What are you messing about at? See below.

Trading Standards letter to City & Guilds 30 April 2001

MIDDLESBROUGH COUNCIL

Ⱶ Harper
Head of Public Protection & Planning

P.O. Box 65, Vancouver House, Central Mews, Gurney Street, Middlesbrough. TS1 1QP
Website: http://www.middlesbrough.gov.uk

Mr T Williamson
The City and Guilds of London Institute
1 Giltspur Street
LONDON
EC1A 9DD

Direct Line:	(01642) 264235
Switchboard:	(01642) 245432
Fax:	(01642) 264199
DX60532	

Our Ref: JPMcC/HS/City
Your Ref:

When telephoning please ask for :
James McCluskey

30 April 2001

Dear Sir

TRADE DESCRIPTION ACT 1968
RE : NATIONAL DISTANCE LEARNING COLLEGE

Following your letter of 7th February, I visited the above company at 102-108 Borough Road, Middlesbrough. I was concerned that your letter stated that "NDLC has agreed to remove these references (to City and Guilds qualifications) in future material until formal accreditation of their courses has been given". In response to my enquiries NDLC showed me a copy of a letter from your organisation dated 19.11.99 and signed by Richard Stott.

This letter states that "City & Guilds is delighted to be associated with NDLC" and later "we confirm the use of the City & Guilds name and logo.... Our only design suggestion is that, as with other City & Guilds adverts, the 'ampersand and lion' symbol is used in the bottom right corner of each relevant course description box'.

This information appeared to preclude any action against the company under the provisions of the above legislation and in some ways the two letters appear contradictory.

I would be grateful if you would clarify the precise relationship between The City and Guilds of London Institute and the National Distance Learning College, and specifically how the City and Guilds logo may be used by the company. I would ask you to treat this as an urgent matter as I am continuing to receive allegations that the courses are misdescribed as 'City and Guilds' courses by use of the logo.

Customer Services
Enquiries Unit
rec'd – 1 MAY 2001
Action:

Now, I'll refer you back to the Sue Thickitt document. They clearly show the Department of Education trying to find a reason to turn our funding off. There were various possible reasons they could use to do that. Could they use the involvement of the News of the World – who'd said that they'd had 25 complaints? In actual fact, when it came out in court they had only had three and that was after trading had ceased! As a performance indicator for any company, that's quite exceptional for 180,000 students. Could they use the situation with City & Guilds? Who knows? They were just looking for a reason. But then you read down this letter and you see the real underlying reasons were to save their political necks because of the mess they had made in running their scheme.

Four paragraphs up from the bottom of the first page, I quote, *"Furthermore, while the press involvement might be irrelevant to a Judge it is far from irrelevant from your point of view in advising ministers."* It goes on to say, *"It seems to me that there is a risk involved in suspending but you will wish to balance that risk against the political risk of not suspending and therefore exposing ministers to criticism should the result of the News of the World article be for the provider subsequently to be shown to be ripping people off."*

It is clear the political agenda was to cover the mistakes made by the Department of Education and they were hoping they could find something dodgy in my business that would deflect their mess up. Read the whole of the document, but I just want to quote the last paragraph, which shows that they were willing to cut my business off because the political risk of me being believed was huge.

I quote, *"In summary, I advise that this is a judgement call with the risk attendant on each of the alternative causes. It is perfectly reasonable, in my view, to give greater weight to the compelling political risks than the narrow legal risk."*

What they are saying is it's better to lie about it and risk Michael Smallman's potential litigation against us than to risk the political connotations. It is my submission, that this document confirms that I had damning information that the Department of Education had made a mistake amounting to many millions of pounds, and they needed me silenced. So, they used the City & Guilds scenarios, and the national press, to portray me as the villain, where, indeed, I was the victim.

It just goes to show that if you are the young lad from Manchester, or Kentucky, or Edinburgh or Berlin jumping up and down begging to have your story told properly, you can beg the press, the State, the police, to look more closely at your provocateurs, but you're never going to be believed when your provocateur is a huge establishment that is beyond reproach. And, within that establishment is a department and, in conversations with that department, the government needs a scapegoat.

I bring you back to the document dated 26th April 2001 – the email to Vivienne Parry of the News of the World. It confirms that a bigwig in City & Guilds, Michael Osbaldeston, has spoken with his colleagues and together they have approved the following statement to Vivienne Parry: *'We have not approved City & Guilds to offer NDLC courses'*.

Obviously, all the above covers around a two and a half year relationship with City & Guilds. I ask you again, right up to the last minute, was there any indication from City & Guilds given to us that they wanted us to stop our marketing? No; on the contrary, the only indications are that we were approved as a Centre and they were continuing to drag their feet, simply to 'cross the Ts and dot the Is'. Do you think that, on 26th April 2001, the statement to the press was the real truth, or was it the lie that began my downfall?

To add to all this, let me put a few things into context here to explain why they were dragging their feet. City & Guilds do not write courses. They are not educationalists. Effectively, they are auditors. They don't teach anybody anything. A college like mine, or a government college, writes the course collating all the information that is needed to teach someone to a tier level. Whether that be a NVQ level 1,2 or 3, a degree, or a PhD, the person – on behalf of the college that writes the course – compiles the course with diagrams and words in explanations.

They will deliver the information of the course through books, printouts, verbal communication, lectures and advice. All these collated deliverables are called optional hours. Each level of qualification has denoted notional hours allocated to that level. For example, to gain a NVQ level 1, it might take 20 to 30 notional hours. To gain a degree it might be 600 notional hours, and everything else fits between.

So a college, like mine, writes the course and it says, 'I have a course which is equal to NVQ level 3, or whatever', then asks City & Guilds [or another body like them] to verify that the course is as the college says it is. Typically, City & Guilds take two to four weeks to do this.

See below the internal City & Guilds email, 2000:

From:	RICHARD STOTT
To:	ANDREW JOHNSTON
Date:	12 December 2000 17:38:00
Subject:	Fwd: National Distance Learning College

Andrew

Attached is email on revised costing assumptions for existing NDLC courses and first shot costings for short courses. Also memo to Carolyn.

From discussion with Paul, suggest we also put in 5 development days for the new business - I had put all into existing business as essentially it will be setting up new courses from existing modules with product operations. I was due to meet Neil tomorrow but will ask him to give you a call.

I will fax up original costing memos. If you need anything else, just let me know.

As per telecon please bring to urgent conclusion. I am glad Glenda has visited NDLC offices and has some positive comments. We should also remember that one of the reasons for progressing with NDLC was to learn about an area of the market where we have little experience, and one thought was to have a stake in the business.

Peter Kenyon is MD (01642 803333). He is visiting USA from Thursday. Suggest make contact with provisional meeting for next week when hopefully you will have everything you need to reach an agreement asap. While City & Guilds obviously needs to meet quality and business requirements, please remember NDLC has a massive mailshot in the works for January.

Good luck
Richard

Our course approvals took longer as we were pioneering. City & Guilds had no other courses like it. Online studying and accreditations were new to the world and they didn't know how to deal with it. These days studying and examinations online are commonplace, but back then very few people did City & Guilds' courses. At that time, they were practical and typically joinery, welding or such like. City & Guilds had noticed a transition that more people were taking office-based jobs; the evolution of industry was changing and NDLC were the leading edge of education. We were ahead of the game and City & Guilds wanted a part in that. If they hadn't have got involved with online access, the number of students they reconciled each year would have reduced as the evolutionary process of education changed.

A little known fact is City & Guilds, Edexcel and the other governing bodies are not a part of the government. They are regulated by the government; by what used to be the Qualification and Curriculum Authority (QCA). This means that the QCA set the standard and City & Guilds, Edexcel and the other bodies, whomever they are, work to that set standard. The crux of this is that the newspapers said that NDLC was a bogus company. It wasn't. It was pioneering and introducing new ideas, which are now commonplace. City & Guilds were taking much longer than normal to accredit because they could not get a grip of what was needed with this new line, this growing form of education. As a result, they let me down, everybody in my business down, and at least 80,000 students down.

I could say I'll leave it there, but, no, I'm not going to. Here are some more documents...

"CHOCOLATE-COATED PIRANHA"

Internal email (two pages) within City & Guilds 01 May 2001

· JOHNSTON - Re: NDLC   Pa

(39)

From:	KEITH BROOKER
To:	FORDE, HENRI; HUMPHRIES, CHRIS; JOHNSTON, ANDREW; NUNKOO,
SHANI; OSBALDESTON, MICHAEL	
Date:	01 May 2001 14:27:21
Subject:	Re: NDLC

Comments as marked in **bold**. Copy to Bob and Mike to keep them in the loop.

Keith

>>> SHANI NUNKOO 30/04/2001 18:11:26 >>>
Dear All,

I have come up with a first draft letter to send to NDLC after reading all correspondence. I have discussed the same with Michael, Hemri and Andrew and I would like to amend it tonight for approval by yourselves tomorrow before we fax the same to NDLC tomorrow afternoon. Andrew states they are impatient for a response.

Having now looked at everything on file - I have the following comments:

1. Richard Stott did respond adequately to the Thanx letter dated 12th January by e mail. **Good**

2. It appears that we have led NDLC to believe that if they are accredited for the Practical Computing course then we will be able to legitimately award the existing candidates certificates - this is what NDLC are expecting - this is wrong. Even if we decided we were happy with the course materials and properly accredited them,this could only be in respect of FUTURE candidates not existing ones who are part way through the course. I would be surprised if our Royal Charter and our obligations re QCA allowed us to retrospectively award certificates to candidates who had taken a course which at the time was not accredited by us. **A couple of points - first it that providing there is good solid evidence that the proper assessments have been properly used and reported and there is an audit trail to these we should be able to take prior evidence. If we believe the systems were not robust enough or the scheme sufficiently developed to facilitate this then we cannot accommodate any historical activity. Second - this is not a QCA accreditted provision but even if it were the requirements for using prior achievement (known as accreditation of prior learning - APL) is still acceptable in an NVQ.**

3. Bearing the above in mind (and I welcome comments on the above analysis) - whatever we do we will not satisfy NDLC and therefore must prepare ourselves for a response form NDLC that would lead to either them taking legal action against us OR they continue to flout our requests on desisting to misuse our logo in which case having come thus far we shall have no real alternative but to pursue them with an injunction thereby opening the litigation door ourselves. Not to do so, would result in us going back to "square one" and being tarred with the same brush as NDLC when other investigations commence.

4. Either way it may be only a matter of time (once NDLC use us to deflect claims against them) when we are investigated ourselves.

Conclusion

We must expect this to be at the worse a costly action which we will have to defend or bring, at best, one in which NDLC eventually give up and walk away from. When they do this, will very much depend upon how things pan out with the press and the investigations by the relevant authorities and how much "heat" they are going to be able to take before involving us.

In the event that the matter escalates we should be prepared to instruct external lawyers to handle the litigation upon our instruction and then to play legal tactics to drag out matters - this will be costly but I see no other option. The matter is unlikely to reach a hearing in two years.

My only worry is that the civil action (if any), is coupled with a criminal action against city and guilds for aiding and abetting a fraud. My criminal law is not great, but it would not take much for investigations

288

to take this line in the light of our inaction for nearly two years. We have really only taken things seriously when the watchdog people became involved. Our only saving grace is that we haven't taken any money.

Our Stance

I firmly believe that we have no option but to maintain that we allowed them to use our name and logo subject to the courses being accredited. We must maintain that they knew this and that we have told them verbally to stop using the name and logo in this way.

This is not a great argument - I have seen the ad that went out on tv but the only one that we can realistically run without deviating from the truth as our intentions have not been fraudulent (although may be construed to be).

I am sorry that this sounds grim - this is the worse case scenario, but I do want to ensure that everyone is prepared for what may happen once we send the letter. They are not fools and are probably preparing their case against us.

Please let me have any comments to the above.

I will of course circulate the letter tomorrow for comment.

This e mail is legal privileged information not to be disclosed as part of discovery in the event of a court hearing.

Shani

CC: COATES, BOB; GREGORY, MIKE

You would think that sometime between the start, in November 1999, and lying to the press in April 2001, City & Guilds would have told us to stop, or told us we were being naughty, called the police, or something. As I said, all they had done was encourage us, gloat on the potential and express their many mistakes within their administration and management.

So, why, on 1st May 2001, are many people from City & Guilds drafting a letter which is going to ask me to stop and end my businesses association with City & Guilds? Now this is an interesting document; read it carefully. Point number two on the document says: *"It appears that we have led NDLC to believe that if they are accredited for the Practical Computing course, then we [City & Guilds] will be able to legitimately award the existing candidates certificates — this is what NDLC are expecting."* Reader, this is an interesting statement and I'm just going to pull it apart for you a little bit.

On 26April 2000, at 8:57am, the NDLC received an email from City & Guilds stating, and I quote verbatim, "We would register existing Edexcel students in the same way planned for new students." But here saying, "We have led NDLC to believe" is a man from City & Guilds talking to senior members of City & Guilds and – not that you need a reminder – but years after this document was created, I was sent to prison for not having permission from City & Guilds and yet here is a confession from them saying that they have 'led my organisation to believe'.

Now in court, it was portrayed that I had led them 'down the garden path' when, to the contrary, it was them leading me. Secondly, it gibbers on about existing enrolled students that would need to be retrospectively accredited to City & Guilds and couldn't be. Poppycock! Let me tell you, if you as an individual taught yourself a subject such as bookkeeping, computers or whatever, you yourself could contact City & Guilds or another accreditation body and say, "I want to be accredited, could you let me know the name of one of your centres or colleges that will let me take an examination. I don't want to do the studying as I've done it already."

City & Guilds (or whoever) would simply say something along the lines of, "Of course! You'll have to pay a small fee to the centre that we direct you to." This shows how pointless and benign this document is regarding the need, legally, for your studying to be accredited, or, for that matter, any course leading to examinations.

In the below excerpt from a letter from City & Guilds to Trading Standards (which also showed my continued good intentions to assist students through this debacle in whatever way I could), you can see exactly what I'm saying here corroborated by City & Guilds below.

that they will be able to obtain a City & Guilds certificate on successful completion of an NDLC course. Whilst it appears that NDLC is not inferring that they are an accredited and approved centre, they are offering to pay for the candidate to take the examination at an alternative local venue which would carry City & Guilds approval. City & Guilds cannot comment on whether the content of NDLC customised courses are comparable to similar examinations at other accredited centres as City & Guilds have no knowledge of the courses NDLC are offering or indeed the content of those courses. However, we can confirm that this approach would provide candidates with an opportunity to take a City & Guilds assessment and provided they reached the required standard against our assessment specification they would receive certification.

Besides that overall point, there is an additional point that the 'existing candidates' City & Guilds were referring to were enrolled during the approved advertisement campaigns with City & Guilds. Thereby showing how City & Guilds didn't give two shits about their commitments when giving approval to advertise to the students.

In point three it says, *"Whatever we do we will not satisfy NDLC and therefore must prepare ourselves for a response from NDLC that would lead to either them taking legal action against us OR they continue to flout our requests on desisting to misuse our logo."* They further express concern about being tarred with the same brush as NDLC. Ask yourself, why are they now saying this? I'll make it very clear later.

Point four in this document sees City & Guilds saying, *"Either way it may only be a matter of time (once NDLC use us to deflect claims against them) before we are investigated ourselves."* Do you think that here they are shitting themselves for their mistakes? You can clearly see from this statement that they were worried about their inaction. You can clearly see that they had led us to believe everything was good. They openly encouraged us to market them as being associated with us.

But when the News of the World got involved and asked the question, 'are these people accredited to City & Guilds and able to offer City & Guilds' qualifications?' their world fell apart. So much so that they chose to ignore the long term relationship that we had had and the good, honest intent I had to produce quality education.

They chose to abandon our joint project. They chose to abandon the tens of thousands of people that had enrolled on one of the NDLC courses. They chose to create a deception-filled smokescreen to cover their total inadequacies. The smokescreen was turned on when the News of the World asked the question. At that point it was just a smokescreen. What would it become?

They go on to say, '*In the event that the matter escalates, we should be prepared to instruct external lawyers to handle the litigation upon our instruction and then to play legal tactics to drag out matters. This will be costly but I see no other option. The matter is unlikely to reach a hearing in two years.*"

Reader, do you think the 'good boys' are City & Guilds? Can you see that City & Guilds are trying to use me and my business to mask their inadequacies and deception? "To drag out matters". The only reason for this is so that I face the firing squad before anything can happen to them, with my litigation and responses. Otherwise, why talk about dragging things out and playing legal tactics to do so? The playing of legal tactics, as they put it, is in order to give them time to work with the newspapers and others to deflect the problem onto me and allow them the momentum of my character assassination to take place.

Once the press had printed City & Guilds say this, that and the other about Smallman and his businesses accreditation, it became the false truth they wanted it to be. After that it was just a case of biding time. They just had to wait for my downfall. Wait for me to be crushed by the press. So that any response from me, legally or otherwise had no weight and I had no time to do it. You can see one after the other... newspaper after newspaper, police on top of the Crown Prosecution Service, on top of the prosecution barristers joining the procession that was fed by these false truths that City & Guilds had manipulated away from the actual happenings.

And, reader – sorry for calling you reader, I wish I knew your name and could talk to you face to face and show you all my documents so you could see my passion and how much I believe in what I'm saying.

So, let's pretend that City & Guilds did ask me to stop, verbally, as they are inferring they did way before the papers got in touch – what do you think my response would have been? Would I have said ok, no problem, I don't mind wasting the millions of pounds that I've spent on marketing, which you approved? Or would I have jumped up and down, in a very 'managing directorial' sort of way, and sued the ass off them for their self-admitted procrastination? Of course, I would have needed to protect my business position, the position of my staff and –most importantly of all – the position of the students, who had enrolled on a course as a result of the approved advertisement campaign.

I certainly would have been concerned more about the students than they appeared to be regarding their commitments based upon these documents and what happened.

Nevertheless, it didn't happen the way I have given in this scenario, I just felt it necessary to express the obvious nature of what would have happened should that scenario have occurred. I didn't take up any legal position until after this; you will see later what happened.

More from this document… it goes on to say, 'My only worry is that civil action, if any, is coupled with a criminal action against City & Guilds for aiding, abetting a fraud. My criminal law is not great but it would not take much for investigations to take this in the light of our inaction for nearly two years.'

The last part of this document on page two says, "I firmly believe that we have no option but to maintain that we allowed them to use our name and *logo, subject to courses being accredited. We must maintain that they knew this and that we told them verbally to stop using our name and logo in this way."* This in itself is saying we didn't tell them. We are 'maintaining' our 'story'. Surely, if they ever had told us to stop, on such a serious matter, they would have put it in writing?

There would be some documents contacting us to ask us to stop? There are none, reader! Can you see in their undertones in this document that the writer was almost begging for everybody to be compliant with the story... "We need to continue to maintain"! ... or... We need the world to believe that we told them to stop. Ask yourself, why use the words in their statement that "we have *no option* but to *maintain* our *story?*" It goes on, and I quote, *"Our intentions have not been fraudulent although may be construed to be."* It goes on, and to quote, *'I am sorry that this sounds grim, this is the worst case scenario, but I do want to ensure that everyone is prepared for what may happen once we send the letter. They are not fools and are probably preparing their case against us'.* I think the biggest, damning sentence in this document is in bold at the end, **"This email is legal privileged information not to be disclosed as part of discovery in the event of a court hearing."** What do you think of that?

On the 10th May, just two weeks after City & Guilds stirred up the barrel of shit and threw it at the fan with the News of the World, they were looking for a reason they could use to terminate the contract with NDLC. The internal City & Guilds email below speaks for itself, but I'd like to point out that, with normal business, a termination of contract would follow an obvious known reason to terminate, hence the termination. There would be no speculation as to what could be used. They were looking to terminate because of the media frenzy – and their part in that – and therefore had to find reasons to terminate the contract that they said they didn't have.

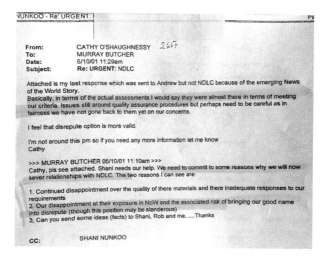

NUNKOO - Re: URGENT:

From:	CATHY O'SHAUGHNESSY
To:	MURRAY BUTCHER
Date:	5/10/01 11:29am
Subject:	Re: URGENT: NDLC

Attached is my last response which was sent to Andrew but not NDLC because of the emerging News of the World Story.
Basically, in terms of the actual assessments I would say they were almost there in terms of meeting our criteria. Issues still around quality assurance procedures but perhaps need to be careful as in fairness we have not gone back to them yet on our concerns.

I feel that disrepute option is more valid.

I'm not around this pm so if you need any more information let me know
Cathy

>>> MURRAY BUTCHER 05/10/01 11:10am >>>
Cathy, pls see attached. Shani needs our help. We need to commit to some reasons why we will now sever relationships with NDLC. The two reasons I can see are:

1. Continued disappointment over the quality of there materials and there inadequate responses to our requirements
2. Our disappointment at their exposure in NoW and the associated risk of bringing our good name into disrepute (though this position may be slanderous)
3. Can you send some ideas (facts) to Shani, Rob and me.....Thanks

CC: SHANI NUNKOO

And further speculation by their press officer... Had they been good guys then they "would be hard pushed to send them on their way"!! Doesn't that say it all? Even this dyslexic can see that's an oxymoron. Everything was good, they had no real reasons to terminate, but we were now seen in the press media frenzy as bad guys – with significant help by them – and so they needed to terminate.

From:	SHANI NUNKOO
To:	BOB COATES; CATHY O'SHAUGHNESSY; CHRIS HUMPHRIES; KEITH BROOKER; MICHAEL OSBALDESTON; MIKE GREGORY; MURRAY BUTCHER
Subject:	NDLC termination letter

This communication is legally privileged.

Dear All

I have mulled over this again and again. I have taken on board all comments and come up with the attached. The important question is to ask ourselves for what reason are we terminating with NDLC. We cannot rely upon the quality of the assessment materials being not up to standard. Having met with Cathy this morning it is clear that NDLC were close to achieving the standard required. For this reason it is not appropriate in my opinion, to go into any detail in respect of the defects of the materials - this provides NDLC with more ammunition to use against us and will generate more correspondence to and from them. We need to put an end to this as it is getting out of hand. Our very valid reason for terminating is the abuse of our brand leading to a public, fraudulent misrepresentation. This is more than enough of a reason to terminate even if we assume we have a contract with them (which I doubt very much). However I have made mention of the fact that they have not met our criteria but this is not the main reason of the termination.

NOTE: had they been good guys then we would have been hard pushed to send them on their way and would have probably been still undergoing the assessment.

I do not think on reflection we should mention the press articles and base our decision to terminate on that - bad press coverage cannot be an excuse on its own to terminate - we should stand on NDLC's behaviour alone - we will give the wrong impression if we are seen to rely on the press as our "policemen".

This letter is not just for the eyes of NDLC - it may be leaked to the press and we may seek to rely upon it in court. Anything we say must therefore be squeaky clean and any of the less salubrious comments and allegations can be thrashed out in the forum of the court (if we get that far).

I would like to send this today or tomorrow morning. Please could you let me have the final comments by then.

Many thanks
Shani

There are many documents, too many to include here, spanning the entire relationship where the NDLC were being told, 'we are almost there on approval of our materials'...but still they were thinking to use quality of materials as an excuse because they had backed themselves into a corner and were now scraping the bottom of the barrel that they had previously stirred.

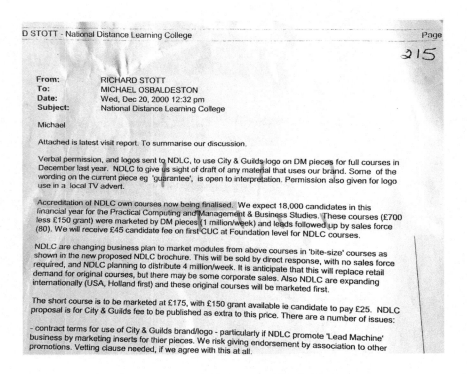

So they send the NDLC a severance letter in May 2001, two and a half years into our relationship, asking us to stop marketing and ending our relationship. Ask yourself this, if there was no contract / partnership/ a dual intent to supply good education through the NDLC leading to a City & Guilds qualification, why would there be any need to sever? Imagine for one second that NDLC was a bogus business, would City & Guilds send a severance letter to sever something that was never created?

10ᵗʰ May 2001

Mr Peter Kenyon

Dear Sir

As you are aware City & Guilds has been in the process of seeking to approve assessment materials submitted by NDLC in respect of NDLC's Practical Computing Course.

Having now completed the assessment procedure submitted by NDLC in respect of this course, we regret that we are unable to approve those materials.

City & Guilds has with every good intention sort to advise and guide your development staff through the necessary stages to produce course and assessment materials of sufficient standard to reach City & Guilds requirements. Despite considerable efforts on our part, we find that your recent submission continues to fall short of our requirements and we can no longer expend our resources in offering further guidance.

You are aware that City & Guilds is an organisation of considerable repute and with an honourable history of some 125 years. In the light of the current developments in respect of your continued abuse and misuse of our brand despite requests to the contrary we no longer wish to be associated with your organisation and formally notify you that City & Guilds hereby withdraws your approved centre status with immediate effect.

Yours faithfully

Murray Butcher

By the time the above severance letter came into existence in May 2001, City & Guilds had done the dirty on me. My name was mud. It was mud in the press. It was mud in every government department associated with us and who'd believe me jumping up and down, shouting, 'Please look closer at City & Guilds, they are lying?!'

Who would believe me – the 'Delboy character' that the papers said I was, against the all-singing all-wonderful reputation of City & Guilds. My name was now, thanks to them, associated with the words "fraud", "conman" and all the other derogatory statements.

Yet clearly from the City & Guilds document you have just read, I should have, at the very least, been listened to. City & Guilds should have been investigated properly at this early stage by the press and by the other organisations. Hey, but who am I? Just a skinny, poorly lad from Manchester! Or, in the words of Vivienne Parry, "some scabby bloke from Middlesbrough".

What do you think I did? Let me tell you. I've got to admit, the pressures and strains were massive. I had promised to students, through my marketing and sales staff, that they would get a City & Guilds qualification and, as you can see, I was working for two and a half years to make that happen. So, when City & Guilds chopped us off, so to speak, to try and cover up their inadequacies, this is what I did. I instructed top barristers from a firm in Newcastle called Dickinson Dees, to bring to the attention of City & Guilds, that, if they did chop us off, the consequences for my students would be devastating and they should honour the contract that we had.

For City & Guilds to say there was no contract is ridiculous. All law whether it be criminal, civil, commercial and so on is based on common law. Common law provides the foundations and in itself dates back to the Magna Carta. This is added to as society gets wiser. Common law would suggest that if something isn't said or written, it doesn't exist, and, if something is said or written, it is. It forms the foundation of a written or verbal contract. I believe there is not a judge at any level that could argue against that.

For example, on 19th November, a letter was written by Richard Stott of City & Guilds to my employee Dr Roy Grimwood. You've read it. It is at least giving us permission to use their logos. We could use the basis of this common law interpretation hundreds of times within the hundreds of documents I possess. A few of the documents you have seen in this book and they show City & Guilds have made extensive negative derogatory statements to the press, to the police, to government departments and to the court which would contravene not only common law but contractual law. Hmmm … Maybe I'll sue them for defamation of character.

I'll let you read the letter from my solicitors to City & Guilds: it speaks for itself.

Solicitors letter from NDLC to City & Guilds 20 Aug 2001

112 Quayside
Newcastle upon Tyne
NE99 1SB

Fax: (0191) 279 9100
E mail: law@dickinson-dees.com
www.dickinson-dees.com
DX No 61191 Newcastle upon Tyne

City & Guilds
1 Giltspur Street
London
EC1A 9DD

Direct Dial: 0191 279 9782
E Mail: alison.tate@dickinson-dees.com
Please quote our reference on all correspondence
Our Ref: /PBM/AT/THA/7/6
Your Ref:

20 August 2001

Dear Sirs

National Distance Learning College Limited

We are instructed by the above named company and have had sight of correspondence passing between you since November 1999. In particular, we have seen your letter of 25 May 2001 in which you state that you formally withdraw NDLC's approved centre status. You also state that NDLC's materials still fall short of your requirements and that is why you have not accredited any courses submitted by NDLC.

It is clear from the correspondence we have seen that the first time you raised any query with NDLC's quality standards was in your letter of 1 May 2001. It is also apparent that, from the outset of your relationship with our client, you understood that our client would be marketing courses to clients for which it sought City & Guilds' accreditation. You allowed our client to use your logo from November 1999 and were aware that courses were being sold as City & Guilds courses prior to the accreditation being completed.

It is clear therefore that your intention from the outset was to enter into a relationship with our client under which those courses submitted by it would be accredited. In fact, clear indications were given to our client both verbally and in correspondence in December 2000 and January 2001 that the practical computer skills course had met your guidelines and would be accredited as soon as all four signatories were able to sign it off.

At no time during the last 19 months have you set out to our client what you consider deficient with our client's courses or their quality systems. Instead, you have continued to reassure our client that its courses were nearing accreditation until May of this year when your stance changed.

299

Continuation

You will be aware that our client will suffer substantial damage as a result of your failure to work with it to accredit these courses. We have had sight of correspondence from you to our client's students. It seems to us that the stance you have taken in relation to these enquiries will simply provoke litigation rather than produce a reasonable and amicable solution.

We are instructed to request a without prejudice meeting with you in an attempt to resolve current problems. Should you refuse to meet with our clients or should this meeting fail to produce a satisfactory outcome our client will have no alternative than to issue proceedings against you for damages for breach of contract.

We would be grateful to receive your response to this suggestion by close of business on 28 August 2001.

Yours faithfully

All of the above, I think, shows what big flipping, whopping lies City & Guilds had told, and that they did truly lie to the press, and it shows their inadequacies. If they had a problem, either with my courses and my staff or, as it really seems to be, problems with their own staff, surely the press release in April 2001 should have been something like this…"I would like to confirm that we have given permission to the NDLC to offer City & Guilds' qualifications and have been working with them very closely for two and a half years and we will continue to work with them in order to resolve any delay issues on our part."

Now, while all that's going on, the Department of Education, which I hasten to add have nothing to do with City & Guilds, had stopped my business funding because I had found a problem in their granting legislation and they wanted me to be silenced. So as in Chapter Nine – 'Downfall Part One', they tried to pass their inadequacies, their mistakes, off on me and had made a statement at some point to the News of the World, that my business was probably ripping off their granting scheme.

Hence the News of the World running the article headed, Mr Big ripped off Tony Blair for £5.8m. This is the point where you can see that the City & Guilds' problem and the Department of Education's problem worked in those two organisations' favour. The smokescreen, having grown large enough, was easily utilised by the Department of

Education for their benefit. The smokescreen acted as a decoy for their inadequately written legislation, with loopholes that even a carpet cleaner could take advantage of. This was 'smoke and daggers' and they could use their relating problems against me, ie the Department of Education saying I was ripping them off when I wasn't, and City & Guilds saying the same.

I refer you back to my 'Downfall Part One', and point you to the two documents that are in that, which clearly show that the Department of Education and the Scottish Executive were clearly satisfied that there was no fraud found in my business and no non-compliance found. They didn't just conclude this once, they concluded it twice over.

Can you see where I'm going? I could stop now, but I'm not; here are some more documents. I don't want to put words in your mouth, but I think you'll agree City & Guilds lied to the press in 2001. Now I'm going to show you a few more documents from City & Guilds' computers that show they also lied to the police in 2003 by giving them false information and withholding the documentation that would prove that my NDLC and City & Guilds had a long-term relationship. This, reader, is where the smokescreen for City & Guilds to try and save their face stops being a smokescreen and it becomes serious criminal deception by members of staff, of City & Guilds in misleading the police.

The three documents below are attendance notes of various City & Guilds employees – from directorship to senior management level – discussing what they were to say in a statement to Cleveland Police.

I'll let you read it yourself, but I'd like to point out a few bits. Why are, in document point 1, City & Guilds discussing who should be a witness for City & Guilds? Surely the police should have access to everybody and take multiple witness statements from everybody who

CHOCOLATE-COATED PIRANHA"

had involvement with my business? They go on to say in point 2 that *"KKS said that her major concern was that the statement was misleading. KKS feared that the police had not understood the C & G accreditation process or C& G's relationship with NDLC."* Point 3 in the document, headed providing documents to Cleveland Police, was that *"KKS felt one of the reasons the witness statement was misleading was that the police did not have all the documents".* KKS explains that *"at the moment the police only have a limited number of documents provided to them by the receivers and the file did not start at the beginning of the relationship".* The question of what should be produced to the police was discussed. KKS pointed out that *"the police could ask for a City & Guilds file if they so desired and if City & Guilds had withheld key documents this could be embarrassing. KKS was concerned that failing to provide missing documents would lead to a misleading statement. There is also a chance that when the police see how much more complicated the relationship is between City & Guilds and NDLC than they currently think, they may decide to discontinue that side of the prosecution to concentrate on NDLC and the ILAs".*

Well, let me put that statement into context. Is it saying, if we tell the truth to the police they'll stop investigation into Smallman and the City & Guilds related scenarios? Is it also saying that the police would then, therefore, have to concentrate on potential ILA fraud? Now we know something that City & Guilds possibly didn't know at the time. I refer you back to the two investigations in which no fraud was found in the ILA audits. Now, does this sentence mean City & Guilds are aware of an agenda within Cleveland police? That they want to get me at all costs? Because as we know – FACT – the judge did say that the funding of the police by the Department of Education was *ultra vires* (abuse of power).

I'm sure once this book is in the public domain that someone with a conscience from City & Guilds reading this will pop out from the woodwork and confirm my suspicion. Maybe you, Mr Stott?

302

As you can clearly see from this, City & Guilds were lying to the police and withholding the true information about our relationship with them. You can also see their deflection away from what is now quite clearly a City & Guilds intent to pervert the course of justice.

Attendance Note of City & Guilds Meeting dated 07 January 2003

ATTENDANCE NOTE

This attendance note records a meeting held at the offices of City & Guilds at 3:30pm on Tuesday 7 January 2003.

Those present: Bob Coates, C&G Director, Sales and Customer Relations ("**BC**")
                Sue Berry, C&G   ("SB")
                Katie Stephen, NR   ("KKS")
                Vicky Jones, NR   ("VJ")

The purpose of the meeting was to discuss the draft witness statements provided by Cleveland Police and C&G's response.

1   **Who should give the witness statement?**

BC said that he was prepared to give the witness statement. KKS asked whether there was anyone still at C&G with a closer link to the matter. KKS pointed out that, if BC is called to give evidence, it might be embarrassing for him to have to admit during questioning that he does not know the full background to the NDLC matter and that there is someone who would have been better placed to give evidence. KKS said it was BC's decision as to who should give the statement but that he should be aware that the prosecution may consider that C&G have something to hide if access to other employees is withheld.

BC stated that most of the people involved with NDLC had left C&G and the only person remaining, Andrew Johnston (AJ), had said he would rather not give evidence and had been reluctant to give reasons for this. BC did not want to push him on the subject unless KKS felt it was very important for AJ to give the witness statement. KKS reiterated that it was BC's decision and he had to balance AJ's wishes with the risks to C&G. BC said he would ask AJ to reconsider, but if AJ refused, BC would explain the reason he is giving the witness statement is that the people most involved with NDLC had since left C&G and that the matter had been elevated to BC as a director.

2   **Drafting the witness statement**

The discussion moved on to the witness statement provided by the police. KKS said that her major concern was that the statement was misleading. KKS feared that the police had not understood the C&G accreditation process or C&G's relationship with NDLC. It was agreed that the witness statement needed to be redrafted and KKS put forward two options:

    1   C&G could hold another meeting with the police in order for the police to redraft the witness statement. C&G/NR could then liaise with the police to reach a statement that was acceptable to C&G; or

    2   C&G and NR could redraft the statement and present it to the police.

KKS stated that she thought the first option could ultimately involve the same expense in terms of time and money as the second, as the statement would probably need to be repeatedly reviewed by NR and sent back to the police. With the second option, C&G and NR could just go ahead and draft the statement clearly setting out C&G's position.

3   **Providing documents to the Cleveland Police**

KKS felt one of the reasons the witness statement was misleading was that the police did not have all the documents. KKS explained that, at the moment, the police only had a limited number of documents provided to them by the receivers and the file did not start at the beginning of the relationship. The question of what should be produced to the police was discussed. KKS pointed out that the police could ask for C&G's files if they so desired and, if C&G had withheld key documents, this could be embarrassing. KKS was concerned that failing to provide missing documents would lead to a misleading statement. There is also a chance that when the police see how much more complicated the relationship is between C&G and

NDLC than they currently think, they may decide to discontinue that side of the prosecution to concentrate on NDLC and the ILAs.

4   Contents of the witness statement

KKS said that a short witness statement should be drafted which includes relevant documents where necessary. It was agreed that the statement should begin with a short explanation of BC's position followed by a brief description of C&G's business.

KKS pointed out that the police have not understood what C&G does nor do they comprehend the accreditation process. The police appear to believe that, because none of the NDLC courses appears on the C&G list, they were not accredited and therefore NDLC was involved in a scam. It should, however, be explained in the statement that it is possible for other courses to gain accreditation. BC emphasised that C&G does not provide courses. C&G approve the quality and delivery of courses and students attain a C&G award having completed an approved course. SB said that non-C&G courses are called 'centre devised' or 'customised' schemes. This should all be clearly explained in the new draft statement.

It was decided that there was no need to talk about the C&G Group companies, such as Pitman, as this is of no relevance.

Discussion moved to the paragraph in the witness statement relating to the C&G accreditation process, which states that only an organisation which has been accredited can offer C&G qualifications. KKS stated that the potential problem with the explanation of how this process should work is that C&G made an exception in the case of NDLC and the paragraph should be drafted to reflect this. BC said that, during the accreditation of NDLC's courses, both C&G and NDLC were slow to progress matters. As NDLC had been through the centre accreditation process without any difficulties, C&G had not anticipated any problems with the further accreditation. BC is happy to admit that a mistake was made in allowing NDLC to use C&G's logo before the courses had been accredited. Given the benefit of hindsight, it had been wrong to allow NDLC to use C&G's name. When C&G realised there were problems with NDLC, it asked for the adverts containing the C&G logo to be withdrawn, but NDLC were extremely slow to comply. It was agreed that the normal accreditation procedure should be set out in the witness statement, followed by how the situation differed in NDLC's case. A mistake was made and when it was recognised, NDLC was asked to stop mentioning C&G in its promotional material. Documentation should be provided to support this.

BC said it was important to point out that a number of oral requests were made to NDLC to desist from using C&G's name. There is no evidence of these, save for threats made in writing by NDLC to C&G in return, showing the pressure put on NDLC by C&G. SB remembers that AJ said at one stage NDLC had offered C&G money, but C&G had turned it down, stating that standards were the issue, not money. She did not think that there were any documents to support this, but it should be made clear that C&G has not gained from its business with NDLC.

BC felt that the delays in the accreditation of NDLC's courses should be explained. As the initial impression of NDLC was good, the amount of time it would take to accredit the courses was underestimated. At the time, C&G also had other internal projects which took priority, including developing its own software.

KKS sought to establish whether there were any students in 2000 taking the courses listed in the original flyer agreed by C&G in November 1999. BC and SB were not sure, but VLJ pointed out an internal e-mail from AJ to Sarah Dhanda dated 6 September 2000 which stated that the first C&G candidates would start asking to take exams in November 2000. KKS added that another problem was that C&G had told their customer service people to answer enquiries regarding NDLC by saying NDLC was a C&G accredited centre, the courses were an NDLC product and candidates successfully completing a course would receive a C&G certificate. This was inaccurate.

BC asked to what extent C&G could discredit the actions of Richard Stott (RS) given that he approached NDLC for a job during the period in question and therefore had an interest in ensuring that NDLC was successful in gaining accreditation at any cost. KKS stated that it would not necessarily assist C&G to discredit RS. At the time, RS was an employee of C&G and was authorised by C&G. Therefore, C&G must take responsibility for RS. BC said that he thought C&G would come across as well meaning incompetents who may have played an unwitting role in NDLC's misrepresentation, but did not make any financial gain from it.

5   **Witness statement for Sue Berry**

KKS mentioned the short witness statement received from the Cleveland Police to be signed by SB. The statement only serves to confirm that SB provided various C&G brochures to the police during the meeting with them in October 2002. KKS said that this statement was unnecessary, not only because the brochures are available to the public, but also the statement could easily be included in the main statement to be provided by BC. KKS felt that the police interest in the list of courses approved by C&G goes back to the misunderstanding by the police of the C&G accreditation process. BC pointed out that the booklet only contains courses available to the public and does not include those for which a particular college must be approached. It is therefore not an exhaustive list of C&G approved courses in any case. KKS said she would revert to the police and ask for the statement to be integrated into that to be provided by BC.

6   **NDLC Ireland**

KKS asked if anything more had been heard regarding the investigation into NDLC's operations in Northern Ireland. SB said that she had left the matter with CXXE who was going to talk to Belfast police in the hope of encouraging them to co-operate with the Cleveland police and agree to the production of a single C&G statement. KKS said she thought the police had said that one statement would not be possible, as the investigations were on two different matters and would therefore require separate witness statements. KKS said that, if it was not possible to provide one statement, the C&G witness statements should at least be consistent. BC to check with C&G staff in Belfast whether they have received any new correspondence from the police regarding NDLC.

Matters arising from the meeting

- BC to speak to AJ about whether he is willing to give the witness statement.

- BC to talk to C&G in Belfast to find out if it has heard anything further about the investigation by the Belfast police into NDLC.

- KKS to speak to police about SB's statement.

- VLJ to e-mail to SB the chronology of documents originally received by NR from Shani Nunkoo.

- SB to check documents held by AJ against those in the chronology and to send NR copies of any NR does not have.

K:\DEPT\CLD\Cxxe\AA47611\Attends\Cit & Guilds 07-01-03.doc

The next document shows notes of a conversation between Cleveland Police and City & Guilds, October 2002. The first point in this document is that the police begin to point out that the case had been passed onto them by the Department of Education. Why would this happen when a year and a half earlier there were two independent investigations which proved my business to be compliant with regulations and non-fraudulent?

Why would they need to begin to rake it all up again? This is simply because I was forcing the pursuance of their mistake. I wanted exoneration, I wanted their multimillion-pound mistake highlighted and put into the public domain. The Department of Education needed me buried and so they abused their power. They paid Cleveland Police [like a private investigator], to trump up anything they could muster against me. This meant that the police were never going to investigate City & Guilds properly, as I was begging them to do when I was in custody.

I draw your attention in particular to the highlighted paragraph on the document where a lady called Katie, on behalf of City & Guilds, makes this statement: *"Katie believes that the police departed happily convinced that City & Guilds hadn't accredited NDLC courses, given permission to use its logos or ever agreed that any of NDLC's assessments would lead to a City & Guilds qualification certificate."* We know the above not to be true, you've seen the documents, so why did the police depart 'happily convinced'? It goes on… *"However, she is concerned that detailed examination by the police of the documents received from the Official Receiver will reveal that City & Guilds was slow in getting back to Smallman with feedback about the course materials that NDLC had submitted. I gather from Andrew that documents had actually been lost by us."* Really, lost?! You can see from all of this that City & Guilds were just continually manipulating the truth and continually manipulating what evidence should be given to the police. They subsequently went on to tell the same lies in court. Turning their criminal deception into perjury.

Note of conversation re NDLC - 22 October 2002.
Cleveland Police – Fraud Investigation Department

Present: Katie Stephen – Solicitor (Norton Rose)
Detective Sergeant Phil Murphy – Cleveland Police
Detective Constable Steve Jermey – Cleveland Police

Di Walster – City & Guilds
Sue Berry - City & Guilds

- Phil Murphy outlined the background to their investigation; it had been passed to them by the DfES.
- The main thrust of the investigation - and Katie Stephen has subsequently confirmed this by e-mail - centres on ILAs and batch claims made by NDLC for non-existent students. – some 42,500. Mike Smallman even told employees to get relatives to sign up for ILAs
- D S Murphy's feeling was, that originally NDLC had set up with a view to offering legitimate courses. The advent of ILAs offered an opportunity too tempting to resist. Apparently, Smallman has ' a history ' sadly, undisclosed to the rest of those present !
- Students were signed up believing that they would get BTEC or City & Guilds' qualifications at the end of their courses.
- There were no *complete* courses (modules had still to be written) and tutors were told not to return work.
- Only one tutor had any qualifications.
- Crests and logos on leaflets/fliers had been made up ' in Smallman's front room.'
- Smallman had a contract with the Post Office to put fliers through every door in the UK
- The Official Receiver apparently has copies of all City & Guilds' correspondence and that of NDLC.****
- We were asked whether City & Guilds had NDLC's **written** agreement to remove our logo from their documents. Di and Sue are convinced that we did not receive anything in writing but will check.
- The police want to know exactly what potential course material City & Guilds received. We have to check this; there are question marks hanging over what was received and its fate when it got to City & Guilds. ****
- The police are keen to have a copy of our complainants' database. We have told them that we require a **written** request for this. They agreed that it would be reasonable for us to write to our correspondents before they are contacted by the police. If we wish, the police will supply us with a data protection form – I believe

**** Katie believes that the police departed happily convinced that City & Guilds hadn't accredited NDLC courses, given permission to use its logo, or ever agreed that any of NDLC's assessments would lead to a City & Guilds qualification/certificate. However, she is concerned that detailed examination by the police of the documents received from the Official Receiver, will reveal that City & Guilds was slow in getting back to Smallman with feedback about the course materials NDLC had submitted. I gather from Andrew that documents had actually been lost by us. Our understanding of this is, that Smallman could therefore contend that he had submitted materials which he could legitimately expect at some future stage to be accredited by City & Guilds and he therefore produced his publicity accordingly.
Katie also feels that, since Andrew has been more immersed in the whole set-up than any of the staff still at City & Guilds, he is clearly the most appropriate person to be asked for witness testimony if this should be required. Customer Services have only been involved since the complaints started to come in.

Sue Berry 23/10/02

To show you how much effort City & Guilds went into controlling the evidence and statements to the police, let me tell you who KKS is; she is a solicitor/barrister who worked for a large legal company called Norton Rose. City & Guilds had employed them to draft and write their singular statement that would be offered to the police. I refer you to one of eight invoices that City & Guilds paid to Norton Rose solicitors to advise them on how to manipulate the truth and how Norton Rose was able to convince the police to accept a singular statement from City & Guilds as opposed to the police going in and interviewing everybody concerned. See below.

IMPORTANT, PLEASE PLACE ON FILE IMMEDIATELY

The next document again, I'll let you read for yourself, but I just want to point out two bits which are highlighted in the documents. The document is a record of a conversation between the police and City & Guilds, and the two highlighted areas show the police intent not to carry out a proper investigation. Why else would the police say *"They intend to nail NDLC"*? Maybe this was because they were being paid to do so by the Department of Education? The other highlighted part shows the police had no interest in looking for the truth. They say, *"We might call in [to City & Guilds] for coffee if there's time."* Can you see what I mean about an underlying agenda? 'We might just call in for coffee'!! Is this just a friendly chat over coffee!! "If there's time"! Surely if the police were doing their job properly they would make time and do a thorough investigation? Now, one last thing. If you were in any doubt that City & Guilds were deliberately hiding things from the police, simply read the last sentence of the document 18 which reads *"Both Di and Sue are very clear that they mustn't provide any gratuitous information to the police".*

RECORD OF CONVERSATION BETWEEN DC JERMY, CLEVELAND POLICE AND SUE BERRY, 31/10/02

- The main thrust of the conversation was DC Jermy's desire for City & Guilds to know that he had obtained 'significant' information from the Deloitte & Touche files which affected the first part of the City & Guilds 'Statement' (based on our discussions of 22/10) faxed to us by DS Murphy on 30 October.*

- He was very keen to know why Richard Stott had left City & Guilds and where he had gone, because ' **where he went to could have an impact on City & Guilds' investigations.**' Of course, SB could not supply this information other than to say what Bob Coates had previously told the solicitors in response to the same question – that Richard's departure was not linked to his dealings with NDLC.

- D C Jermy estimated that roughly a quarter of the way through negotiations, between City & Guilds and NDLC, Richard had sent his CV to NDLC together with a letter expressing his interest in pursuing a job at NDLC . My impression was, that he hadn't applied for a specific post but rather, expressed his interest in a general way **

- DC J feels that, if NDLC 's use of City & Guilds' logo was based on permission given (in a letter written as long ago as 1999) by someone at City & Guilds, who subsequently sought a job from NDLC, it compromises NDLC's, rather than City & Guilds' position.

- The Police will want to see us again – in around three weeks - to go through all the documentation they have.

  *   **We have protested the use of the word 'statement.'**
  **   **Copies of the letters to be delivered when they arrive.**

05 NOVEMBER 2002 – RECORD OF CONVERSATION BETWEEN KATIE STEPHEN & SUE BERRY

- Letters were supplied by DC J on 01 November and copied to Bob Coates and Katie Stephen.

- Katie S telephoned 05 November; she says that the 'statement' is ' **all over the place** ' and also she is concerned that the Police have got out of context some facts on which they intend to nail NDLC. Katie herself, was still not completely clear as to what City & Guilds means by 'Scheme Approval.' S B explained this to her.

- K S is debating whether, if she now drafts a letter to the Police re the statement, it should come from Norton Rose or from City & Guilds. Further, since Bob C is to be the signatory to the statement on behalf of City & Guilds, she suggested (tactfully) that maybe she should be dealing directly with Bob rather than with anyone else.

- Most importantly, she wonders whether we should be telling the Police that, since Richard Stott started off the whole NDLC saga, they should be contacting him.

- DS Murphy has e-mailed S B to say that he and DC J will be in London on Thursday 07 November and would like to call by for coffee. After first discussing this with Di, S B has agreed to this. Katie was not consulted about what really did look to Di and Sue as a ' We might call in if there's time ' type of arrangement ! Katie wondered whether she should be present but both Di and Sue are very clear that they mustn't provide any gratuitous information to the Police.

Sometime after this, the police interviewed Richard Stott. He was the first man we met from City & Guilds back in 1999 and we're now in 2003 and 2004. I have in my hand at the minute his police interview statement, it's falling apart physically and there are about 12 pages of it. I'm just going to highlight a couple of points. In the next document, on page two of Richard Stott's statement to the police, it says, *"The NDLC negotiations due to this particular interest in the matter"* [the interest was probably due to the fact that the NDLC was likely to be a big account with great potential and City & Guilds were looking to move into this area]. *"I recall that Mr Coates had spoken of the possibility of C&G taking some form of equity stake in the distance learning business, a market that City & Guilds currently was not reaching."* It really makes me laugh to read this, two and a half years of working with them and them saying my business was accredited, then turning against us for their inadequacies, whilst all the time they were thinking of buying a chunk of my business!

Paragraph 17, page four of his statement says, *"I believe that the basis of the decision to allow the use of the C&G logo in marketing by NDLC to precede C&G's approval of its courses was due to the following factors, the recognition of the business opportunity that the NDLC arrangement offered, the need for the marketing to proceed in the interest of speed and the assumption that due to NDLC's existing relationship and accreditation arrangement with Edexcel, the requisite quality for City and Guild's purposes would be there. I felt that the decision for NDLC's marketing to precede C&G approval of NDLC courses was due to the fact that C&G was reluctant to lose out of the considerable opportunity the NDLC arrangement offered".* They were just being really greedy, weren't they? They had jumped on my business and then didn't follow up with their part of the arrangements. Even if they had any concerns about the courses, there had been plenty of time to communicate that and to follow up with changes. As I've said before though, the courses themselves do not require accreditation for City & Guilds certificates to be given to those who pass examinations.

So finally, to cut through all the crap of his statement, I take you to page 12, paragraph 57 of Richard Stott's statement. *"It is my belief, that from the beginning City & Guilds entered into negotiations with NDLC with the full intention of accrediting NDLC courses."* So why didn't they? Especially when my college had already surpassed the legally required standards and this was verified by the Edexcel approval and the continuing excellent results that we had obtained with Edexcel's independent external invigilator. Mr Mike Dolan had given us a triple A star rating at each invigilation.

Pages 2,4 & 12 of Richard Stott's statement to the police

the NDLC negotiations due to his particular interest in the matter. This interest was pr___ry due to the fact that NDLC was likely to be a big account with great potential and because __ was looking to move into this area. I recall that Mr Coates had spoken of the possibility of C_ taking some form of equity stake in the Distance Learning business, a market that C&G currently was not reaching.

[means]

6   In October 1999, I attended the IDP exhibition in Harrogate on behalf of C&G. As one of the C&G members staffing our stand, I received an approach from Dr Roy Grimmond, Director of Human Resources at NDLC. Dr Grimmond asked me about the opportunities offered by C&G in relation to the accreditation of centres and courses, stating that NDLC would be interested. I had never heard of either Dr Grimmond or NDLC before and was not aware of the existence of any prior relationship between C&G and NDLC.

7   I subsequently received a telephone call from NDLC from Dr Grimmond and Syd Hutchinson (the Group Sales Director of NDLC), suggesting a meeting with C&G to discuss business prospects. They said that they were currently accredited with Edexcel, but were looking to develop their business in this regard and would like to seek C&G accreditation.

C&G accreditation

8   By way of background to C&G's business, in order to obtain full C&G accreditation, two types of approval must be granted by C&G. The first is so-called "centre approval", a process to establish that a particular institution meets C&G's standards and has the ability to deliver C&G accredited courses. The process by which an institution may be awarded "accredited centre status" by C&G involves an investigation into the financial standing of the institution, the training of its assessors, its internal verification system and its human resources personnel.

9   Once a centre is "approved", that centre is entitled to use the C&G logo in its marketing materials, without necessarily offering C&G courses. Such use of the logo should be within C&G guidelines, but there is no real control over the use of the C&G logo as these guidelines do not tend to be enforced or published in any great detail. However, this has never been an issue until now. Centre approval involves the payment of a one off fee by the institution to C&G. There is no process or payment for re-approval, but the certificate is renewed annually.

send materials for approval

15   On 18 ~ ~ 1999, I sent a note to Bob Coates attaching a draft leaflet and national advertising design sent to me by NDLC, which would require C&G approval prior to its circulation. The NDLC advert was subsequently approved by Mr Coates.

16   On 19 November 1999, I sent a letter to Dr Grimmond at NDLC, confirming the use of the C&G name and logo as it appeared in the draft leaflet supplied to us. The statement in the NDLC advert that candidates would receive a C&G certificate at the end of the course was therefore not correct at this time. The plan was for C&G to sign off on the courses within a period of six to eight weeks, during which time NDLC was to send the relevant material to the Pitman Qualification Arm within C&G to duly examine, make any suggestions for improvement and to eventually approve the courses for C&G accreditation.

17   I believe that the basis of the decision to allow the use of the C&G logo in marketing by NDLC to precede C&G's approval of its courses was due to the following factors; the recognition of the business opportunity that the NDLC arrangements offered; the need for the marketing to proceed in the interests of speed; and the assumption that, due to NDLC's existing relationship and accreditation arrangement with Edexcel, the requisite quality for C&G's purposes would be there. I felt that overall the decision for NDLC's marketing to precede C&G's approval of the NDLC courses was due to the fact that C&G was reluctant to lose out on the considerable opportunity the NDLC arrangements offered.

18   As I stated in my letter of 19 November 1999 to Dr Grimmond at NDLC following my visit to NDLC's premises in Middlesbrough, both Linda Steel (Quality Controller at the Pitman Qualification Arm within C&G) and I were very impressed by NDLC's operational and quality assurance systems. During our visit to NDLC we observed staff dealing with individual candidates, with managers present to oversee the quality control aspects of assessment.

19   Both Dr Grimmond and Brian Dowd (the NDLC's Director of Education) were present when I visited the NDLC premises and I am convinced that they understood that the accreditation process was very real and that, prior to any contractual arrangements being put in place, the accreditation process was something which had to be gone through. We explained the

CLD-#669601-v1 (PPH) (CYG)   4

~ clear to NDLC at the time that C&G's name ~ ~r wit ~ ~ ne ~ ~ any form could not be used within any promotional material for the bite-sized courses until the full course had been accredited.

57   It is my belief that from the beginning C&G entered into negotiations with NDLC with the full intention of accrediting the NDLC courses. In the relation to the bite-sized courses, it was always made clear to NDLC that it would not be able to market   courses with either C&G's name or logo on the marketing materials until the full courses ha been approved.

I believe that the facts stated above are true.

Signed ....
Richard Stott

Date ....

Was I guilty of not being able to provide my students with City & Guilds qualifications? Did I do everything I could? Did City & Guilds lie to the police? Did the police investigate properly? Did City & Guilds, the News of the World and the press, together with the Department of Education and the police, have their own private agendas? Was the judge balanced and unbiased as the law provides?

YOU DECIDE!

And if in doubt take a look at what my managing director said to the press after being found not guilty.

City and Guilds accused over College collapse

THE conspiracy of the "chocolate-coated piranha" was one of several explosive claims made during the mammoth college fraud trial.

Allegations of cover-ups, stitch-ups, spin, lies and betrayal abounded.

They were levelled mainly against educational body City and Guilds, accused of scapegoating the NDLC and its founder Michael Smallman.

It was alleged that they cut the college adrift and conned News of the World consumer crusader Vivienne Parry, who ran a scathing exposé condemning Smallman as a "sleazeball" tycoon.

Their damning press statement was described in an internal City and Guilds email as "short and sweet like a chocolate-coated piranha".

NDLC managing director Peter Kenyon cleared by the jury of fraud, said: "They stitched us up like a kipper."

Former City and Guilds Director-General Christopher Humphries was quoted as saying that City and Guilds had not been as robust in some of their procedures as they should have been.

A City and Guilds

STITCH UP: Cleared Peter Kenyon, left, blamed City and Guilds

Picture by ANDREW GRAY

spokeswoman said: "Process controls have now been tightened to ensure that there can be no repetition of this historical abuse of the good name of City and Guilds."

Smallman also blamed the government for the death of his companies as the Department for Education and Skills (DfES) scrapped its troubled Individual Learning Account (ILA) grants scheme in 2001.

But senior civil servant Peter Lauener told how the £200m system was stopped because of escalating abuse and fraud, not overspending.

Just before you finally decide whether I was guilty or not, I'm sat here writing the book and I'm surrounded by approximately one thousand pieces of paper from City & Guilds' own computers and, similarly, the Department of Education's computers, some of which were in the evidence presented strategically late to the court and, therefore, never saw the light of day. I couldn't use them in my appeal. Nearly every piece of paper proves my innocence. I can't put them all in the book due to the massive volume of them and the impact upon its flow, but if you're hungry for more I've stuck a few bits in an appendix on the book's website www.chocolatecoatedpirhana.co.uk. Be my guest.

Quite some time ago, about 29 years old, I was soon to get married. I was brought up as a Church of England boy, my wife-to-be was a Catholic. That meant me going for religious instruction on six consecutive Sundays with the priest who was to marry us. We sat in this wooden cabin type room. On the last session, the priest said with his deep brawl Irish accent:

"Michael, marriage is based on love, true love. Pure love. The sort of love that God and Jesus gives…and you should only be getting married if your love for each other is that sort of love."

He goes on: "Now, I've asked this question for 25 or 30 years, this question I'm going to ask you, in a minute, no-one has ever got the answer right."

He looked at us both and said, "I don't expect you to get it right, but I expect you, when I tell you the answer, to understand what it means and to try to apply it to each other."

He went on to say, "Now, Michael, the question is… what is the definition and the most important, number one thing for true love?"

Needless to say, the priest was a bit taken aback when I offered him, for the first time in his 25, 30 years, the correct answer. I think it disappointed him because I suppose in some ways he wanted to keep control of the situation – to give a jaw dropping moment. But it was his jaw that dropped and hopefully your jaw, whoever you are, will drop when I give you the answer that I got right on the day. The most important thing, the fundamental thing that makes love, perfect love, true love, is this… it's the ability to forgive someone for anything that they may have done.

All of you, that have been involved in my downfall in any way, I just want to say this to you now. That all you succeeded in doing is building me up to be able to tell this story and hopefully to share it with the world in order that others can gather strength from their adversities. I hope you gather strength too.

And to all those people, even if you caused my downfall deliberately for your own gain, I truly forgive you. Not only that, if I was to meet you, Mick Bowman, I'll hold you to what you said to me when you first arrested me… and we will go and have that pint.

POSTSCRIPT

T his book takes you from 1963 to June (ish) 2012 and I'm now sat on my blue butterfly couch and it's late June 2023. So there's a lot of time that this book doesn't cover. Similarly, within that time that we don't cover, hell continued to ensue. More prison, more super-ups and super-downs and they will all come out in the sequel to this book. However, I feel the need to tell you what life's like now. The good bits, because there are some, but also the adversities, because there are still a lot of them...

You know I'm 59 years old now. I'm 60 in two months, one week and one day which was pointed out to me yesterday. Although I am still only looking like a 42 year old!!. You look in the mirror every morning, that is, I do and I really do. It sometimes gives me something to think about in my pink coloured mankini – not really, only joking – cos it's joking that's kept me going. For the most part it's the outward vision that you'll see of Mike.

I make a joke out of anything, I make a joke out of nothing; poo jokes, sexual jokes, some slightly tainted with racism – but it's not racism really – it's just a bit of fun and some jokes are about myself. I have a joke for every minute, a joke for every occasion, but really, what are the jokes for? They are there to put a face on me. If you took the mask off, took the jokes away, what you'll find is an exceptionally lonely, tired, frightened individual who doesn't know what tomorrow brings. Every click of a door, every sound outside doesn't bring an image of a friend coming to visit, it brings an image of a policeman, or two, or more of them, coming through the door. Not because I've done anything wrong, but because I do expect retribution for this book and some of the things I've said about one or two people in other ways. These expectations are based on what's happened in the past. The nasty stuff when I was a kid. The nasty stuff when I was a young adult. The nasty stuff that happened in prison. The building up of the large empire and even though there were good years in building that, it wasn't easy. To give you a comparison of where I am today, I take on a job to fix something for someone, a window or whatever it would be. For everybody else, who would do that sort of thing, it would be – generally speaking – straightforward. With me it turns into a chore, a disaster in some ways, because I can't find the things I want. My mindset is so put to one side with everything that's happened, there's not much space to concentrate on a normal thing. So I work extra hard, many hours' overtime to get a straightforward, simple thing correct.

Another thing, people's opinion of me. I knock on a potential customer's door because I have an appointment with them. What they see is a 59-year-old bloke, charming, laughing and joking, knowledgeable and they get great confidence in me. My conversion rate for business is very good, but then they say "what's your full name?" and I tell them, within hours the business can be down the pan cos they don't want somebody with a history like mine working in their garden, in their house or wherever it would be. What they've done is googled me. You can google me too. Most bits have fell off Google by now, but if you dig deep enough though you'll find all the lies that Google says, the writings from all the newspapers and court reports which, to some extent, this book puts straight. Even you, having read the book, will have some doubts. It'll always be there, it'll always hang around. If you have done some of these things yourself, you'll have paid your price by going to prison. That, in itself, is some form of 'deservedness' and some form of closure, but let me tell ya, when you're one hundred percent certain, as I am, that I have done nothing wrong, other than be ambitious, the 'deservedness' is unacceptable. It is unacceptable to be sent to prison and the closure is non-existent. You're forever thinking, 'How can I prove myself innocent? How can I prove myself not to be the person that the newspaper reports within Google portray me as?'

Most people's lives are very straightforward and simple and they don't realise that conspiracies like the one I have experienced take place. They don't understand that governments and police and other authorities have the aptitude to lie. There is an acceptance, generally speaking, that Google carries mountains of information that is untrue. Donald Trump invented the phrase 'fake news'. It exists, it's everywhere. People can understand that fake news exists but still ignore its existence when they read what's on Google and believe it. Then it has a direct effect upon that person, or persons, that it's about. Having belief in yourself, in itself, can be a burden in my situation. Having mountains of belief in myself, knowing all the things that have gone wrong in the past, but also knowing the vast majority of the people that the news reaches to don't have belief in me anymore. And that is a burden. It's contrary to me makeup, it's alien, it makes me feel exceptionally uncomfortable.

The experiences of going to prison and things that happen in prison, the manipulation by the state and its system, and the control it has on you. When you do become free you still live in those zones. Locked behind a closed door, not allowed this, not allowed that.

Personally, every night I wake up feeling like I'm still in prison and for the most part I am. I think for seconds that I'm in my cell and I ask myself when can I actually move on with my life?

Then I realise I have been released and I'm in my bedroom and I ask myself again, when can I actually move on with my life? It's not much different. So, mentally, I'm not free. Physically I am free. The restrictions that life puts on me because of false reports on Google, because of restrictions that I put on myself, because I want to be the person I used to be, it makes life extremely hard. It's painful. It's difficult for anyone to understand unless they've been through something similar themselves. Wanting to move forward, to be successful, to tell your story and make a positive effect on other people is held back by the possible consequences or the retribution of people that caused the problems in the first place. What do you do? Where do you go? How do you do it?

I'm continually told not to be thinking of the negative things because it puts things out to the world. To some extent I agree that someone who thinks negatively can put things out to the world and those negative things take place and come back on them, but let me tell you, there's absolutely nothing negative about me. Sinking or swimming I aim to move forward every single minute of every single day. There are no rules as to whether I do it with a smiley face or a bit of anger or a statement that I could go and kill someone if it doesn't happen. Obviously, I say that phrase, it doesn't mean that people will get hurt, but we say these kind of things in anger. Anger is not a negative, anger is a positive. It's simply a statement that you're not going to put up with the shit that is going on about you, bearing in mind, there is shit every single day...

Underneath all the anguish, and all the layers of trepidation lies my core. It's the core that I had when I was born, I had as a child, as a young man, as a father, a husband, and as a friend to many. Just like Earth has a core of molten iron, thousands of degrees hot and full of energy, waiting to explode, my core is the same. It is, in itself, potentially massively destructive or massively creative. Controlling the rate of energy released is the frustrating part. Holding back the real energy that forms the passion and desire to help, by influencing others in getting over their problems. This book is there to help do that. Someone who reads a part of it or all of it should get inspiration that anyone can get through anything. My desire to take my stories around the world in a thousand different ways is there and hopefully the experience of that is imminent. Not for a justification of my innocence, but simply to inspire others to deal with and work through their adversities. Most of this, and certainly the drive to do so comes from the core. However, you can't do it on your own, so some of the pleasures that exist in my today's world is when my influences do begin to affect others. From the smile on their face through to their activity in helping my actions and intent to come to fruition.

The balance of adversity and my core are the extremities of hope. This is reflected in the poem that I wrote when incarcerated...

WITH OR WITHOUT HOPE

Date: 2nd January 2009

Location: Holme House Prison, Middlesbrough

With Or Without Hope was written in less than six minutes from inside the walls of my prison cell, just weeks after arriving at Holme House prison on the eighth of December 2008. It is a true expression of my utter despair and a complete void of hope. Yet, at the same time, somewhere digging deep within my soul I could access a seed of hope.

The transformation of any individual from hopelessness to being full of hope is six minutes long.

A poignant note: I came out of prison for the last time, exactly 10 years to the day that this message of hope was channelled through me

When life is without hope it is hopeless.

**When life is without hope, desperation
sets in and desperate things begin**

**When life is without hope it becomes
discouraging, unpromising and fruitless**

When life is without hope it's impossible,
bleak and you are doomed to failure

When life is without hope you become anxious, worried, distressed

When life is without hope life distracts you into
fraught, gloomy, daunting despondency

When life is without hope it's dispiriting, disappointing,
creating doubt about yourself and others

When life is without hope it's to live without prospect,
it's off-putting, dubious and unproductive

When life is without hope you become useless,
unrewarded, wasted, desolate, dreary and miserable

When life is without hope you are ill-fated,
dammed, condemned, ruined, futile

When life is without hope you misplace concern,
become restless, fearful, apprehensive, unhappy

When life is without hope you are unfocused, side-tracked,
diverted, agitated, burdened, loaded, weighed down, laden

When life is without hope it's overcast, dull, dismal,
intimidating, off-putting, discouraging, scary,
frightening, overwhelming, you are lost

However, if you can sew the seed of hope in your mind,
it flourishes, and puts itS roots down into your heart,
spreads itS branches to fill your soul, lifting your spirits

Then hope becomes the life force, your drive, your reason to live

When life is with hope it expects, anticipates,
wishes, looks forward to

When life is with hope it has expectation,
optimism, anticipation

When life is with hope it's what you're
waiting for, what you're expecting

When life is with hope you can imagine, suppose, guess,
foresee, await, predict, be hopeful of, think likely

When life is with hope, you have desire, aspiration,
yearning, longing, craving, fancy, belief, optimism

When life is with hope, there's prospect, probability, possibility,
inclination, cheerfulness, confidence, buoyancy, sanguinity

When life is with hope, it has expectation, keenness,
eagerness, all are peppered with enthusiasm

When life is with hope, you can have fanaticism, intensity,
devotion, dedication, fever, passion, gusto, zeal and zest

When life is with hope, it's with strength, with
power, with force, with greatness and desire

When life is with hope, it's longing, yen,
hunger, thirst, ache, craving,

But above all, hope is you

And what makes you what you are and who you are

It's how people see you and what you show
and give to others and to the world

Hope is life and life is hope

And life with no hope is no life

So, heed these words and get some hope and begin to live
and breathe all the great things hope brings to you

Hope for your friends

Hope for your family

Hope for your neighbour, whether friend or foe

Hope for the world and the dust upon it

Hope for me

And OF COURSE, hope for yourself

Through hope, grow wise, grow strong,
never give up, never give in

AFTERWORD

I t's fair to say that helping to bring this book about has been a journey for me. It has made me laugh and cry. It has opened my eyes to many things that I didn't realise were happening in this small island of the United Kingdom and no doubt in many places of the world.

One thing I can say, here and now, is that this entire story and the journey of this book has been a heartfelt journey of support for a person that has been persecuted in many ways. I am happy to continue with this support and one of the ways that I have enjoyed a collaboration with Mike is the cover materials he has designed and painted for books that I am to make public very soon. Until then I would like to add that Mike is an exceptional artist and a lot of his work is depicting many levels of awareness within the subtle layers of their construct.

He is painting, and has painted, many great pieces that are available to see at www. House-of-Art.co.uk. I wish him great success in his ventures and I look forward to many days of recordings for his next books to be. Time and space is all that is required. Mike has done his time.

He works under the name of Passive the artist and although this is not obvious during the story, he is a well-established artist in his own right through many different works, including 'The People's Door' a favourite of mine that depicts No. 10 and the relationship that we have with our government and its leaders.

I know this book appears in some way derogatory towards that, but I'd like to add that Mike is always offering kindness and genuine heartfelt openness to all those that he is mentioning in his story. I hope you have enjoyed this book and reading it as much as I enjoyed the collaboration with Mike in pulling this together.

Peace is in the mind and always in the will to sit down and share the human experiences without any intent to continue the stories that have created the current day experiences, but to let them go with forgiveness and a little bit of Mike magic.

Andrea (also known as Meher Anna)

Printed in Great Britain
by Amazon

47033659R00185